*The American
Immigration Collection*

Laughing in the Jungle

LOUIS ADAMIC

Arno Press and The New York Times

NEW YORK 1969

Laughing
in the Jungle

Laughing in the Jungle

The Autobiography of an Immigrant in America

By

LOUIS ADAMIC

Harper & Brothers
New York and London

To
MADSEN

Contents

Author's Note

THIS book is a narrative of the influences which, in 1913, prompted me as a boy of fourteen and a half to leave my native country in Europe and go to America, and of things within my experience as an immigrant living in various parts of the United States that seem interesting or significant, or merely amusing to me personally, and give themselves to telling at this time. It does not pretend to be a complete autobiography (if such a thing is ever possible).

Immigration was a large factor in the upbuilding of America. The immigrant flood during the last seven or eight decades, and especially from about 1890 to 1914, included large numbers of my countrymen—"Bohunks," or "Hunkies": Slavs from the Balkans and from eastern and central Europe—whose contribution as workers to the current material greatness and power of the United States, albeit not generally recognized, is immense. ". . . Much of our work and our strength is frozen in the buildings of New York, and in the buildings of other cities, and in the railroads and bridges of America. . . ."

On the other hand, of course, immigration is in no small way to blame for the fact that the United States today is more a jungle than a civilization—a land of deep economic, social, spiritual, and intellectual chaos and distress—in which, it seems to me, by far the most precious possession a sensitive and intelligent person can have is an active sense of humor.

Immigration now is ended. The United States is pulling down the "Welcome" sign. This fact appears to me one of the most significant in America's national existence today. Hence, perhaps, it is not inappropriate for, or presumptuous of, me at this time to add a volume to the rather meager shelf of autobiographical books by immigrants.

Yaddo,   Louis Adamic
October, 1931

PART ONE

Why I Came to America

CHAPTER I

Amerikanci *in Carniola*

I

As A boy of nine, and even younger, in my native village of Blato, in Carniola—then a Slovenian duchy of Austria and later a part of Yugoslavia—I experienced a thrill every time one of the men of the little community returned from America.

Five or six years before, as I heard people tell, the man had quietly left the village for the United States, a poor peasant clad in homespun, with a mustache under his nose and a bundle on his back; now, a clean-shaven *Amerikanec*, he sported a blue-serge suit, buttoned shoes very large in the toes and with india-rubber heels, a black derby, a shiny celluloid collar, and a loud necktie made even louder by a dazzling horseshoe pin, which, rumor had it, was made of gold, while his two suitcases of imitation leather, tied with straps, bulged with gifts from America for his relatives and friends in the village. In nine cases out of ten, he had left in economic desperation, on money borrowed from some relative in the United States; now there was talk in the village that he was worth anywhere from one to three thousand American dollars. And to my eyes he truly bore all the earmarks of affluence. Indeed, to say that he thrilled my boyish fancy is putting it mildly. With other boys in the village, I followed him around as he went visiting his relatives and friends and distributing presents, and hung onto his every word and gesture.

Then, on the first Sunday after his homecoming, if at

all possible, I got within earshot of the nabob as he sat in the winehouse or under the linden in front of the winehouse in Blato, surrounded by village folk, ordering wine and *klobase*—Carniolan sausages—for all comers, paying for accordion-players, indulging in tall talk about America, its wealth and vastness, and his own experiences as a worker in the West Virginia or Kansas coal-mines or Pennsylvania rolling-mills, and comparing notes upon conditions in the United States with other local *Amerikanci* who had returned before him.

Under the benign influence of *cvichek*—Lower Carniolan wine—and often even when sober, the men who had been in America spoke expansively, boastfully, romantically of their ability and accomplishments as workers and of the wages they had earned in Wilkes-Barre or Carbondale, Pennsylvania, or Wheeling, West Virginia, or Pueblo, Colorado, or Butte, Montana, and generally of places and people and things and affairs in the New World. The men who returned to the village, either to stay or for a visit, were, for the most part, natural men of labor—men with sinewy arms and powerful backs— "Bohunks," or "Hunkies," so called in the United States —who derived a certain brawny joy and pride from hard toil. Besides, now that they had come home, they were no longer mere articles upon the industrial labor market, "working stiffs" or "wage slaves," as radical agitators in America referred to them, but adventurers, distant kinsmen of Marco Polo safely returned from a far country, heroes in their own eyes and the eyes of the village; and it was natural for them to expand and to exaggerate their own exploits and enlarge upon the opportunities to be found in America. Their boasting, perhaps, was never wholly without basis in fact. . . .

4

I remember that, listening to them, I played with the idea of going to America when I was but eight or nine. My notion of the United States then, and for a few years after, was that it was a grand, amazing, somewhat fantastic place—the Golden Country—a sort of Paradise —the Land of Promise in more ways than one—huge beyond conception, thousands of miles across the ocean, untellably exciting, explosive, quite incomparable to the tiny, quiet, lovely Carniola; a place full of movement and turmoil, wherein things that were unimaginable and impossible in Blato happened daily as a matter of course.

In America one could make pots of money in a short time, acquire immense holdings, wear a white collar, and have polish on one's boots like a *gospod*—one of the gentry—and eat white bread, soup, and meat on weekdays as well as on Sundays, even if one were but an ordinary workman to begin with. In Blato no one ate white bread or soup and meat, except on Sundays and holidays, and very few then.

In America one did not have to remain an ordinary workman. There, it seemed, one man was as good as the next. There were dozens, perhaps scores, or even hundreds of immigrants in the United States, one-time peasants and workers from the Balkans—from Carniola, Styria, Carinthia, Croatia, Banat, Dalmatia, Bosnia, Montenegro, and Serbia—and from Poland, Slovakia, Bohemia, and elsewhere, who, in two or three years, had earned and saved enough money working in the Pennsylvania, Ohio, or Illinois coal-mines or steel-mills to go to regions called Minnesota, Wisconsin, and Nebraska, and there buy sections of land each of which was larger than the whole area owned by the peasants in Blato. . . . Oh, America was immense—*immense!*

5

I heard a returned *Amerikanec* tell of regions known as Texas and Oklahoma where single farms—*renche* (ranches), he called them—were larger than the entire province of Carniola! It took a man days to ride on horseback from one end of such a ranch to the other. There were people in Blato and in neighboring villages who, Thomas-like, did not believe this, but my boyish imagination was aflame with America, and I believed it. At that time I accepted as truth nearly everything I heard about America. I believed that a single cattleman in Texas owned more cattle than there were in the entire Balkans. And my credulity was not strained when I heard that there were gold-mines in California, and trees more than a thousand years old with trunks so enormous that it required a dozen men, clasping each other's hands, to encircle them with their arms.

In America everything was possible. There even the common people were "citizens," not "subjects," as they were in Austria and in most other European countries. A citizen, or even a non-citizen foreigner, could walk up to the President of the United States and pump his hand. Indeed, that seemed to be a custom in America. There was a man in Blato, a former steel-worker in Pittsburgh, who claimed that upon an occasion he had shaken hands and exchanged words with Theodore Roosevelt, to whom he familiarly referred as "Tedi"—which struck my mother very funny. To her it seemed as if some one had called the Pope of Rome or the Emperor of Austria by a nickname. But the man assured her, in my hearing, that in America everybody called the President merely "Tedi."

Mother laughed about this, off and on, for several days. And I laughed with her. She and I often laughed together.

6

II

One day—I was then a little over ten—I said to Mother:
"Some day I am going to America."

Mother looked at me a long moment. . . . She was
then a healthy young peasant woman, not yet thirty,
rather tall, with a full bust and large hips; long arms
and big, capable hands; a broad, sun-browned, wind-
creased Slavic face; large, wide-spaced hazel eyes, mild
and luminous with simple mirth; and wavy auburn hair
which stuck in little gold-bleached wisps from under her
colored kerchief, tied below her chin. She had then four
children, two boys and two girls; later she bore five more,
three boys and two girls. I was the oldest. Years after I
came to America my oldest sister wrote me that there was
a story in the village that Mother had laughed in her
pains at my birth—which probably is not true; mother
herself, who is still living, does not remember. But I know
that when I was a boy she had—and probably still has—
the gift of laughter in a greater measure than most people thereabouts; indeed, than most people anywhere. Hers
was the healthy, natural, visceral, body-shaking laughter
of Slovenian peasants in Carniola, especially of peasant
women—variable laughter; usually mirthful and humorous, clear and outright, but sometimes, too, mirthless and
unhumorous, pain-born, and pain-transcending. . . .

"I am going to America," I said again, as Mother continued to look at me in silence.

I imagine she thought that I was a strange boy. Now
and then she had remarked in my hearing that I worried
her. Often she looked at me with silent concern. In some
respects I was a self-willed youngster. I usually had
things my way, regardless of opposition.

Finally, Mother smiled at me, although I do not doubt

7

that what I said frightened her. She smiled with her whole face—her mouth, her wrinkles, her eyes, especially her eyes.

I smiled, too. I was a healthy boy, tall and strong for my age. Physically, as Mother often remarked, I resembled Father, who was a peasant in body and soul; but evidently I was not made to be a peasant. If necessary, I could work hard in the fields, but I very much preferred not to. I liked to move about the village, roam in the woods, go to neighboring villages, stand by the side of the highway, and observe things.

With a little catch in her voice, Mother said: "To America? But when are you going?"

"I don't know," I said. "When I grow up, I guess. I am already ten." I had not thought of it in detail, but had merely decided to go some day.

Mother laughed. Her laughter was tremulous with apprehension. She could not make me out.

I realized then that she would not like me to go to America. A cousin of hers had gone there twenty-odd years before, when she was still a little girl. She scarcely remembered him, but had heard other relatives speak of him. The first year he had written a few times. Then Heaven only knew what became of him. And, as it occurred to me later, Mother knew of other men in Blato and the vicinity who had gone to America and had sunk, leaving no trace, in the vastness of America. She knew of men in villages not remote from our own who had returned from the United States without an arm or minus a leg, or in bad health. There was an *Amerikanec* in Gatina, the village nearest Blato, who had come home with a strange, sinful, and unmentionable disease, which he later communicated to his wife, who, in turn, gave birth to a blind child. There was a widow in Podgora, another

8

village near by, whose husband had been killed in a mine accident in the United States. Mother had only a faint conception of what a mine was; there are no mines in Lower Carniola; but she dreaded the thought that some day one of her children might work underground.

III

All of us, parents and children, slept in the *izba*—the large room in a Slovenian peasant house—and that night, soon after we all went to bed, Mother called me by name in a low voice, adding, "Are you asleep?"

I was awake, and almost answered her, but then it occurred to me that she probably meant to discuss me with Father. I kept quiet. The bed which I shared with my brother was in the opposite corner from my parents'.

"He is asleep," mumbled Father. "Why do you call him?"

"I want to tell you what he said to me today," said Mother, in a half-whisper, which I heard clearly. "He said he would go to America when he grew up."

Father grunted vaguely. He was heavy with fatigue. He had worked hard all day. He was one of the better-to-do peasants in Blato, but, with Mother's aid, did nearly all the work on the farm, seldom hiring outside help. He was a large, hard man, in his late thirties; blue-eyed and light-haired; a simple, competent peasant.

He grunted again. "America? He is only a child. How old is he, anyhow?" he asked. He was too busy to keep up with the ages of his children.

"He is ten," said Mother. "But he is like no other boy in the village."

"Only a child," Father grunted again. "Childish talk."

"Sometimes I am afraid to talk with him," said Mother. "I don't know what is going on in his head. He

9

asks me questions and tells me things. Nothing that occurs hereabouts escapes him. And he reads everything he finds in the village."

They were both silent a minute.

"I'll send him to city school, then," said Father, "even if he is our oldest." According to custom in Carniola, as the oldest son, I was supposed to stay home and work on the farm, and after my father's death become its master. "He isn't much good on the farm, anyhow," Father went on. "I'll send him to school in Lublyana"—the provincial capital. "Let him get educated if he has a head for learning."

"That's what Martin says we should do, too," said Mother. Martin was her brother, the priest in charge of the parish of Zhalna, which included the village of Blato.

"They say children are God's blessing," said Father, after a while, "but——"

"Oh, everything will be well in the end," Mother interrupted his misgiving. "There is little to worry about so long as God gives us health." She was a natural, earth-and-sky optimist; a smiling, laughing fatalist. Then, after a few moments, she added: "Maybe—maybe, if we send him to school in Lublyana, he will become a priest, like my brother Martin."

Father said nothing to this. Mother was silent, too. By and by I heard Father snore lightly, in the first stage of his slumber.

Mother, I believe, did not fall asleep till late that night. She probably smiled to herself in the darkness, yielding her consciousness to delicious thoughts. It was absurd to think that I should go to America! I was only a child, and one should not take seriously a child's chatter. . . . They would send me to Lublyana; that was settled. Then, after years of schooling, I would become a priest and the

10

bishop might send me to the parish church in Zhalna.
"Oh, that would be beautiful!" she exclaimed to herself,
half aloud. I heard her clearly, despite Father's snoring,
and I imagine that this is what she was thinking to herself. She probably figured that by the time I would be
ordained a priest, Uncle Martin would have been promoted to a bigger parish than Zhalna, making a vacancy
for me.

In common with many peasant women in Carniola,
Mother was not deeply religious in the ordinary sense. I
believe that she scarcely concerned herself with the tenets
of the Catholic faith. She was innately pagan. In her
blood throbbed echoes of prayers that her ancestors—Old
Slavs—had addressed a thousand years ago from their
open-air sacrificial altars to the sun and to the wind- and
thunder-gods. What largely appealed to her in Catholi-
cism, although, of course, she was not conscious of the fact,
were the ritual and the trappings. She loved the vest-
ments that her brother and other priests wore at mass.
She loved the solemn processions with bells tolling long
and sonorously on big holidays or on hot, still days in
midsummer when drought threatened to destroy or harm
the crops. She loved the jubilant midnight mass at Christmas. She relished the incense, the smell of lighted candles,
the pictures, the stations of the Way of the Cross, and
the statues of saints at the main and side altars, and the
organ music on Sundays. She sang in the choir with a
strong and clear, although untrained, voice. Sometimes,
when she sang solos, her fellow parishioners from Blato
said they detected a ring of laughter in her singing. She
did not care for sermons, not even her brother's; at least,
so far as I know, she never praised a sermon; but I think
it was deeply satisfying to her to see Uncle Martin stand
in the pulpit and read the Gospel and preach. . . . And

11

some day, perhaps—perhaps, I, her son, would stand in the pulpit at Zhalna and preach! She would be so proud of me. All the people of the parish would be proud of me, just as they were proud of Uncle Martin, who was also a native of the parish and a peasant's son.

In my father's life, too, religion was of no great moment. He was essentially a practical man who had serious and constant business with the ancient earth. He went to church on Sundays and prayed to God every evening with his family, but I think he did so more because that was the conventional thing to do than because he felt it necessary. Basically, like most peasants in Carniola and elsewhere, he was a hard realist, a practical man, a fatalist, possessing a natural, almost biological good sense and a half-cynical earth knowledge older than any religion or system. . . . However, he probably figured, if a son of his was cut out to be a priest—why, well and good. Priests were an important part of the scheme of things. To have a priest in the family added to one's prestige. Father knew that. He felt that even now peasants in the parish showed him a special sort of deference because his wife's brother was a priest. To have his own son become one, he possibly said to himself, would be even better. At any rate, he decided to send me to city school which—for the time being—was agreeable to me.

IV

Late in the spring of 1909, four months before I was taken to school in Lublyana, and six or seven months after I had first announced my intention to go to America, there returned to Blato a man who had been in America for more than twenty years.

He was Peter Molek, brother of Francé Molek, a rather well-to-do peasant who was our nearest neighbor. Peter

12

had no property in the village, and so he went to live in Francé's house. His brother had not heard from or of him for eight years. He had thought him dead. None of the returned *Amerikanci* had seen him in America. Then, of a sudden that spring, there came a letter from him that he was "coming home to die."

Peter Molek was an unusual *Amerikanec* to return to Blato.

At the supper table the day after his homecoming, I heard my parents discuss him. Father said that he remembered when Peter had gone to America. "He was one of the sturdiest and lustiest young men in this parish, even stronger and taller than Francé," who, although in his fifty-seventh year, was still a big and powerful man. "Now look at him!"—and Father shook his head.

Although not yet fifty, Peter Molek was a gaunt, bent, and broken man, hollow-eyed, bald, mostly skin and bone, with a bitter expression on his face; suffering from rheumatism and asthma—two diseases till then all but unknown in Blato. He was eight or nine years younger than Francé, but only a shadow of his brother.

"America is an evil place," said Mother, glancing at me concernedly, although I had not spoken of going to America again. "They say Peter came home almost penniless. I guess Francé will have to keep him till he dies."

Which, to me, was the most extraordinary aspect of Peter Molek. With my ideas about America, I could not understand how anyone, after spending twenty years in that country—in the midst of abundance—could return home in such a state. And it doubtless was true what people said about Peter Molek having no money. He brought no presents even for his closest relatives. He did not go to the winehouse, nor talk about his adventures in America with anyone. He kept, for the most part, to himself.

13

All day long he sat in the sun on the bench in front of his brother's house. He read books and papers which evidently were American publications. He took slow walks in the fields. Sometimes he coughed for ten or twenty minutes at a spell.

Peter Molek's cough was a great sensation among the children in Blato. When the asthmatic spasm seized him, his face turned purple, his deep-sunken eyes bulged and looked wide and terror-stricken; and bending over, he held his chest in desperation. The first two or three weeks after his return, as soon as one of the boys heard him cough, there was much yelling in the village and, with the heartless, unthinking curiosity of youth, ten or a dozen husky, barefooted urchins came dashing from all sides to Molek's house, to watch the strange *Amerikanec* choke, and listen to the wheezing sound that issued from his tortured chest. When he emitted an especially long wheeze, the boys looked at one another in wonder and smiled.

In this respect I was no better than the other boys, until Mother forbade me to go near Peter Molek when he coughed. Then I watched him from the distance. Our house was only a couple of hundred yards from Molek's.

But occasionally, when he was not coughing, I walked by him. I wanted to talk with him, but could not work up enough courage to address him first.

One day he smiled faintly and said to me, "You are the neighbor's boy, aren't you?"

"Yes," I said. "My father remembers you when you went to America."

Peter Molek nodded his head. "That was a long time ago," he said.

"Why do you cough like you do all the time?" I asked.

Peter Molek did not answer for a while. He stared at

14

me in a way that made me uneasy. Then he looked away and swung one of his large bony hands in a vague gesture. "America," he said. ". . . America."

I did not know what he meant.

"How old are you?" Peter Molek asked me.

"Ten," I said. "Soon I'll be eleven. I am going to city school in the fall."

Peter Molek smiled again and nodded his head. "You are *all right*." He said "all right" in English.

"I know what that means—'*all right*,'" I said, eagerly. "It means 'good' in the American language. I have often heard other men who came from America say '*all right*.' I also know other American words. '*Sure Mike!*' . . . '*Sonabitch.*' . . ." I was pleased with my knowledge.

Peter Molek peered at me from under his eyebrows. He seemed to want to touch me, but probably was afraid that I might draw away from him because he was a sick man. "You are *all right*," he said again.

I was delighted with his approval.

On the bench beside him I noticed some papers and books. I stepped close. "What are these?" I said.

"Books and papers from America," said Peter Molek. "I brought the books with me. The papers I get by mail once a week."

The newspapers were copies of the *Appeal to Reason*, a radical sheet then printed at Girard, Kansas. One of the books was *The Jungle*, by Upton Sinclair.

"Are there pictures in them?" I asked. "Pictures of America?"

"No," said Peter Molek. "But I have some pictures inside. Wait; I'll bring them out." He went into the house and presently returned with some photographs, postcards, and newspaper clippings.

I sat beside him.

15

"This," said Peter Molek, showing me the first picture, "is a coal town in Pennsylvania. Forest City. This, which looks like a mountain, is a pile of coal, dug out of the ground—thousands of feet below—mostly by our people from Carniola. Nearly all the miners in Forest City are Slovenians. I worked in one of the mines there for seven years."

He showed me the next picture. "A steel-mill in Pennsylvania. Once I worked here awhile, too. Most of the time I worked in the mines. I worked from one end of the country to the other—not only in Pennsylvania, but in Ohio, in West Virginia, in Illinois, in Montana, in Nevada—in places you have never heard of."

"I have heard of Pennsylvania"—pronouncing it *Panslovenia*—"and Ohio and ——"

Peter Molek smiled wanly. He liked me, and I was happy that he did.

"This is New York," he said, showing me another picture. "You see these buildings? Some of them are many times higher than the highest church tower in Carniola."

"I know about the buildings of New York," I said.

"They are building them higher every year. *Skyscrapers*, they call them. You know what that means?"

"No," I said.

Peter Molek explained to me why the tall buildings in America were called skyscrapers. It was the most interesting talk I had ever heard.

Then I said, "Some day I am going to America."

Peter Molek looked at me, startled. He was about to say something, when another asthmatic spasm seized him.

v

"This is what America did to me," said Peter Molek, after he had stopped coughing.

16

"What does this mean?" I said, pointing at the title of a book on the bench.

"*The Jungle,*" said Peter Molek. "That means *dzhungla* in Slovenian."

I did not even know what *dzhungla* meant. The forests around Blato were neat, thinned-out, idyllic groves where one went to pick berries or gather mushrooms.

"A jungle," Peter Molek explained, "is a wild place, a great forest, all tangled up with vegetation, everything growing crisscross, almost impenetrable, mysterious and terrible, infested with beasts and snakes, and spiders bigger than my fist. . . . This is a book about the United States, although there are no jungles in the United States, so far as I know. But the whole of America is a jungle. This is a story about people like me—foreigners —who go there and are swallowed by the jungle. Understand?"

I nodded in the affirmative, but I did not really understand.

"America swallowed me," continued Peter Molek, "but she did not digest me." He smiled, as if to himself, a peculiar, mirthless smile.

Peter Molek went on: "America the jungle swallows many people who go there to work. She squeezes the strength out of them, unless they are wise or lucky enough to escape before it is too late; unless they work in the mills or the mines only a few years and save every cent they can and return home, or buy themselves a piece of land where land is still cheap."

My understanding of Peter Molek's words was scant, but I listened and remembered everything he said.

". . . I was there too long," he was saying. "I worked too hard. Here is New York," pointing at the picture he

17

had shown me before. "I—we helped to build these buildings—we Slovenians and Croatians and Slovaks and other people who went to America to work. We helped to build many other cities there, cities of which you have never heard, and railroads, and bridges, all made of steel which our people make in the mills. Our men from the Balkans are the best steel-workers in America. The framework of America is made of steel. And this smoke that you see here—it comes from coal that we have dug up; we from the Balkans and from Galicia and Bohemia. We have also dug up much ore. I myself worked for a few years in the iron-mines of the West. I lost my health in the mines. Miners get asthma and rheumatism.

"Three times I was in accidents. Once, in Colorado, I was buried for four days three thousand feet underground. There were seven other men buried with me—three of them Slovenians like myself, two Poles, one Dalmatian, one American. When they dug us out, the Dalmatian and I were the only two still living. Once, in Pennsylvania, a rock fell on me in a mine and broke my right leg. The leg healed and I went back to work. I worked two months, and another rock fell on me. It almost broke my left leg.

"For many years I did not understand America. Then I began to read and understand. . . .

"The day before I sailed for home I walked in these streets"—he pointed at the picture—"where the buildings are tallest. Steel buildings—and I looked up, and I can hardly describe my feelings. I realized that there was much of our work and strength, my own work and strength, frozen in the greatness of New York and in the greatness of America. I felt that, although I was going home to Blato, I was actually leaving myself in America."

18

That spring and summer I had more sessions with Peter Molek. Between asthmatic spasms he talked to me of the vast jungle that he conceived America to be. His view of the country, as I remember it now, was one-sided, bitter. He told me of accidents in the mines and iron-foundries which he had witnessed or of which he had merely read or heard; of labor upheavals; of powerful capitalists who owned immense industries and whom he sketched as "the beasts in the jungle"; of rich people's orgies in Chicago and New York at which, as reported in socialistic prints, men smoked cigarettes wrapped in hundred-dollar bills; of millionaires who wore diamonds in their teeth and had bands playing while they bathed in champagne; and of slums where people lived in rags and misery.

I listened open-mouthed.

"But for some people America is not a bad place," said Peter Molek one day. "Many foreigners have greatly bettered themselves there, but these fortunate ones are few when compared with the multitude of immigrants who, I believe, would be better off had they remained in the old country. American industries use them, then cast them off."

"More people go to America all the time," I said. Lately I had read in a newspaper to which my father subscribed that four thousand more persons had emigrated from Carniola to the United States in 1908 than in 1907.

"Yes," said Peter Molek. "They go because each thinks that he will get the better of America and not America the better of him. They listen to the few who return home from the United States with two or three thousand dollars. They hear that some one else who stayed there has

19

succeeded on a big scale. And they think they will do the same. America is the Land of Promise to them. She lures them over by the thousands and hundreds of thousands— people from many countries, not only from Carniola. She needs their hands even more than they need her dollars, and makes use of them. Once upon a time immigrants were called 'dung' in America; that was a good name for them. They were the fertilizer feeding the roots of America's present and future greatness. They are still 'dung.' The roots of America's greatness still feed on them. . . . Life in America is a scramble. More people are swept under than rise to riches."

All of which, on top of what I had previously heard and thought of America, tended to bewilder me.

CHAPTER II

"*Do Not Go to America!*"

I

WHAT country schooling I had received in Blato qualified me to enter the pre-*Gymnasium* class in the primary school in Lublyana (Laibach) from which I advanced, the following year, to the *Gymnasium*, or "Latin school."

The first three years of my student life in Lublyana, if compared with my later years, especially those in America, were, while not uninteresting, almost uneventful. I was a fairly good student, passing the examinations with ease. I did my homework during rest periods in class, so that after school I could wander—usually alone—through the streets of the city, over the castle-crowned hill which dominated the town, along the river Lublyanica which flowed through it, or by the ancient crumbling Roman wall around it, and look at things. The first year I found the little provincial city, with its forty thousand inhabitants, interesting, even mildly stirring; the second year less so, and the third year hardly at all. In all that period I made no especially pleasing or exciting personal contacts. Occasionally I went to lectures, theatrical performances, and sporting events, and always read a good deal.

Mother, in her simple way, was a happy woman. She warmly told me that I was a good boy. When, every other month or so, she came to see me at the students' boarding-house in the city, bringing me fruit and home-made *potica* —Carniolan cake—or when I came home to Blato at Christmas, Easter, and summer vacations, she glowed with parental pride at sight of me. I imagine she was saying

21

to herself over and over what a nice young priest I would make twelve years hence.

For a time there was a vague and tacit understanding between Mother and myself that at the end of my eight years of *Gymnasium* studies I would enter the seminary of the Roman Catholic Church in Lublyana, and four years later be ordained a priest. In common with my parents, whose attitude toward religion I have described, I had not a deeply religious nature in the orthodox sense. In the basic phases of my character I was (and still am) essentially a Slavic peasant; but during the first and perhaps a part of the second year in the city school I thought, with a mingling of adoration for and a sense of duty toward Mother and a youthful peasant cynicism, which was half fatalism, that I might as well enter the priesthood to please her—although perhaps deep down in me I knew or felt all the time that I would never become a priest.

I recall that I had momentary misgivings about entering the holy orders even before I went to the city schools. Later I remotely admitted to myself, off and on, that I still wanted to go to America no less than I had wanted to go a year or two before. But then I said to myself, with a glow of filial virtue, that, things being as they were, I had to choose between going to America and fulfilling Mother's wish to see me ordained a priest. Subsequently, however, when I learned that not a few young Slovenian clerics emigrated, to take charge of Slovenian churches in various parts of the United States, I decided to do both —become a priest, to please Mother, and after a few years of ministerial service at home apply for transfer to America. Mother, I thought, might not object to my going there as a clerk of the Church.

At vacation time in Blato I still talked with Peter

22

Molek, whose health appeared to be slowly improving, or rather I listened to his talk. His fondness for me was palpably increasing. I did not tell him that I meant to become a priest. I had an instinctive feeling that he would not approve of my intention. His words often verged dangerously upon heresy; he was a socialist and, as I learned later, an atheist. He was the most exciting person I knew then. I could have listened to his version of America forever.

In the city, too, I pricked up my ears every time I heard mention of the United States. I read such books as *Stric Tomova Koča* (*Uncle Tom's Cabin*) and *Zadnji Mohikanec* (*The Last of the Mohicans*), and numerous American dime novels, translated into vile Slovenian.

II

At the beginning of my fourth student year, when I was going on fifteen, I struck up a close and satisfying friendship with a youth a year older than myself. His name was Yanko Radin. Like myself, he was a tallish, healthy, avidminded, active boy. He hailed from a little town somewhere in the province of Istria, north of Trieste, which then was an Austrian seaport. We lived in the same students' boarding-house. We were third-*Gymnasium* students and classmates.

Yanko had a brother in America, who was three or four years older than himself. The brother's name was Stefan, but in his infrequent letters to Yanko, most often only brief notes, he signed himself "Steve." Now and then he sent Yanko copies of *Narodni Glas*, a Slovenian newspaper published in New York, which Yanko and I read together. Nearly every issue contained a picture of some scene in America. Every now and then the cut was a photograph or an architect's drawing of New York's new-

23

est and tallest skyscraper, which always gave us a great thrill.

One day Yanko said to me: "You know, some day, I think, I'll go to America, too. Maybe after I finish *Gymnasium*. My brother Stefan went there too soon. Three years ago. He was only sixteen then. He ran away from school in Trieste and stole aboard a Dalmatian barkentine bound for America which happened to be in port, and concealed himself in the vessel till she sailed. He landed in New York. But I think he was foolish. He had had only two years in the *Gymnasium*. He should have acquired more education before venturing to America. I believe that if one has some education, one does not have to be an ordinary laborer in the United States."

I narrated to Yanko some of the things that Peter Molek had told me of America.

To this Yanko remarked: "That may all be true. I know that *Narodni Glas* often writes about accidents and labor strikes in the American mines and factories in which men are hurt and killed. For many people, I don't doubt, America is a bad place, but I am not afraid of the country. I am sure it doesn't get the better of you if you are smart and know how to go about things. America is a new country—very inviting! Enormous! Carniola, and for that matter all of Europe, are old and set. Life here is no longer vital. Recently I read somewhere that in America everything is, more or less, 'in the process of becoming.' "

"Some day, perhaps, I'll go to America myself," I said. I had not previously told Yanko that I meant to become a priest, to please my mother, and I said nothing about it now.

"Perhaps we can go together, eh?" said Yanko, eagerly.

I nodded.

Of a sudden I was happy to talk this way with my friend. I forgot all about becoming a priest. We spoke of New York, of the buildings and bridges of New York, and of Cleveland and Chicago and Pittsburgh, all of which places we meant to see when we went to America.

III

Adventurous as we both were, early in our third *Gymnasium* year, Yanko and I joined a secret students' political club, affiliated with the general revolutionary Yugoslav Nationalist Movement that had sprung up in the South-Slavic provinces of Austria five or six years before the outbreak of the World War.

For a little while I found life in Lublyana very fervid. Yanko and I attended secret meetings of our group, listened to impassioned speeches by adult leaders and agitators of the Movement, many of whom were sought by the Austrian police. We joined other boys in trampling upon the Hapsburg emblems and singing ribald parodies of the Austrian anthem. At night we prowled through the city, armed with sticks of chalk, and upon the walls and on the sidewalks in front of government buildings wrote insulting words after the name of the Emperor Francis Joseph. Frequently we were chased by the police, and we reveled in this fact.

Generally, we behaved in the manner of romantic, daft devotees of the goddess Liberty, although I recall that I never intensely believed in the idea behind the Movement. Nor, I suppose, did Yanko. We were both peasant lads from fairly well-to-do homes, as were one or two of the other boys in the club, and as such we actually cared little whether our fathers and brothers tilled the soil under the Austrian domination or within the borders of a Yugoslav country ruled by the king of Serbia. We were in the Movement, as I might put it now, for the fun of it—because it was perilous and heart-swelling.

Every once in a while the question of emigration to America came up at our secret meetings. The leaders of the Movement who addressed us were opposed to people emigrating to the United States. Down with Austria! Down with America! Austria drove the good Slovenian peasants to America, and America ruined them. True, a deal of money came from the United States, but (asked the propagandists) was it worth the price? America broke and mangled the emigrants' bodies, defiled their souls, deprived them of their simple spiritual and æsthetic sensibilities, corrupted their charming native dialects and manners, and generally alienated them from the homeland. The peasants (said the agitators) were lured to America by her dollars and so-called opportunities because at home the Austrian oligarchy denied them the soil which was their birthright, and on which they might have made decent livings. Emigration and America, in other words, were issues in the Movement. Indeed, one could hardly do anything or go anywhere in Carniola without coming upon something that had to do with the United States. Our people had already begun emigrating in the 1870's.

A widely read book in Carniola at that time, sponsored by the Yugoslav Movement, was *Obljubljena dezhela* (*The Land of Promise*), an anonymous novel dealing with the unhappy voyage of a small party of honest, simple Slovenian peasants to the falsely called Land of Promise, and their brief and heartrending sojourn within its borders, where, swindled by sharpers out of all they possessed, most of them perished from hunger, thirst, and exposure in a desert. The dreadful tale ended with these words: *"Ne v Ameriko!"* ("Do not go to America!") . . .

"DO NOT GO TO AMERICA!"

The author, in all likelihood, had never been in the United States, and his story, perhaps, had meager factual basis, but Yanko and I believed that it was essentially true. Only we did not take to heart the advice at the bottom of the last page. The horrible story, on the contrary, stimulated our passion for America. It would be, we thought, exciting to live in such a country. Yanko and I were not ignorant peasants. We were educated. We would be careful. We were confident that "land sharks," such as described in the story, could not sell *us* worthless land in the desert. Indeed, we imagined that it would be great sport to guard ourselves against such characters, to outwit them. . . .

IV

Soon after Yanko and I got into it, the Yugoslav Movement in Lublyana began to come defiantly and recklessly into the open. In broad daylight, mobs of students dashed through the streets, pulling down German signs from above the entrances to stores and the Austrian double-headed eagle from government buildings, breaking windowpanes, staging small demonstrations. Occasionally a few of them achieved the status of heroes and martyrs within their respective groups by getting their heads bloodied in encounters with the police.

One afternoon fresh from a mass-meeting at which the Austrian rule had been rhetorically defied by the speakers, several hundred youths marched through the streets of the city, singing, shouting, waving the Slovenian colors. They had no permission for the "parade" from either the municipal or the local military authorities.

One of the boys carried a huge brass cuspidor tied to the top of a long pole. It dangled over the heads of the mob bound for the courthouse square. The idea was to "crown" with the cuspidor the large white-marble statue of the Emperor Francis Joseph in front of the courthouse.

Yanko and I were in the mob, burning with excitement. He held my arm as we marched.

"Look!" cried Yanko.

But before I had a chance to turn where he had indicated, a detachment of Austrian cavalry, of which two regiments were garrisoned in the city, charged the mob from a side street, where it had been waiting for us in ambush. In a moment the mounted soldiers were upon us with drawn sabers.

Then one of the hotheads from our midst hurled a rock at the lieutenant leading the detachment, whereupon that officer commanded:

"*Fire!*"

The soldiers not wielding sabers commenced to fire at will, creating a panic in the mob which until then had been full of mischief and fighting spirit. We retreated in all directions before the shooting soldiers. Some of the boys sought safety in stores, cafés, and in doorways of private residences.

Suddenly Yanko, who was running ahead of me, dropped. He was dead, a bullet in his head. I suppose he never knew he was hit.

I stumbled over him and fell, scarcely knowing what had occurred.

Then the firing ceased. The total casualties were two dead and four or five wounded, all of them students. The whole thing happened in perhaps less than two minutes.

Aside from a few bruises, I was unharmed. I knelt beside Yanko's body, still but dimly realizing what had transpired, when a *gendarme* yanked me up and arrested me. I was one of a score or more who were imprisoned.

For three days, in the city jail, I was in a daze. The

28

whole affair was too terrible to think about. Only now and then, for a few minutes at a time, I fully allowed myself to realize what had happened. Yanko was dead, and I remember that I wept. One of the jailkeepers, who was sympathetic to the Yugoslav Movement, slipped a newspaper into the cell that I occupied with three other boys, and we read of the tremendous funeral that the city of Lublyana had given Yanko and his fellow victim. They were national heroes. We also read that most of us who had been arrested were to be expelled from *Gymnasium* and in the future forbidden to enter any educational institution conducted by the Imperial and Royal Government.

What would I do in the event I really should be expelled from school? . . . Inevitably the thought of America began to buzz in my mind again. I would go to America, without Yanko. And then I bawled again, while my cellmates—youths, like myself, in their mid-teens— who appreciated the friendship that had existed between Yanko and myself, tried to console me.

v

The fourth day after the bloody incident, the day following the funeral, most of us were turned out of prison.

At the boarding-house, Mother, Father, and Uncle Martin were waiting for me.

Mother smiled, although no doubt she felt more like crying, and embraced me. Father and Uncle Martin looked stern.

"What have you done, son?" said Father in a hard voice. He had been informed, he added, that I was expelled from school and that thereafter he would personally be held responsible by the Imperial Authority for my future political activities till I attained majority.

"I haven't done anything, Father," I replied, "except——" I gave them my version of the Yugoslav Movement and the demonstration.

"But why did you have to be in the demonstration?" said Mother, barely able to keep back her tears.

"Because my friend Yanko Radin was in it," I said.

"And I suppose your friend Yanko Radin was in it," said Uncle Martin, "because you were in it."

Then we all smiled, even Father. They all felt, no doubt, that it was an outrage for Austrian soldiers to ride down and kill Slovenian students, no matter what we had done or tried to do.

"What do you think you will do now?" asked Father.

I hesitated. I almost said, bluntly, that I wanted to go to America, but then changed my mind and said, instead, "I don't know, Father."

Mother said: "Uncle Martin thinks that maybe, if the Lord is willing, with the aid of some of the reverend priests here in the city whom he knows, he can get you admitted into the Jesuit School, so that even if you have been expelled from the government school you won't lose any time."

The Jesuit School! A vague shudder went through me.

"Would you like that, son?" said Father, gruffly.

Mother looked at me imploringly. Her smile was irresistible. Obviously, she wanted me to say yes. "Then you would be a priest, surely," she said.

I shivered again.

I said, "I don't know, Father." I tried not to look at Mother, "I ——"

"You don't know what?" snapped Father.

Then Uncle Martin said: "Let me explain it all to you, my boy. You know where the Jesuit School is, don't you?"

"Yes, Uncle," I said.

The Jesuit School was in the most ancient part of

30

Lublyana. It was immediately behind the Jesuit Church; indeed, it was a part of it. All the buildings were over six hundred years old, inclosed by a high, thick wall, which was black with grime and age. Here and there the wall was crumbling. In spots the stones were covered with bright-green moss. I had been inside the Jesuit Church a few times. I had entered it from curiosity. It was a dim, damp, musty edifice. The atmosphere in it had made me shudder. Once, when I had gone in, I had seen a group of boys—students in the Jesuit School—dressed in uniform robes, kneeling in a semicircle around the main altar, chanting prayers.

"I have friends in the Jesuit Order," Uncle Martin went on, "and, as your mother has said, I think I can induce them to use their influence in your behalf. I believe I can convince them that you are a good boy and a serious, diligent student in spite of what has just happened. Only exceptional boys who wish to dedicate themselves to God are taken in. In other words, it will be an honor to you and your parents, and to myself as your uncle, should you be accepted. . . . Besides, your father will no longer have to pay your expenses while you are being educated. You will be provided with everything by the institution— food, shelter, clothing, books, *et cetera*. Of course, as you probably know, the students never leave the school; they never come into the outside world until they are ordained. In your case, since now you are only in the third year of *Gymnasium*, it means that you won't come out of the institution for nine or ten years. But your father and mother, of course, and myself, will be allowed to come to see you on certain days. . . . Understand?"

"Yes, Uncle Martin."

Mother smiled to me again. "I'll come to see you as often as possible," she said.

I looked at her. Then at Father. Then at Uncle Martin. There was a long silence. All sorts of thoughts flashed through my mind. The Jesuit School—that would be like going to jail for nine or ten years! I had no coherent anti-religious views, as I recall, but I instinctively rebelled against spending a number of years within the walls of the Jesuit institution. I thought of America . . . Peter Molek . . . Yanko Radin . . . Yanko's brother Steve, who was in America. . . .

"Well?" said Father. In his eyes I was a *spriden student*—a "ruined student." Now I was not good for anything unless I went into the Jesuit School. The government schools were barred to me, and I was useless for work on the farm.

Mother's looks and smiles implored me.

Uncle Martin said: "If you want to enter, I shall go to see my friends among the Jesuit fathers at once, and next week, or in ten days, you may continue your studies. Shall I go?"

"Yes," I said. "Thank you, Uncle."

Whereupon Mother burst into tears, she was so happy. She hugged me and then held my face in her hands, looking at me for a long time, as she used to when I was smaller. For a moment, loving her and thinking how beautiful she looked in her simple way, I was glad that I had consented to go into the Jesuit institution.

VI

All this occurred about the middle of November, 1913.

I went home to Blato. There, waiting to be notified, through Uncle Martin, whether or not I was acceptable to the Jesuit fathers, I began to have attacks of deep regret for having consented to enter the Jesuit School. Nine— ten years! I understood that there were gardens and playgrounds within the Jesuit walls, but I would see no fields or mountains or forests in all that time. Could I change my mind? Hardly. Mother would be hurt. Father would rage. Uncle Martin had already gone to so much trouble to get me admitted. He was sure the Jesuits would take me in; there were just some formalities that required a few days.

Miserable, I roamed through the barren autumn fields and woods outside the village.

I talked with Peter Molek, but I noticed that, since he had heard that I might be going to the Jesuits, he spoke less freely to me. However, he told me that his health had improved so much in the last three and a half years (and he unquestionably looked much better) that he was thinking of returning to America. He had some friends in Pennsylvania and elsewhere, who, he believed, would send him money for passage back.

"I think I belong there," he said. "I am grateful to Blato for giving me back my health which I lost in America, but—" He shrugged his shoulders. I suppose he thought that I understood.

The wild idea to go to the United States possessed me strongly once more. Peter Molek was returning there! Why couldn't I go with him? . . . America! . . . The word and the meaning of the word, rich with the things I had heard of the country, pulsated in my brain.

VII

Finally, one day word came from the city that I was acceptable to the Jesuits. I was to come to Lublyana at once.

My parents and Uncle Martin were very happy. Perhaps it was all for the better, they philosophized, that I had been expelled from the government *Gymnasium*. Living in student boarding-houses in the city, they said, I had been exposed to the influences of bad companions; now, in the Jesuit institution, I would be safe; my immortal soul would be carefully guarded and developed for the service and glory of the Lord. Of course, what appealed to Father most of all was the fact that thereafter my education would not cost him a penny. This, excusably, was no small consideration in his mind.

Mother smiled and nodded when Uncle Martin remarked that under the benevolent auspices of the Jesuit priests I would keep out of mischief; that eventually I would get used to living in the institution; that I would not be lonely because I would always have plenty to study; and that the Jesuits were famous throughout the world for their learning, their saintly asceticism, and their accomplishments in the cause of God.

The next morning Father and I were on the way to Lublyana. In the train Father tried to make conversation, but I was unwilling to talk. I looked out of the window at the passing autumn landscape. A cold, clammy sensation held me. Those high walls and the dim, musty old church! My whole being rebelled against spending ten years in the institution. My mind whirled.

In the city, Father, wanting to be nice to me, despite my sullenness, took me to a wineshop where peasants from Lower Carniola were wont to stop to feed their horses and refresh themselves. He ordered food and a bottle of wine. The place was full of better-to-do peasants, several of them mildly drunk.

Father said it was a great honor indeed for me to be accepted by the Jesuits. I was a lucky boy. But I scarcely heard him and barely tasted the food and the wine.

Then, in the middle of the meal, following a blind and sudden impulse, I rose from the table and mumbled that

34

I had to go out. Father naturally assumed that I was going to the lavatory and would return in a few minutes.

I paused in the courtyard. There was a good, healthy smell about the place; a mingling of the odors of wine and fresh-cooked food from within, and of horses and dung, hay and oats, and tobacco smoke and peasant bodies. A newly arrived team of horses neighed exuberantly at the prospect of being fed. It was a nice day. The autumn sun shone brightly. Peasants were feeding their animals, and chewing, smoking, spitting, joking, laughing, discussing their businesses in the city. They were big solid men from the fields and the woods, valley men and hill men, with strong, hard bodies, brownfaced; simple, matter-of-fact fellows like my father. They talked to their horses, reproached and chided them gently for spilling their oats or scattering hay on the ground, and affectionately slapped the animals' rumps and stroked them under the bellies.

My mind was made up. I would not go into the Jesuit School! Let Father sit in the wineshop. He was wrong. Everything in me insisted that I was not for the priesthood. I felt hard inside, and a cruel feeling of satisfaction welled up within me. Let him sit in there!

I slowly sauntered across the yard, among horses and wagons and peasants. A horse flipped me with his tail.

I came into the street, and there, turning the corner of the inn, I began to run as fast as my legs could carry me. Having run out of breath, I started to walk at a fast pace. I was headed out of the city, taking the highway that goes through Lower Carniola, through fields and forests and frequent villages.

No more school for me. I was going to America. I did not know how, but I knew that I would go.

35

VIII

In Lublyana, Father searched for me all afternoon.

I walked but a few kilometers on the highway, when a peasant came along in his wagon and gave me a ride all the way to Blato. His destination was some distance beyond our village.

It was already dark when I arrived home. Father had returned by train an hour or two before.

The moment I appeared a storm broke loose. Father burst into a rage and wanted to beat me, but Mother begged him to leave me alone. She told me to go to my room in the attic.

I went. Presently Mother brought me some supper. She was hurt, upset, and sad, but tried to be as sweet to me as ever.

"Eat," she said. Then she left me alone.

As I ate, Father was slamming the doors below, and the younger children, frightened by his anger, were crying. I could also hear Father shout at Mother, who was trying to pacify him.

After a while Mother returned to my room.

"But what do you want to do, son?" she asked me, quietly.

"I want to go to America."

She looked at me startled, frightened.

"Don't worry, Mother," I said. "Nothing will happen to me in America." I thought of Yanko Radin and our talk about the United States. "For some people, I know, America is a bad place, but I can take care of myself there."

"You mustn't go to work in the mines—underground," she said.

"Of course not." I saw that she was already willing to let me go.

"But how are you going?"

"Maybe I'll go with Peter Molek," I said. "He is going back, now that his health is so much better. Perhaps Father will loan me the money for the passage. I'll send it back to him from America."

Mother was silent, looking at me. Fatalist that she was, she probably thought to herself that there was no way of stopping me; I seemed to know what I wanted. Now I would never be a priest; and she—no doubt—had told other women in Blato that I might become one. She was disappointed, chagrined. But, peasant-like, she recovered almost at once.

Late that night, as I lay sleepless in the attic, I heard Father and Mother talk below.

In the morning everything was quiet again. The storm was over. Father and Mother bore their parental misfortune with the unconscious dignity of simple people. The effect upon them of my expulsion from school and my subsequent balking at going into the Jesuit School was essentially the same as had been the effect of a severe hailstorm early the previous summer, which, in a few minutes late one afternoon, had ruined most of our growing potatoes and young corn. On that occasion I had seen Mother stare at the swirls of hailstones beating upon the young plants. She had wept and sprinkled holy water from the doorway, while Father, standing by her side, had prayed and cursed in the same breath. But then the storm had passed and in a few minutes the sun had come out, and Mother had ceased weeping and Father had stopped praying and cursing. A half-hour afterward they had walked in the fields, inspecting the ruins. I had walked with them. Suddenly, Mother's sad face had lighted up. "Look," she had said, "here the hail did almost no harm. It passed over. This will grow yet." She had smiled at Father, then at me. "Yes," Father had agreed, "this will grow again." . . .

When I came down that morning, Mother said, simply:

"Father says he will give you the money and you may go to America, and God bless you, son."

CHAPTER III

I Go to America

THE *Niagara* sailed from Le Havre, France. She was an old ship, rather small, carrying mostly immigrants. Most of the steerage passengers were Poles, Slovaks, Czechs, Croatians, Slovenians, and Bosnians, with a sprinkling of Jews, Greeks, Turks, Germans, and Austrian Italians; young men and middle-aged men, women and children of all ages, some of them wearing colorful native costumes— all of them headed for the Land of Promise. A few of them were returning to America from visits to their old home- lands. Most of these traveled second-class.

Peter Molek and I were the only two Slovenians aboard not traveling steerage. Molek had feared that the bad food and lack of ventilation "down below" might play the devil with his health again, and my father, in his pride, had then insisted on buying me a second-class ticket, too. Molek and I occupied a tiny room together.

The first day on the ocean I had a heavy feeling in my midriff. Through my mind went loose thoughts of home, of Yanko Radin, of Blato and Lublyana, of everything that had lately happened to me.

The best part of the trip, aside from the thrill of being on the ocean for the first time, were the lessons that Peter Molek gave me in the meaning and pronounciation of American words and phrases.

The day before we reached New York Harbor, Molek said to me in English: "You'll be all right in America, even if it is a jungle," which I understood with but slight help from him. He added in Slovenian: "You are going to America for excitement and adventure. Don't fear; you will not be disappointed; you will find plenty of both."

I did not know what to say to that. The heavy feeling in my midriff had left me completely. I ceased thinking of people and things in the Old Country.

II

The morning of December 30, 1913, in New York, was clear and cold. There was snow on shore.

Molek and I were on deck as we passed the Statue of Liberty, the size of which momentarily impressed me. My gaze strained toward the skyline of lower Manhattan. Molek was talking to me, but I remember little of what he said. I was quivering all over.

"Those are the buildings," said Molek. "There—in the mist—is the Woolworth Tower. See?"

I nodded. I was in a chaos of visual sensations. I experienced a curious elation when the *Niagara* blew a passing-signal to a vessel ahead of us. I wanted to yell as loud as that whistle.

Now and then I glanced at the noisy, picturesque, garlicky crowd on the steerage deck: people of perhaps a dozen nationalities milling among the capstans and steam-hissing winches, pushing toward the rails, straining and stretching to catch a glimpse of the new country, of the city; lifting their children, even their infants, to give them a view of the Statue of Liberty; women weeping for joy, men falling on their knees in thanksgiving, and children screaming, wailing, dancing.

We docked somewhere in the East River, and I began to hear the distant rumble of the city's traffic.

Near by, too, I saw the great span of Brooklyn Bridge.

It looked huge and superb against the clear winter sky, with vessels passing under it. Steel! There was steel all about.

III

I had written Stefan ("Steve") Radin, brother of my late friend Yanko, whose address in Brooklyn I happened to have, that I was due in New York on December 30th, and would he meet me on Ellis Island, which Peter Molek had told me was the clearing-house for immigrants? In my letter I explained that I had witnessed the killing of his brother and had, as a result of my participation in the demonstration with Yanko, been imprisoned and expelled from school. . . .

From the ship we were transferred on a lighter to Ellis Island, where I received a telegram from Steve that he was coming for me the next afternoon, when he had learned from the immigration authorities I was to be released, assuming I was found admissible.

The day I spent on Ellis Island was an eternity. Rumors were current among immigrants of several nationalities that some of us would be refused admittance into the United States and sent back to Europe. For several hours I was in a cold sweat on this account, although, so far as I knew, all my papers were in order, and sewed away in the lining of my jacket were twenty-five dollars in American currency—the minimum amount required by law to be in the possession of every immigrant before entering the country. Then, having rationalized away some of these fears, I gradually worked up a panicky feeling that I might develop measles or smallpox, or some other such disease. I had heard that several hundred sick immigrants were quarantined on the island.

The first night in America I spent, with hundreds of

41

other recently arrived immigrants, in an immense hall
with tiers of narrow iron-and-canvas bunks, four deep. I
was assigned a top bunk. Unlike most of the steerage immigrants, I had no bedding with me, and the blanket
which some one threw at me was too thin to be effective
against the blasts of cold air that rushed in through the
open windows; so that I shivered, sleepless, all night, listening to snores and dream-monologues in perhaps a dozen
different languages.

The bunk immediately beneath mine was occupied by a
Turk, who slept with his turban wound around his head.
He was tall, thin, dark, bearded, hollow-faced, and hook-
nosed. At peace with Allah, he snored all night, producing
a thin wheezing sound, which occasionally, for a moment
or two, took on a deeper note.

I thought how curious it was that I should be spending
a night in such proximity to a Turk, for Turks were tra-
ditional enemies of Balkan peoples, including my own
nation. For centuries Turks had forayed into Slovenian
territory. Now here I was, trying to sleep directly above
a Turk, with only a sheet of canvas between us.

Soon after daybreak I heard him suddenly bestir himself. A moment later he began to mutter something in
Turkish, and clambered out of his bed in a hurry. He had
some difficulty extricating himself, for there was not more
than a foot between his and my bunk, and in his violent
haste rammed a sharp knee in the small of my back. I
almost yelled out in pain.

Safely on the floor, the Mohammedan began to search
feverishly in a huge sack which contained his belongings,
and presently pulled out a narrow, longish rug and carefully spread it on the floor between two tiers of bunks.

This done, he stretched himself several times, rising on
his toes, cleared his throat, rubbed his beard, adjusted his

42

turban, which was slightly askew; whereupon, oblivious
of my wide-eyed interest, he suddenly crashed to his knees
on the floor with a great thud. Next he lifted his long
arms ceilingward and began to bow toward the east,
touching the carpet with his brow, the while mumbling his
sun-up prayer to Allah.

At first I did not know what to think of the Mussul-
man's doings. Then, slowly realizing what it was all about,
the scene struck me as immensely funny. Sleepy and cold
though I was, I had to pull the blanket over my head, lest
the worshiper hear me laughing.

IV

Late in the afternoon of the last day of 1913 I was examined for entry into the United States, with about a
hundred other immigrants who had come on the *Niagara.*

The examiner sat bureaucratically—very much in the
manner of officials in the Old Country—behind a great
desk, which stood upon a high platform. On the wall above
him was a picture of George Washington. Beneath it was
an American flag.

The official spoke a bewildering mixture of many Slavic
languages. He had a stern voice and a sour visage. I had
difficulty understanding some of his questions.

At a small table, piled with papers, not far from the
examiner's desk, was a clerk who called out our names,
which, it seemed, were written on the long sheets of paper
before him.

When my turn came, toward dusk, I was asked the
usual questions. When and where was I born? My nationality? Religion? Was I a legitimate child? What were the
names of my parents? Was I an imbecile? Was I a prostitute? (I assume that male and female immigrants were

subjected to the same questionnaire.) Was I an ex-convict? A criminal? Why had I come to the United States?

I was questioned as to the state of my finances and I produced the required twenty-five dollars.

What did I expect to do in the United States? I replied that I hoped to get a job. What kind of job? I didn't know; any kind of job.

The inspector grunted vaguely. "And who is this person, Stefan—Stefan Radin—who is meeting you here?"

I answered that Stefan Radin was the brother of a friend of mine, now dead.

Then the inspector waved me out of his presence and the clerk motioned me to go back and sit on one of the benches near by.

I waited another hour. It got dark and the lights were turned on in the room.

Finally, after dozens of other immigrants had been questioned, Steve Radin was called into the examining-room and asked, in English, to state his relationship to me.

He answered, of course, that he was not related to me at all.

Whereupon the inspector fairly pounced upon me, speaking the dreadful botch of Slavic languages. What did I mean by lying to him? He said a great many other things which I did not understand. I did comprehend, however, his threat to return me to the Old Country. It appeared that America had no room for liars: America was glad to welcome to its shores only decent, honest, truthful people.

My heart pounded.

Finally it occurred simultaneously to me and to Steve Radin that the man must be laboring under some misapprehension. And, truly, before another minute elapsed

44

it turned out that the clerk had made a mistake by entering on my paper that I had declared Stefan Radin was my uncle. How the mistake had occurred I do not know; perhaps the clerk had confused my questionnaire form with some one else's.

Finally, perceiving the error, the examiner's face formed in a grimace and, waving his hand in a casual gesture, he ordered me released.

Steve Radin picked up my bag and, in the confusion, I barely remembered to say good-by to Peter Molek, who was going to Pennsylvania.

I was weak in the knees and just managed to walk out of the room, then downstairs and onto the ferryboat. I had been shouted at, denounced as a liar by an official of the United States on my second day in the country, before a roomful of people, including Steve Radin, whom, so far, I had merely glimpsed.

But the weakness in my knees soon passed. I laughed, perhaps a bit hysterically, as the little Ellis Island ferryboat bounded over the rough, white-capped waters of the bay toward the Battery.

Steve Radin gaped at me. Then he smiled.

I was in New York—in America.

PART TWO

Greenhorns

The names of some persons, places, and newspapers in the ensuing chapters are disguised.

The stories of certain men and women I have known in America I record with greater detail than is usual in autobiographical books. The reason that I make so much of other people in my personal narrative is that these persons were definitely a part—indeed, one of the most important parts—of my American experience. At various times they all deeply interested me and, directly or indirectly, did things to me, or rather to my ideas about America. Through them and their stories, which I learned in most cases without intending to write them, I experienced—somewhat vicariously, it is true, but nevertheless keenly—certain phases of American life. My life in America has been largely an adventure in understanding, and these people—foreign-born and native American—and their histories have been a vital factor in that adventure.

CHAPTER IV

Steve Radin

I

WHEN I came to the United States, Steve Radin was not quite twenty years old. He had been in America three and a half years.

He was unlike his brother Yanko; rather short, compactly made, with a large torso and thin, wiry legs on which he moved with springy ease. He had a darkish, lively, attractive face. His small brown eyes flashed alertness. His manner was somewhat hectic, self-conscious, self-dramatizing, amusing.

Yanko had told me that Steve had run away from school in Trieste and stowed away on a New York-bound barkentine. When I came to the United States, Steve himself told me (along with his experiences since his arrival in America) that he had left Trieste on a sudden impulse, after having listened for two years to Yugoslav, Italian, and German seamen talk of America. Their talk, I imagine, was similar to that of the *Amerikanci* I had heard in Blato.

II

The barkentine (as Steve told me) was an old, slow vessel. She sailed under the Austrian flag, but her crew were all Dalmatians from the Adriatic coast. Her cargo were Croatian *rakija* (a species of brandy) and Balkan prunes.

When Stefan was discovered, the second day out, the boatswain made him work on deck. Soon his fine student's clothes were in tatters. Before reaching New York Har-

49

bor, seven weeks later, he sold his watch, which was his sole possession of value, and purchased from members of the crew odd pieces of clothing, including a suit of blue dungarees slightly too large for him, a tiny English sailor's cap much too small for his head, and a pair of clumsy Breton wooden shoes. Heaven only knows how these things happened to be on a Dalmatian vessel.

Thus attired, before daybreak the morning after the barkentine's arrival in America, Steve—he had already been called Steve by sailors at sea who knew a little English—slipped off the ship with a dollar in his pocket. The vessel was moored somewhere in Brooklyn.

All morning he walked in the streets of Brooklyn, not a little confused by the traffic and turmoil. His wooden shoes clattering on the pavement added to the noise, and passers-by, amused, paused to grin at him. This suffused him with a pleasant glow. People seemed very kind in America.

The fact that he was a stranger in a great city lay lightly on his consciousness. In the afternoon he came to a large open space amid buildings near a railroad, in the center of which stood an immense tent decorated with flags and banners. A circus. The place teemed with workmen and onlookers. Steve tried to ask for a job, but no one connected with the show appeared to understand Slavic, German, or Italian, while he as yet knew no English beyond a half-dozen seagoing words he had picked up on the barkentine from Dalmatian sailors who had made previous trips to the United States.

Steve ate, then bought himself a ticket to the circus. In the tent, he sat behind a thick pole, but by stretching his neck he missed no part of the performance. He was most fascinated by the clowns and the enthusiastic response that they evoked from the public.

After the show, he walked around some more. Now and then he caught himself making funny faces and doing clownish steps with his clattery wooden shoes. People paused to look at him; some laughed, others seemed mildly perturbed. For a few minutes he collected a crowd, but then a colossus in a blue uniform came and dispersed it, and told him to go on.

It was dark, a light drizzle began to fall, and Steve spent his last quarter for supper. At first he did not mind the rain; he scarcely noticed it. So far his experiences in America had been very wonderful. But presently the rain soaked through his rough dungarees, and his wooden shoes got full of water. The season was mid-autumn, and he began to feel cold and tired and a little afraid.

The ship's whistles and the foghorns blew in the harbor, and Steve's thoughts went back to the barkentine, to Trieste, and even back to his village in Istria. He stood in the doorways and walked around all night. He passed bakeries in the morning, and the odors of fresh bread caused saliva to flood his mouth. From a milk-wagon, while the milkman had run into a house, he stole a bottle of milk and drank it.

At dawn Steve returned to the waterfront. Through the dense veil of raindrops he glimpsed the gray outline of the Manhattan skyline across the river. It looked dismal, vast, and magnificent. It frightened Steve.

Finally he found the dock where he had left the barkentine, but the ship was gone. He almost burst into tears.

He walked the length of the dock, and on the other end of it came upon a youth who evidently was a sailor and a little older than himself. Steve shivered in his rain-soaked garb; the other boy was dry, buttoned up to his neck in a German sailor's water-proof jacket. He leaned against the wall of a shed, out of the rain, reading a New York German newspaper.

"*Guten Morgen!*" ventured Steve, hopefully. He spoke passable German.

The young sailor returned the greeting matter-of-factly, then, after looking at Steve a moment, an amused grin lighted up his stolid German features. Steve's disorganized spirit promptly began to collect itself.

Steve explained that he was from Trieste, Austria, a sailor on the barkentine which had been moored at this dock yesterday, when he had last seen her; that he had got lost in the city and, in consequence, failed to return before the ship left.

The young German understood Steve's plight and, smiling as though it were all a mild and commonplace joke, suggested that he come with him to a sailors' boarding-house near by, adding that he was putting up there himself. It was run by a German woman who, he scarcely doubted, would take Steve in, regardless of the fact that at the moment he had no money. She was a good soul, and would wait till he got a job and was in position to pay her.

The idea appealed to Steve and, adding that he really did not care if he ever saw the barkentine or not, went with the young man, who said his name was Karl Zimmermann, recently of Hamburg, in America not quite three weeks. Karl explained that he had jumped his last ship because he wanted to live in America, and later, penniless, strayed into this boarding-house. Then Steve told him the truth of his adventure, too; that he was not actually a sailor on the barkentine, but had come over as a stowaway. He and Karl became friends even before they reached the boarding-house.

Mrs. Schmidt, of the boarding-house, was an excessively kind German woman, a widow, and immediately took a liking to Steve.

By and by Steve and Karl got jobs together as deck-hands on a small passenger steamer running between New York and Boston. They worked on it for a year and a half, with Mrs. Schmidt's house in Brooklyn as their head-quarters, where they received their mail from the Old Country.

When the ship was at the dock overnight, either in New York or in Boston, Steve and Karl usually went to see a motion picture. Those were the days of slapstick comedies and cowboy melodramas. They developed a taste for striped shirts and fancy ties, the kind that they saw the swells wear in the movies. They wanted to lose no time in getting Americanized, and thought that to dress in American fashion was the initial and most important step in that direction.

The kind Mrs. Schmidt thought they were good lads; only she hoped they would settle down and work at steady jobs ashore, so that some day, perhaps, one of them would marry her daughter Mathilde, who was about their age and a nice, competent girl. But Steve and Karl—and Steve more than Karl—were restless young men in an un-settled, dynamic new world. Steve was rapidly learning the American language and ways. He read American newspapers and *Narodni Glas*, published in New York. The movies fascinated him more every month. Most of them presented American life west of the Hudson—stir-ring life in the far West.

One day, a year and a half after their first meeting, Steve and Karl strolled on the dock in New York where their ship was tied. They were killing time, discussing the last Western bad-man thriller they had seen in a Boston film-house, two nights before.

There was a pause in their discourse, when, of a sudden, Steve stopped before Karl. "Say," he said, characteristically, on the impulse of the moment, "let's quit this job and go West." By now they both spoke only English as they knew it. Steve, having had a little more education in the Old Country than Karl, handled the language somewhat better than his friend.

"All right," grinned Karl. "Ve go Vest, Steve. Dat's O.K. mit me."

They quit their jobs that afternoon, each receiving thirty-two dollars in wages. They went to a costume-shop in Manhattan and bought two large cowboy hats. Steve figured that when one went West one might as well look like a Westerner.

But that evening, before starting West, they "picked up" a couple of girls who had made eyes at them, took them to a restaurant for supper, after which the girls suggested that they go walking on Broadway. They laughed at the boys' hats and at Steve's tales of life in the West. He spoke of the great herds of buffalo that roamed the vast open spaces of Texas and Oklahoma. He boasted of his and Karl's marksmanship, bareback riding, and other Wild Western accomplishments he had seen in the pictures. The girls giggled at his and Karl's peculiar English. Steve explained that that was how people spoke in the West.

Suddenly, walking on crowded Broadway, the girls excused themselves—they had another date—and they disappeared in a Subway entrance.

A few minutes later Steve and Karl discovered that except for a few nickels apiece they had no money. The charmers were a couple of pickpockets, specializing, perhaps, on just such victims as Steve and Karl.

After the first flush of anger, Steve laughed. "We go

54

West, anyhow," he said. "We hop train. See?" He had
seen hobos in the movies.

But Karl was more prudent. He induced Steve to give
up the idea of going West and return to Mrs. Schmidt's
till they found new jobs.

Mrs. Schmidt was glad to have them back.

Before long Karl got a job on a coal-barge and Steve
found work in a Brooklyn shipyard.

III

The next two years of Steve's life were uneventful. He
worked ten hours a day. He became a rigger, and made
what for one so young was considered good money. The
process of his Americanization went on. Once a boss in the
shipyard referred to him half-disparagingly as a Hunky,
whereupon Steve silently resolved to learn the language
and the manners of the country, so that no one would be
able to tell him from a native American.

He went to the movies twice a week, and read the *New
York American.* He wore better clothes from season to
season, and occasionally stepped out with the fellows of
the neighborhood—most of them American-born or else
Americanized immigrants—for a Saturday night's good
time. Now and then, after he had seen some specially
thrilling film, he still thought of going West. Off and on
he was tempted to join the army or the navy. But one
thing or another held him in Brooklyn.

One of the things was that he was getting rather fond
of Mathilde. He took her to the movies. Infrequently, he
thought of matrimony. He was strong and made a man's
wages, and his job was a steady job; while Mathilde,
whom he saw daily, was a fine girl, with a healthy round
body, a mass of pale-golden hair, a pair of soft blue
eyes; not excessively pretty, as Steve observed in his

55

thoughts, but nice and plump, kind-hearted like her mother, and an eager worker, handy around the house; the kind of girl that would make a good wife to a workingman. Also, she was ever ready to admire Steve's neckties and socks; and when he acted for her and her mother, as he frequently did, imitating Charlie Chaplin and other movie comedians, she was convulsed with appreciative laughter. All this tended to sentimentalize Steve to the verge of a proposal. . . . But he hesitated. He did not want to get tied down. . . .

One day (about six months before I arrived in the United States) during the lunch hour at the shipyard Steve involved himself in an argument with another workman, a Dane by the name of Oluf Tallaksen. (When Steve told me of the incident, he did not remember what the argument was about; no doubt, about some trivial matter.)

"Aw, hell," said Oluf when Steve obstinately maintained his position in the tiff, "you're nothin' but a greenhorn! A Hunky. You don't know nothin'."

At the time "Battling" Nelson, a Dane, was at the height of his pugilistic career, which caused many Danes in America, including Oluf Tallaksen, to be tough and pugnacious.

"If I'm a greenhorn," returned Steve, sore, but holding himself in check, "you got me beat. There's nothing so thick as a thick squarehead."

Oluf turned pink with anger. He had been in the United States nearly ten years and had the natural Nordic pride. "Greenhorn," to say nothing of "thick squarehead," was the worst name one could call him.

Steve and Oluf exchanged a few more insults and finally mixed in a fist fight. Oluf was nearly a head taller than Steve, and much heavier, but, to his own great surprise, Steve landed a wallop that knocked Oluf senseless. After Oluf revived, he was so weak and groggy that he had to knock off work for the afternoon.

Steve became a hero in the yard.

Oluf avoided him for a few days; then, a week or so after the incident, came to him and said, casual-like: "Say, you're some fighter, Steve. I tell the cock-eyed world! You pack a wallop, boy—yes, sir! Never been hit like you hit me in all my life. Ever thought of gettin' in the ring?"

Steve shook his head.

Oluf continued to admire Steve's style of fighting. Finally he proposed that Steve become a fighter and let him manage him.

"I tell you," said Oluf, "you can become a crackeryack of a boxer. Battlin' Nelson is a countryman of mine, but he ain't got nothin' on you. You're a crackeryack!"

Having licked him, Steve, of course, had no grudge against Oluf, and after a while he said: "O.K.," and put himself into Oluf's hands.

For weeks then Steve skipped rope, ate raw meat, ran around the block from ten to fifty times every morning before going to work, until one day Oluf came to him with the news that he had just matched him with an "easy one."

Oluf said: "You know, you're a crackeryack, Steve, but I don't want you to tackle too gooda guy the first time, because if he licks you bad, maybe then you lose confidence in yourself; and you're too good to ruin. See? You yoost leave it to me, eh, Steve?"

"O.K.," said Steve.

"You know, Steve," Oluf went on, "a fighter's manayer he's got to use his head!" He informed Steve that the fight was to come off as a preliminary number, week after

57

next at the bouts in the Saturday Night Club, near Williamsburg Bridge in Brooklyn, a hangout for dock-workers and waterfront toughs and gangsters. The Club was run by a small-time politician, Joe Riley by name, who was a cog in the Tammany Hall machine, in connection with his saloon downstairs. "I told Yoe Riley," Oluf went on, "that you was a crackeryack. See?" . . .

On the night of the battle Steve stepped into the ring at the Saturday Night Club and the referee introduced him to the "easy one." The "easy one" was an Irish gorilla, even bigger than Oluf—a stevedore used to rolling barrels on the docks ten hours a day.

The purse was five dollars, the winner getting three, the loser two—and, to make a long and cruel story short and mild, when Steve came to, late in the evening, in one of the back rooms of Joe Riley's saloon, some one handed him two dollars, and he learned that he had been knocked out in the first round.

Oluf sat beside Steve, buying him drinks and talking about what a "ham" the big Irishman was. "If he whipped you, Stevey-boy," he said, "it yoost is hard luck, that's all; and maybe, too, because you didn't use the right tictacs. I yoost *know*, Stevey-boy, that if you mix with the big stewbum again, and you listen to me like I tell you, and use a little science in your punches and footwork, you'll make hash of 'im. See? You're a crackeryack fighter. Ain't he there, Yohn?"—turning to a countryman of his, who readily agreed with him.

Oluf talked on and bought Steve more drinks until, not quite himself, Steve got sore at the Irishman, who sat with his fellow barrel-rollers in the next room, spending the three dollars, and then and there challenged him to a return bout next Saturday night or any other night.

Joe Riley signed them up again; and, to make another

long and tragic story short and not too sad, Steve once more collected two dollars out of five.

He began to suspect that something was wrong with Oluf's "dope." Finally it occurred to Steve that the Dane had "framed" him, to get even for the beating he had given him at the shipyard six weeks before.

The fighter and the manager parted company. But the ring appealed to Steve. He liked to have a hallful of people watch him dance around, punching his opponent and getting punched.

Joe Riley took a liking to Steve and let him fight at the Club every other week, and before long Steve became known in the Williamsburg Bridge neighborhood as a pretty fair "ham-an'-egger." He became popular. With his big chest and short, skinny legs, he looked funny in the ring. Sometimes, too, when he figured that his opponent was an easy victim, and occasionally even if he happened to be getting the worst of the bout, he used to clown in the ring, and the fans—stevedores, petty gangsters, sailors, shipyard-workers, and their girl friends— roared and screamed, which meant more to Steve than getting the decision and collecting the greater part of the purse. The fans liked him. He became locally famous as "The Clown."

It was at this point in Steve's career that I arrived in America.

CHAPTER V

New Year's Eve in New York

I

ON THE ferry from Ellis Island to the Battery, I told Steve Radin of the students' demonstration in Lublyana two months previous, in which his brother Yanko had been killed. Steve listened, but, obviously, was not deeply interested.

"Yes," he said, "I read about it in *Narodni Glas*. It certainly was a terrible thing to do, wasn't it, to shoot into a crowd of boys like that." But he spoke without passion. What I said and what he said about things in the Old Country evidently had no real, immediate, or personal significance in his heart and mind.

For a minute I felt outraged—or perhaps I should say that I thought I was outraged. After all, I said to myself, he and Yanko had been flesh-and-blood brothers. But then, curiously, I ceased to be provoked by his indifference. I realized that, albeit Yanko and I had been the closest of friends, his death and nearly everything else that had happened during my life in Carniola did not mean much to me at the moment, either. I was in New York, in America. Although I vividly remembered everything I had seen and experienced there, the Old Country now was very remote in my feelings. All my thoughts and sensations about it were becoming abstracted. They were not unlike a clearly remembered dream from which one awakened an hour ago. America, the immense, awesome America, was beating, pounding on my senses. Even my mother and father, as I realized a little later, had sud-

60

denly become almost irrelevant, without significance, to me.

And the same, I supposed, was true of Steve; only more so, because he had been in the United States longer. His dead brother was perhaps scarcely more than an abstraction in his mind and in his emotional system.

We dropped the subject.

II

It was growing dark as the ferryboat neared Manhattan. Thousands of windows in the tall office-buildings on lower Broadway and along the Battery were lighted. In the sky over the harbor was the gray afterglow of a winter's sundown.

"What do you think of it, eh?" said Steve, grinning, waving a hand at Manhattan. The expression of awe on my face amused him.

"I don't know," I said.

We reached the ferry slip, and for half a minute I interestedly watched the men at the chain-wheels on the dock making the boat fast.

Outside the ferryhouse I asked Steve, "Where are we going?"

"Are you hungry?" he asked.

"No," I said, although on Ellis Island I had scarcely eaten anything.

"But *I* am," laughed Steve. "We eat first. Then, I guess, I'll take you to where I live"—to Mrs. Schmidt's. "I got a room there for you. Of course, you won't have to stay unless you like it."

It was about five-thirty and most of the lunch-rooms along the Battery were filled.

"I guess we would best go to a Croatian place I know

61

near here," said Steve. "It is a saloon with a restaurant in back. Would you like that?"

"Yes; all right," I said in English, and laughed, self-consciously.

Steve looked at me, and laughed, too.

From the Battery we walked up lower Broadway, crowded with home-going office-workers. Steve insisted on carrying my bag.

I felt a sudden rumble under the sidewalk.

"What is that?" I asked.

"Subway," said Steve, in English.

"What?"

"Underground railway," he explained, in Slovenian.

Peter Molek, apparently, had forgotten to tell me about the Subways of New York. I had never heard of them before. A block or two later I saw crowds of people, all in terrific haste, going down steps into a hole over which there was a blue light.

I caught sounds of their talk, which I did not understand, except now and then the phrase, "All right," or some word that Molek had taught me on the ship.

"All right, all right," I repeated the phrase, to Steve's amusement. I felt a delight in uttering English words.

Steve told me the names of various streets and structures: Wall Street, which Molek had often mentioned to me . . . Trinity Church, which I could barely discern in the half-light . . . the Singer Building . . . the Woolworth Building, off in the distance, hundreds of its windows aglow, making a queer checkerboard pattern of light and darkness against the dark sky. . . .

For minutes at a time, walking with Steve through the deep canyon of downtown Broadway, I hardly felt, saw, heard, or thought anything. I was a blank. The sensation of being in New York, in the midst of America's tallest

buildings, with trains thundering under my feet, was so
overwhelming.

III

The Croatian saloon-café where Steve took me for supper
was near a corner of Cortlandt and West Streets. Above
the saloon was a shabby hotel, under the same manage-
ment, for Yugoslav immigrants coming to America and
returning to the Old Country. In the vicinity were several
Slavic steamship agencies, which sent their customers to
the hotel to wait for the sailing dates. But in the wintertime comparatively few people came over or went back,
and this evening the place was poorly patronized, with
only seven or eight Croatians at the bar, shaking dice,
speaking a mixture of Croatian and English.

In the café, a room adjoining the barroom, only three
tables were occupied. A large music-box was grinding out
harsh, mechanical tunes. Steve and I ate, and he told me
some of the things about himself which I gave in the preceding chapter. We drank a few glasses of wine apiece,
and were in a high mood.

"Now," said Steve, "I'll show you New York. This is
New Year's Eve. There is nothing like it anywhere else.
You'll see—you'll hear!" He enjoyed himself talking to
me and watching my reactions to America. Being over his
greenhorn period, he felt infinitely superior to me.

We walked awhile in downtown New York. The city
was in a roar long before midnight. Firecrackers exploded
under my step. The truck-drivers tooted their horns. People in cabs blew whistles and trumpets, and yelled and
swung rattles out of windows. Overhead, here and there,
now and then, the "L" thundered, the wheels screeching
on the rails.

Some one knocked off my cap with a snowball.

Steve laughed at my momentary indignation. "Never mind," he said in English, which I understood; then continued in Slovenian: "This is New Year's Eve. It's all in fun. You don't want to wear that old cap here, anyhow. You are in America. You have twenty-five dollars; buy yourself a new cap and a suit of clothes." He was having a good time with me. I realized this, but did not mind it.

He took me into several big American saloons on and off Park Row. These were gorgeous places, lighted like cathedrals in the Old Country, only much livelier, and full of friendliness and hearty conversation, which I was dying to understand. Sleek, courteous, smiling men in spotless white moved briskly behind the bars. Here and there music-boxes operated full tilt; only they were better, less cacophonous than the one in the Croatian place. The brass cuspidors and footrails seemed almost too nice for their respective purposes. Bottles of all shapes and colors, most of them picturesquely labeled, were symmetrically arranged against huge mirrors, in which all this glory was brilliantly reflected. I was tall for my fourteen years and a half, and the bartenders had no reluctance in serving me drinks.

IV

Steve and I took the Third Avenue "L" and got off at Canal Street. Here the noise was even louder than downtown. The sidewalks teamed with boys exploding firecrackers, shouting, battling with snowballs.

Steve took me to a cheap Jewish clothing-store on Rivington Street. For fifteen dollars we bought a suit of clothes and a cap. I changed in the store.

"Now you look like an American," said the Jew, which Steve translated for me.

This pleased me very much. Outside, I stopped before

mirrors in store entrances to look at myself. I compared myself with Steve and the boys I saw in the streets. Steve laughed at me.

We went down Delancey Street. Here the sidewalks were jammed with strange humanity. I noticed the hunched-over, melancholy, bearded old men in long black overcoats. They walked slowly or stood passively against the walls, with indrawn looks in their eyes. Somehow they did not seem to belong here. "Old Jews," said Steve. But the young people along the sidewalks appeared to belong. Some of them manifested intense energy—American energy. They participated in the tumult of New Year's celebration. I imagined that probably they were the sons and daughters, or the grandsons and granddaughters of the old men.

My olfactory centers were assailed by an amalgamation of smells, most of them strange to me. The sidewalks were lined with pushcarts, and the peddlers, their bearded faces shining in the lurid light of acetylene lamps which fluttered above them, cried their wares in Yiddish and Yiddish-American. The pushcarts were piled with no end of things: cheap clothes, neckties, shoes, candy, needles and buttons, shoe-laces and shoe polish, pickles, fruit, vegetables. There were stands selling hot sweet potatoes and chestnuts.

On one of the pushcarts, besides apples and oranges, I noticed a pile of long yellow fruit. I remembered that I had seen the same fruit on stalls in Le Havre before sailing for America.

"What are those?" I asked Steve.

He laughed. "Bananas. Didn't you ever hear of bananas?" He bought a small bunch and handed me one.

I looked at it. I smelled it. Then I bit into it, skin and all.

Steve roared. "Peel it!" he cried. "Peel it! That's the skin! You greenhorn!"

I blushed and peeled the banana. Then, eating it and liking it, I laughed with Steve, who offered me more bananas.

We walked a little farther and boarded a street-car, which took us across an immense bridge. After crossing it, we rode a long time in Brooklyn, and Brooklyn was no less noisy than Manhattan.

I thought we were going to Mrs. Schmidt's boarding-house, but Steve said he had changed his mind; there was no hurry about going there, and my bag, which he still insisted on carrying, was not heavy. This was New Year's Eve and we should celebrate it in American fashion, even though I was but a greenhorn—and Steve laughed.

Somewhere in the Flushing section we got off the street-car and were presently in another Bohunk saloon. Its proprietor was a corpulent Slovenian, and his patrons were for the most part Slovenians, too.

Steve, since he was becoming a popular prize-fighter in Brooklyn, was rather well known in the local Slovenian "colony," and the minute we entered the saloon there was much eagerness along the entire length of the bar to treat us. "Come on, Steve! Come on! Have one on me, you and your young friend! . . . Come on, Steve!"

A few of the men were mildly drunk, and when Steve told them of my attempt a while before to eat a banana without peeling it, they all roared. Within a few minutes everybody in the saloon, including the bartenders, knew that I was a "greener," and there was no end of laughing at my expense.

But at the same time, since I did not resent their laughter and also because I was with Steve, my countrymen accepted me as one of them. No one asked me how old I was, and upon his own accord Steve lied that I was eighteen. I was tall enough to be that age, and I leaned against the bar, my foot on the brass rail, and shook dice with Steve's friends and acquaintances, and when I lost I paid for a round of drinks.

v

To carry my initiation into American ways, or rather into the life of my countrymen in the United States, a little farther, toward midnight Steve and I wound up at a lively Bohunk house party in Flushing.

When we got there the clock had just struck midnight and everybody—twenty-odd men and women and boys and girls in their late 'teens and early twenties—was shouting, "Happy New Year!" The unmarried young people were on one another's necks and there was much kissing, in which even I was made to participate.

Some of the girls were American-born, but spoke Slovenian. The fact that I was a greenhorn amused them. Steve, of course, told the banana story and everybody had a good time, including myself. Ten minutes after I had come into the house I was elected to go to the saloon on the corner to fetch two big buckets of beer, fifteen cents each.

One of the men at the party with whom Steve was acquainted was the editor of *Narodni Glas*. When Steve introduced us, he asked me:

"What do you intend to do in America?"

I said I would get a job. I did not know what kind of job—perhaps any kind at all to begin with.

He nodded his head, contemplating me. Then he said: "What did Steve Radin say your name was? There was so much noise in the room that I didn't understand him when he introduced you."

67

I told him my name.

"Weren't you in that riot in Lublyana two months ago?" he asked.

"Yes."

"So I thought," he said. "I saw your name in the Lublyana newspapers, which we get at our office. You were one of the boys who were imprisoned, weren't you? . . . Tell me about it."

His journalistic interest stimulated my recollections of the incident, so that I gave him a very graphic account of it.

"Could you write this up in a little article?" the editor asked me. "I should want it presented in some such way as you just told it. I would pay you for it—two or three dollars, depending on how well you do it."

I said that I thought I could write it; at any rate, I would try. I told him that back in Lublyana, as a *Gymnasium* student, I had once submitted an essay to my professor of natural history, who considered it so good that he gave it to a juvenile magazine, which printed it.

"Fine," said the editor.

Steve, who happened to overhear part of the conversation, said to the editor, "If he can write, couldn't you give him a job on the paper, or something?"

"We'll see," said the editor. "Come to my office in New York. Steve knows where it is. And bring your story with you."

CHAPTER VI

The Jungle

I LIVED at Mrs. Schmidt's in Brooklyn for only two weeks.

On New Year's Day, after I had slept a few hours, I wrote my story for *Narodni Glas*, and the next day, when I went to the office of that newspaper, the editor took me to his boss, the publisher, and induced him to give me a job in the mailing department—the only job available. I became assistant to the mailer at eight dollars a week, wrapping and bundling newspapers and packing them into mail-bags, then carrying the bags down two flights of stairs and piling them on the truck outside. But the paper —a daily—had no more than seven or eight thousand circulation and this work took only a few hours a day. The rest of the time I helped in the circulation office, addressing and stamping envelopes, filing correspondence, running errands, filling the other clerks' ink-wells, and attending to other such trifles. In my spare time I wrote short sketches of New York as it looked to me, some of which found their way into the paper.

The editor—his name was Mr. Frank Zemlar—took a liking to me. He was an elderly man, a former teacher in the Old Country, who had come to the United States twenty-odd years before. He had a family and his salary was small—thirty-five or forty dollars a week.

Soon after I came to America the Zemlars moved from Brooklyn to an old brownstone house in the Yorkville section of New York. One day Mr. Zemlar asked me to lunch, and in the course of the meal mentioned that he had an extra room in his new flat. Would I care to move in? He thought that living in Brooklyn, as I did, was not very convenient for one who worked in New York. His wife, he added, would be glad to have me. She was a good cook.

That evening I asked Steve about moving. Opportunist that he was, he thought at once that it might be a good idea in the long run, for then Mr. Zemlar would perhaps be more inclined to favor my advancement on the paper.

And so I moved from Mrs. Schmidt's to the Zemlars'.

Mrs. Zemlar was a fat, kindly, talkative Slovenian woman. She had been in the United States as long as her husband, but she did not like New York. She was full of gentle complaints. One did not dare open a window, she said, there was so much dust and grime in the air all the time. It was impossible to keep things clean. She spoke no English, but understood it fairly well. They had three children, rather typical middle-class American youngsters—two boys and a girl. But for them, said Mrs. Zemlar, she would insist that her husband take her back to the Old Country. She shrugged her shoulders fatalistically. "The children were born in America. I suppose they belong in America."

For two dollars a week I had a small, windowless room, which was not bad in the winter and the early spring, but almost unendurable in the summer. For two additional dollars Mrs. Zemlar gave me breakfast and supper. I had four dollars left for car fare, lunch, clothes, and incidentals.

The *Narodni Glas* office was all the way downtown, in a dilapidated old building on Barclay Street. I rode to work on the "L," and frequently left Yorkville a half-hour or an hour earlier than was necessary, so that I might walk around awhile and look at things.

The morning crowds downtown fascinated me. I continued to develop the muscles of my neck, looking up at the skyscrapers on lower Broadway and in Wall Street and Broad Street. I vaguely perceived the aspect of tremendous, terrible power of these thoroughfares.

II

Gradually I got over the agitation which had seized me upon my arrival in New York. But America continued to be vastly interesting, profoundly mysterious; indeed, more so from day to day.

New York was a stupendous place, with its awesome structures downtown, its sharp, mechanical tempo, its ceaseless drive and hustle and noise, its amazing bridges and transportation systems, its austere mansions on Fifth Avenue and on Madison Avenue, and its narrow streets and alleys of huddled-in dwellings, tenements and stores, with ragged clothes and dirty bedding hanging out of their windows and over the fire-escapes, and pale-faced, underfed children playing among the ash-cans and swill-barrels.

Now and then, on Saturday afternoons or Sundays, I walked through the Bowery and foreign sections of the lower and middle East Side. On New Year's Eve, in my romantic-greenhorn frame of mind, going about with hectic, laughing Steve Radin, things had seemed glamorous to me even in the slums around Canal and Delancey streets. A week or two later, however, as I went around by myself in the daytime, the glamour largely diminished or utterly vanished for me in many sections of the city.

I found myself thinking of Blato and of Lublyana, comparing them with New York. Blato, it seemed to me, was in its own way a perfect little place. It belonged exactly where it was. It was harmonious with its vicinity. Indeed, looking at it from a distance, it enhanced the

71

beauty of the region of which it was a part. Like most communities, large and small, in the Old World, it was an elemental and sympathetic feature of the region.

New York, as a whole, was not lovely. Parts of it were hideous and crazy. The city, as I perceived it then, was a monstrous, incongruous heap of hard brick, stone, cement, and steel; here clean and even magnificent, if one managed to forget the rest of it for the moment; there heavy and ugly with musty, garlicky odors of crowded poverty. A city of sharp, cruel contrasts.

For a minute, now and then, I recalled the picturesque, eager crowd of immigrants on the ship on which I came over. Some of them were peasants from eastern and southeastern Europe. In the Old Country they lived in poor but clean thatch-roofed houses, with plenty of elbow room. Here they came to this—some of them—to be compelled by their poverty to live in crowded, ill-smelling tenements. I remembered what Peter Molek had said to me: they were "dung" in America. There was no question about this in my mind.

III

The news of America that I read in *Narodni Glas* and other Slavic papers was chiefly of violent doings—murder, rape, robbery, bloodshed in labor troubles—no end of them—and fraud and graft, gang feuds and catastrophes of all kinds . . . and every once in a while, perhaps not often, when I paused in the midst of this vicarious experiencing of the country and inquired of myself what it was all about, and got no reply, there settled on me a deep and heavy sense of bewilderment.

I began to grow serious.

One day Mr. Zemlar said to me: "Is there anything the matter? My wife remarked to me this morning that she was afraid you were not satisfied boarding with us. She said you used to laugh a lot; now you don't laugh so often any more."

I assured him that I was quite satisfied living with them. I said, "Maybe it is just that I am not altogether used to America yet."

Mr. Zemlar looked at me. "Oh, you'll be all right," he said.

For a time I was not entirely sure that I would be all right. I said to myself that I had but the vaguest notions of the real significance of anything in America. Would I ever orient myself? I became self-conscious.

Off and on, walking about in New York, I thought of Peter Molek's characterization of the United States as a vast jungle; but then I still had only an imperfect conception of what a jungle was, and hence could not wholly appreciate Molek's analogy.

To know and understand America, it was obviously necessary that I learn the American language, and with this purpose in view I enrolled in a night school in Yorkville.

Our teacher was a thin, unhealthy-looking, undersized native American, perhaps of foreign parentage, who, I felt, was terribly ill at ease before this assemblage of thirty-odd Dagoes, Dutchmen, Jews, and Bohunks of all ages, many of them doubtless better educated in their native tongues than he was in English. In the daytime, I think, he taught children their a-b-c's; in the evening, to earn an extra few dollars, he became a stirrer of the melting-pot, an Americanizer.

At the beginning of each session he required us to rise, salute the American flag, and pledge allegiance to the country for which it stood. Even the first evening this seemed somewhat absurd to me.

Then he delivered a speech, perhaps prepared for him, as it occurred to me later, by some patriotic society interested in the Americanization of foreigners, on the Constitution of the United States, the Declaration of Independence, or the American form of government, or tried to make us sing "America" or "The Star-spangled Banner," while in adjoining rooms other stirrers of the melting-pot were similarly engaged.

If he started a grammar or spelling lesson, some would-be American made his life miserable with questions, foolish and profound; and to suppress such disturbers he distributed among us an armload of third-grade histories and made us copy chapters on the voyage of the *Mayflower*, the Boston tea party, Paul Revere's ride, or Abe Lincoln the rail-splitter.

On the fourth or fifth evening it occurred to me that sitting in that stuffy, overheated room ten hours a week was not a profitable way to spend my time, but I stuck it out for about a month and a half, anyhow—mainly to please Mr. and Mrs. Zemlar, who appeared to think that it was good for me.

Then, luckily, one fine day in early spring, the Zemlars' fifteen-year-old daughter Angela, a girl of delicate charm who appealed to the mooncalf in me, lost her dog, and for a week or so after that, instead of going to night school, I roamed the streets from the Sixties to the Nineties between Central Park and the East River, looking for the mutt. The lovely one had promised that should I find it she would reward me with a kiss. I searched for a week, as I say, but, alas! with no success. Finally I gave it up, convinced that Mr. Zemlar or Angela's oldest brother, both of whom hated the dog, had drowned it in the river.

But while looking for the animal, I discovered a better

74

method of learning the English language than that practiced by the teacher in the Yorkville night school. At first
unconsciously, then consciously, I picked up many new
words from the shop signs and billboards, and at the same
time caught slightly enlightening glimpses of American
life. I had a fair acquaintance with German and a smat-
tering of Latin and Greek, which I had studied in the
Gymnasium in Lublyana, and so had no great difficulty
in getting at the meaning of English terms, while Angela
and her two brothers took a sympathetic interest in my
pronunciation.

The result was that I stopped going to night school, and
thereafter read and learned by heart the advertisements
in the Elevated trains as I rode to and from work.

IV

War broke out in Europe; but while I was concerned with
what was going on over there, especially in the Balkans,
my interest in America was even greater. Here things
were happening at a terrific rate. It was impossible to
keep up with them.

I did not even understand most of the things I read in
Narodni Glas. I could not relate them to anything basic.
My awareness of places and things west of Hoboken was
extremely faint. There, somewhere, it seemed, was Washington, D. C. And there was Woodrow Wilson. There,
too, was William Jennings Bryan, a great and picturesque figure. And farther on, in the West, was a mighty
man by the name of Jess Willard, whom they called the
"White Hope" because he might defeat a black man, Jack
Johnson, boxing champion of the world. And what was
all this excitement about a sport called baseball? And
where was Colorado, the scene of these bloody battles between labor and capital? I looked at the map, but that

gave me no satisfaction. Colorado was one of many states in the Union, one larger than the other, one greater—in its diverse potentialities—than the other. . . .

Occasionally I asked Mr. Zemlar about some of the things I read in the paper of which he was the editor, but he seldom knew how to enlighten me. By and by I began to notice that my questions annoyed him. One day he grumbled at me: "How should I know all that? All I know is what there is in the papers. How can I explain? America is a madhouse, that's all! That explains it!" Thereafter I ceased asking him; he obviously was in the dark about most things in the United States. That America was a "madhouse" was not a satisfactory explanation to me.

Toward the end of 1914, however, I began regularly to read American newspapers and magazines—the *New York World* and *Everybody's,* for example—but for some time my knowledge of the country and its language was too scant to enable me to understand anything thoroughly.

The motion pictures that I saw, one or two a week—mystery serials, cowboy melodramas, and rural comedies—only made America more fantastic in my mind, giving me frequent brain-whirls.

I spent a good part of my spare time with little Angela Zemlar and her two brothers and their friends—boys in their mid-'teens, all American-born—but their knowledge of America, aside from sports, I discovered, was no greater than mine; and their interest in the country certainly did not measure up to mine in avidity, or even in intelligence. I read books that they read: yarns by Horatio Alger and other such writers, books that told me nothing and meant nothing to me. All that the boys could teach me was how to play baseball.

As for Steve Radin, I spent several hours a week with him in Brooklyn, or he came to see me in Manhattan, but he was too disorganized, too hectic mentally, too American—paradoxically—and at the same time still too much a greenhorn, interested only in local and immediate things, to be able to tell me anything about New York or America that I could not discern myself.

Peter Molek lived in Forest City, Pennsylvania, nearly two hundred miles from New York, which seemed to me a great distance. He had a job there as watchman at a colliery. Now and then he wrote to me, but very briefly. He was no help to me.

v

So far as my understanding of America was concerned, I was left almost entirely to myself. My knowledge of English improved and, with the aid of a little Slovenian-English dictionary, I read nearly every spare minute I could find. I had, however, no definite idea to "improve" myself, but tried merely to satisfy my natural curiosity and mentally gear myself to America.

One day, early in 1915, I bought a copy of the old *Metropolitan Magazine* and came upon an article about a bloody labor disturbance in Bayonne, New Jersey, which, I understood, was not far from New York. There was a strike, during which the police and "gunmen" engaged in battles with the workers. Men were killed. The article ran to several pages, which took me hours to read and comprehend. It was written by John Reed—since dead and buried in Russia—and illustrated by Boardman Robinson. It gave me a flash of understanding of the Bayonne situation that I had not received when I followed the same events in the *World*, in the Bohunk newspapers, or in the New York *Call*, a Socialist paper. With the aid of Robinson's drawings, it read almost as if Peter Molek himself were talking to me, explaining an actual situation, instead of only generalizing, as he had done in Blato a year and a half ago.

Of a sudden I perceived that America was a veritable battleground of tremendous and savage forces. People were shot down, killed in open warfare. And then I began to understand—not quite, of course, but it was a beginning—such incidents as the so-called Ludlow massacre in Colorado in 1913, and the dynamitings in Los Angeles and elsewhere in the preceding few years, that I had seen referred to in various papers and magazines.

One evening some time later Angela Zemlar—of whom I continued to be very fond—and I were walking in the little park at the foot of the Eighties along the East River, and I said to her that I would like to lay my hands on a "real book."

"What do you mean—'a real book'?" said Angela.

"Oh—a *real* book—not anything like Horatio Alger," I said. "I don't know just what I want. I probably wouldn't know till I'd read it."

We spoke partly in Slovenian and partly in English.

Angela suggested that I go to the public library. There was a branch near by. She offered to come with me and, perhaps, help me find something. She had a borrower's card.

Walking to the library, I suddenly remembered the book I had seen on the bench beside Peter Molek in Blato the first time he spoke to me, more than five years before.

"Did you ever hear of *The Jungle*?" I asked Angela.

"*The Jungle?* Who wrote it?" she inquired.

"I don't know."

"I don't think I ever heard of it," she said.

Ten minutes later we had Upton Sinclair's novel about

78

the Chicago stockyards. I began it that evening and finished it the next morning in the "L" on my way to work. It was simply written, obvious in the extreme, and I understood nearly every word of it.

I was young, just sixteen, and the book made a deep impression on me. So *this* was America! For a few days I felt a sharp hatred for the whole country.

CHAPTER VII

Steve Radin—(Continued)

I

DURING my first two weeks in America, before I went to live with the Zemlars, I spent nearly all my spare time with Steve Radin.

Since I was a friend of Steve's, Mrs. Schmidt was glad to make room for me in her crowded boarding-house. Steve was her favorite, and was popular, too, with the other men living there. The few times that he and I stayed home evenings, Mrs. Schmidt was a happy woman. "We all laugh and have a good time when Steve is home," she said to me in German. And Mathilde, her daughter, also was happy. Several other boarders gathered with us in the parlor downstairs, and Steve entertained us with his mimicry of motion-picture comedians and of people he met in everyday life. He delighted in our laughter.

"Oh, he is funny enough to be on the stage!" cried Mrs. Schmidt. Mathilde was doubled over with laughter.

Every second or third night Steve and I went to a vaudeville or a movie show. Once or twice he took Mathilde along; she was a simple, wholesome maiden, deeply appreciative of Steve. After the show, we sometimes walked around Brooklyn for a few hours, but presently the sameness of the streets with their box-like dwellings—block after block—began to oppress me.

Steve seemed incapable of talking seriously, connectedly. Questions which he could not answer he dismissed with some funny gesture. He was interested only in immediate and local things and notions. In this respect (and

80

in some others), as I later perceived, he was already a typical American. An opportunist, and individualist, in all things, he wanted to "succeed," to get on, to get on, without knowing just what he really wanted. He was impulsive, vain, blindly ambitious, as yet unaware of the muddle of his shortcomings, conceits, inadequacies, complexes, and misconceptions about the environment in which he lived. Neither he nor I knew then, as we did later, that he was in the grip of a great ambition to be appreciated by multitudes of people in some such way as Mathilde, her mother, I, and some of the other boarders at Mrs. Schmidt's appreciated him.

One evening Steve took me to Joe Riley's saloon in the Williamsburg section, where he said he liked to hang out. Riley was a big, round Irishman with three chins, large, pudgy, hairy hands, a thick gold chain across his vast belly, and a pair of shrewd, small blue eyes. He and Steve, obviously, were close friends.

Steve told him of my attempt, a few days before, to eat a banana without first peeling it (telling about it was then his favorite pastime), whereupon the great bulk of Riley commenced to heave and rumble. His shoulders rapidly went up and down, and his eyes wrinkled into tiny slits of merriment. He laughed and laughed. He rolled and boomed with laughter. He told his bartender what he was laughing about; then he and Steve and the bartender had a great time talking about me in English, which I could not understand, except occasional words: . . . "greenhorn" . . . "banana" . . . "America" . . . "all right" . . . "beer." . . .

II

The first Saturday after my arrival in the United States, Steve was scheduled to fight a bout at Riley's Saturday

Night Club. He wanted me to see him and procured me a ringside seat.

In the Old Country pugilism was then practically unknown, and these were the first prize-fights I witnessed. During the initial preliminary number, when the boxers began to pound one another, I barely managed to breathe, such was my excitement. At first it seemed almost inconceivable to me that such things should go on. It was absurd and worse. But also immensely thrilling.

The hall, once a livery-stable and still smelling like one, was filled to capacity with rough men—dock-wallopers, sailors, and other such workingmen, and gangsters and waterfront "rats"; Irishmen, Italians, native Americans, with a thin sprinkling of American-born Jews and a few other nationalities, most of them young men—"tough guys." Here and there were a couple of shiny-faced, white-toothed negroes.

Hundreds of men scattered through the hall emitted blood-curdling yells. The blows which the boxers dealt to one another, leaping in the strong glare of the huge incandescents over their heads, seemed to me terrific. I winced at every wallop. But the majority of the customers wanted more action. The fighters' puffed eyes and swollen lips were not enough for them.

"Come on, you bums! Blood! We want blood! . . . Come on, Mickey-boy, sock that shiny! . . . Slam that wop! . . ."

Such, I imagine, were the fans' calls that night; such, at any rate, were the yells at prize-fights that I witnessed in similar places now and then years later, when I understood the English language, including the lingo of ring fans.

Steve was in the third preliminary number. He crawled into the ring wrapped in a long bathrobe, with a pair of

short trunks underneath. He evidently knew several people at the ringside. He waved greetings to them. He
looked at me and winked.

I was half crazy with excitement from the previous
two bouts. My heart kicked hysterically at my ribs. My
throat was parched. Every nerve in my body twitched.
For a time, watching Steve, who almost immediately discarded his bathrobe, I forgot the mob behind me.

"In this corner," bellowed the referee, who acted also
as announcer, "is Steve Radin the Clown ———"

The fans howled savagely, calling out Steve's name.
Steve rose swiftly from his stool, lifted up his arms, and,
clasping his hands overhead, bowed for half a minute in
all directions, grinning, evidently at the height of glory.
Finally he executed a few comical gestures which set the
fans to roaring and booing. He looked at me again and
winked, as if to say, "See how popular I am?"

The referee announced Steve's opponent, a young Italian lad. The lights went out in the hall, except the powerful lamps over the ring; the bell clanged; the fight was
on—and my heart was in my neck.

"Come on, Steve, do your stuff!" yelled the mob, or
something to that effect.

Steve did his stuff. He unquestionably was funny. His
body, with its large torso, thickish neck, long arms, and
thin, extremely agile legs on which he danced and bounded
all over the ring, had a decidedly comic aspect. His whole
personality was rather incongruous. Besides, he made
funny faces at his antagonist and grinned at the referee.
Once or twice during the four rounds he attempted, with
considerable success, to imitate the walk of Charlie Chaplin, at which everybody roared.

To Steve the fight palpably was a slapstick proposition, and yet—to my supreme satisfaction—he evidently

83

had the better of his opponent from the outset. I did not know then, nor for long afterward, that the bout was nothing more than a vaudeville or circus act, calculated by the astute Joe Riley to regale the mob. That this was so Steve told me years later. It was, I believe, his first framed fight; previously Steve had fought "on the level," but his subsequent bouts were nearly all mere clown acts.

III

During the two weeks that I lived at Mrs. Schmidt's, the old lady indicated to me that she was much perturbed by Steve's interests and doings. She did not want him to become a prize-fighter. She had an instinctive fear that fighting might lead him into bad company; that by and by, perhaps, he would be unfit to marry Mathilde.

I moved from Brooklyn to Yorkville, and soon thereafter, alas! Mrs. Schmidt's fears about Steve commenced to materialize. First he got in the habit of laying off at the shipyard for two or three days at a spell. He began to develop an aversion to what Mrs. Schmidt called "honest, steady work." Then he quit his job altogether and started to loaf with a gang of young toughs in the Williamsburg Bridge neighborhood.

The gang had its main hang-out in a pool-room, which they called their "club," not far from Joe Riley's saloon and the Saturday Night Club. Steve took me there a few times after I began to speak some English. The boys for the most part were in their late teens and early twenties, all sporty dressers, with avid leers for girl-flesh.

I never felt quite at ease among them. I had instinctive misgivings about most of them. They tolerated me because I seldom appeared and was Steve's friend. Steve, because of his standing with Riley, was highly popular in the group. He laughed at me. "You're soft! Can't you try to be a regular guy?"

Toward the last of 1914, Steve moved from Mrs. Schmidt's into a room over the saloon that Joe Riley had urged him to take. Mrs. Schmidt wept, but Steve said to me that he thought it would be to his advantage to live in the Williamsburg area. All his interests were there, and he did not want sentiment, which for some months had caused him to continue living at Mrs. Schmidt's, to interfere with his future. Joe Riley made him assistant manager of the Saturday Night Club, and Steve was beginning to consider himself a "big shot." . . . As I look back now, he was swiftly becoming a gangster of the type that not many years later became dominant in the underworld of the larger American cities. . . .

Steve and I remained friends, although the Zemlars discouraged me from seeing him. I went to the fights whenever he fought, or rather clowned, in the ring. He always had money and dressed flashily. He had a girl, gambled, and tried to teach me crap-shooting. But I had no aptitude for the game. "You're hopeless!" he said. We continued to go to the movies together. He liked me because occasionally I laughed at his wisecracks. He insisted on paying for our movie tickets and suppers. He laughed at the idea that I should be working for eight dollars a week. He liked to exhibit his bankroll.

IV

While the war raged on in Europe and *I didn't raise my boy to be a soldier* was a popular song in America, the hundred-percenters, under the leadership of Theodore Roosevelt and Leonard Wood, preached preparedness. On the other hand, "the lunatic fringe," as Roosevelt called the radicals, spoke and wrote against the idea. Emma

Goldman and Alexander Berkman held meetings on Union Square. Down with war! Down with militarism! In the poorer sections of Brooklyn and Manhattan, anti-pre-paredness soap-boxers held forth nightly, some of them attracting large crowds of sympathetic and curious prole-tarians, mostly foreigners.

At the same time young toughs and hoodlums, à la Steve, were being hired by mysterious agents of the pa-triotic Preparedness cause to heckle and otherwise harass the pacifist agitators. The boys were given to understand, as Steve later told me, that it was their duty, no less, to do so. They were assured that the police would be blind to anything they might do to the Reds, short of murder.

One night, when I was in Brooklyn, the boys in Steve's "club" had received instructions, through a man who ap-peared to be a friend of Joe Riley's, to "pick" on a fellow who spoke every third evening on a corner near Riley's. His audience consisted mainly of sailors and dock-workers. He had a powerful, dynamic voice; one could hear him two blocks away over the din of early-evening traffic on Wil-liamsburg Bridge. He attracted big crowds.

Steve asked me to go along. "We'll show the guy where he's gettin' off at," he said.

"But why?" I asked him.

"Oh, the guy's a radical," he answered. "Anyhow, I guess, it's Joe Riley who wants 'im to stop beefin' off there. Between you and me and that lamp-post, these guys around here—stevedores and sailors—instead of goin' in to Riley's and drinkin' like they used to, they listen to the guy on the corner. Joe don't like that."

Besides Steve, four or five other young toughs came to the corner to annoy the speaker. One of them had a paper bag of over-ripe tomatoes. He passed them out among his colleagues.

The soap-boxer's bull voice boomed over the crowd around him. He was describing the horrors and high cost of war.

By-and-by, two of the gangsters—not Steve—began to heckle him, but he paid no attention to them. He could outshout any man.

I saw Steve looking at him with a confused sort of admiration in his eyes.

Suddenly, a soft tomato struck the soap-boxer *tsmock* square between the eyes. The juice and seeds ran down his nose and cheeks and over his mouth, into the stubble of his beard. The bull voice ceased and its owner, dramatically calm, took out his handkerchief and slowly wiped his face. Then he shoved the handkerchief back into his pocket and said to the crowd:

"Comrades and friends, none of you, I suppose, was raised in a school for young ladies or educated for a gentleman at Princeton or Yale or Harvard, so I think you won't mind the language which I am about to use."

After which he turned in the general direction whence the tomato had come, and said, "I can lick the son of a b—— who threw that tomato."

For a few moments, no answer.

Steve, as I knew, had not thrown it, but some perverse impulse in him (which, later, he was unable to explain to me) suddenly moved him to say:

"I threw it. What about it?"

"Oh, you did, did you?" asked the soap-boxer.

"Yeah," said Steve.

The pacifist stepped off his box, and with several "Excuse me, please, comrades," made his way to Steve.

The crowd was silent, expectant.

"You threw it?" the soap-boxer asked Steve again.

"No, he didn't," I said.

The man looked at me. His simple, direct personality emanated strength and purpose. He was short, no taller than Steve, but built with the harmonious compactness of a prize bull, broad as a barn door. He had a powerful, stolid face, small, wide-apart brown eyes, and a great crop of curly dark-brown hair. He was in his late thirties, obviously a workman in one of the skilled trades. I was nearly half a head taller than he, but my knees quaked for fear of what he might do to Steve, or perhaps even to me.

"He said he did it," asserted the man.

"Sure, I threw it," said Steve. He turned to me belligerently: "You mind your own business!" Then, turning back to the soap-boxer: "I threw it, and what the hell!"

I noticed that the other gangsters were edging away.

"What do you mean—'what the hell'?" said the pacifist to Steve, his subdued voice dinful with power.

"I mean, what the hell!" said Steve. "That's what I mean!"

"Well, if that's the case," said the soap-boxer, grinning, and made a swift pass with his right at Steve's face —*biff!* As Steve observed later, it was like getting hit by a pile-driver.

Steve hit back, but his blows were tantamount to the strokes of a wooden mallet upon a rock. The pacifist made no attempt to defend himself. He let Steve hit him, but Steve could not budge him.

Then the fellow grinned again. "Stop when you get tired," he said.

Some men in the crowd laughed.

Steve stopped.

The radical's face assumed a stolid, unsmiling expres-

88

sion. Steve desperately swung once more at the man's face, but the man parried the blow as if chasing off a fly.

Then he seized Steve by the throat with his left hand and, reaching into his own pocket with his right, pushed him against the wall of a building.

"Here," he said in a low whisper, shoving a paper-bound booklet into Steve's coat pocket, "take this and go straight home—this minute, understand?—and as soon as you feel a little better read it three times. Understand? Three times!"

Steve was wiping the blood from his mouth.

"If you don't read it," the man went on, "and I ever lay my eyes on you, I'll punch the livin' hell out of you." His whisper softened: "All right; now beat it, boy! You, too!" turning to me.

Whereupon, just as calmly as he had stepped off it, the pacifist remounted his soap-box and said:

"Now, comrades and friends, where was I?" The comrades and friends broke into laughter. Then he resumed his harangue against war and capitalism.

Steve and I went away.

v

The book which the pacifist had pushed into Steve's pocket was entitled: *"War Is Hell"—Let Those Who Want Hell, Go to Hell!* The author and publisher was one Robert Twombley.

Steve asked me to leave him alone. He said he was going home, to his room over Riley's saloon. He obviously was affected by the experience, not only by the terrific blow in his face, but otherwise.

I went home to Yorkville.

Two days later, at six in the evening when I was

through with work, Steve came to the *Narodni Glas* office. He wanted to talk to me.

Outside, he told me that he had read the booklet. He was impressed; more than impressed. It was the first book he had read since leaving school in Trieste. He had read it three times, just as the pacifist had told him he must. He agreed with the author—let those who want hell, go to hell! The turn of the phrase appealed to him. He thought it was immensely clever. Indeed, the whole book was clever. A great book. It was a revelation to him. War certainly was a crime. The whole "sytem" was awful.

He told me that after reading the book a second time he had walked in the streets of Brooklyn for hours, thinking about it. "Let those who want hell, go to hell!" He thought about capitalism, militarism, imperialism, injustice, poverty, the profit motive—all of which were simply and trenchantly discussed in Robert Twombley's booklet.

"You know," he said, "I think I'm a radical myself. I wish I could talk like the guy that punched me in the face and gave me the book. I wanna talk like that——"

"Why don't you?" I said.

"Think I could?"

"Sure."

He asked me to come with him to Brooklyn. He wanted to talk to me some more. He was full of anti-war feelings and ideas. He thought he was through with boxing and clowning, through even with Joe Riley, whom he liked personally, but who, as he now realized, was part of the evil capitalistic system.

I went to Brooklyn with him and accompanied him to the fatal street corner. After the meeting Steve approached the pacifist and told him that he had read the book. "Three times," he said, grinning.

The soap-boxer looked at him. "Good!" he said, smiling. "I remember you. You're the lad . . . yes, night before last. Come on, let's all have some beer. I'm dry as hell. You get dry talking like this in the open air."

In a near-by saloon, not Joe Riley's, where the three of us went, Steve was amazed to learn that the man was none other than Robert Twombley himself, the author of the anti-war pamphlet. He told us that he was a brickmason by trade, a Socialist in politics, "a more or less educated workin'-stiff," as he put it, "havin' lotsa fun talkin' to folks on street corners who don't know what the hell it's all about." He was a native of a small town upstate. He had written the little book in his spare time and published it at his own expense.

All three of us became good friends, drinking beer that night, especially Steve and Bob, as he insisted that we call him. I liked the man, but felt that, somehow, he was a little fantastic. I kept quiet most of the evening while he and Steve talked.

"I didn't hurt you much the other night, did I?" Bob asked Steve.

"No," answered Steve, and laughed—"that is, you hurt me, all right; you can hit like nobody's business. I been in the ring for a year and a half and never been hit like you hit me—but I'm glad you biffed me."

Bob smiled. "Three more," he called to the bartender.

"It did me lotsa good," said Steve. "It opened my eyes. Say, this little book is an eye-opener." He was all excited. "Say, Bob, I—I wanna——"

"What?"

"I wanna do what you're doin'," said Steve. "I think I'm a radical, too, like you—and wanna talk on street corners against war—against—" He could not quite put his idea into coherent words. "War is a crime."

Bob gave Steve a long, intense look. Then he poured

91

into himself a full mug of beer. "Talkin' makes me dry as hell," he observed. "Drink up," he said to Steve and me. "We'll have 'nother one apiece."

"I see it all now," Steve went on. "Your book opened my eyes."

"Well, I'm glad to hear that," said Bob, modestly. "I'll get you to join the party, if you want to. I guess you're O.K. Then we'll see what you can do. . . . Three more."

I said I had to work the next day and had to go home to get a little sleep. I left them in the saloon.

VI

Some days later Comrade Steve moved from Joe Riley's place to Comrade Bob's flat. Bob had two rooms and a kitchen; he "batched."

They became partners in radical propaganda. Steve joined a Brooklyn local of the Socialist party. He hardly ever saw anyone of his old crowd any more, and steered clear of Riley's saloon and the boxing-arena altogether.

In the daytime, while Bob worked at bricklaying, Steve went from house to house in the poorer sections of Brooklyn with *"War is Hell"—Let Those Who Want Hell, Go to Hell!* and sold from twenty to forty copies a day, which, of course, pleased Bob, the author, very much. In three months the little volume went through three printings. From this neither Bob nor Steve made a cent. It was all for the Cause. Bob provided Steve with food, shelter, and car fare.

By and by Steve began to speak on street corners, too. He surprised both himself and Bob. He said scarcely anything that was not in Bob's booklet or in some other piece of Socialistic literature, but he enlivened the anti-militarist and anti-capitalist arguments with picturesque phrases and clownish pantomime which attracted crowds even greater than Bob's and, to his supreme satisfaction, evoked much laughter.

Steve was noticed by other radicals in Brooklyn, and even at the Rand School in Manhattan. He was a go-getter, young, energetic, enthusiastic, eager to excel himself. In connection with his book-selling, he induced dozens of persons to join the Socialist local in Brooklyn, and subsequently, when the local, spurred by Steve's success, launched a membership drive, he secured in a few weeks nearly a hundred new members, for which he received mentions in the *Appeal to Reason* and in a New York Socialist journal. Once, at the Rand School, he was introduced to Comrade Gene Debs, who embraced and kissed him.

In the summer and fall of 1916, Steve worked in a factory making automobile gears. Its owner was an obese, pompous old German-American, Ludwig Augustus von Heygendorff—Von, for short—employing several hundred men at standardized machine tasks. They worked ten hours daily, with straight pay for overtime, and from the men's point of view the wages were low.

There was much grumbling in the plant. The men wanted more pay and shorter hours, with double wages for overtime, and certain sanitary improvements. Some of them thought this was the opportune time to make their demands. With the war going on in Europe, the factory was rushed with orders. Von Heygendorff, as a German, did not sell his gears directly to the Allies, but indirectly through American manufacturers of trucks and automobiles.

Steve, inevitably, became the leader of discontent. He was then twenty-three years old, and every day he seemed to look more like Napoleon. He was developing a little

93

paunch. People told him that he looked like Bonaparte. He began to affect the Napoleonic gesture. He let a lock of hair fall over his brow. This and his great vitality made him stand out immediately as a personality wherever he appeared. As a soap-box speaker he had lost all reticence. (I saw him infrequently then. As I shall tell a few pages hence, I was out of New York a good part of the time. But later he told me about his last adventure as a fighter in the American class struggle.) . . .

One day at lunch-time in the factory yard he found himself in the midst of a group of men, telling them to organize the shop and then, through a properly elected committee, officially present their demands to the boss in a business-like manner. Some of the men urged him to call a meeting, which, flattered, he did at once. He had for some time been imagining himself a natural-born leader.

He hired a hall and, addressing his fellow workers, made a great impression upon them. A committee was elected to call on old man Von, and Steve, as chairman of the committee, was at the pinnacle of his glory and self-satisfaction. A leader of men! He knew that the men would do anything he said. The shop was nearly a hundred-per cent organized. He could call a strike. All the machines in the factory, should Von decline to grant their demands, would stop instantly at his (Steve's) say-so.

The committee called on Von, and Steve, as its spokesman, told him their demands.

The old man probably was expecting them. He controlled his temper and was polite to the committee, but Steve knew that, inside, Von hated the sight of him.

"Shentlemen," said Von, and his double chin shook, he was so provoked by their coming—"shentlemen, I fill giff you mein reply tomorro' morgen."

"Very well, sir," said Steve, and Napoleonically bowed himself and the committee out of the office.

The next morning Von told the committee that he would grant them a five-per-cent raise and shorten the day to nine and a half hours, which was less than half of what they had asked for. He agreed to the necessity of bettering the sanitary conditions, but said nothing about double pay for overtime.

Steve perked up, his right hand on his chest *à la* Napoleon, and informed Von that the workers whom he had the honor to represent wanted him to grant *all* their demands. This caused the old man to lose his temper. His face trembled like jelly, and he yelled and shook his fist at Steve.

"Oudt!" he said. "I fire you all! Oudt!"

But before Von could effect a lockout, Steve called a strike. At eleven that same day every machine in the shop stopped. It gave Steve a grand feeling. He was the whole strike.

The strike lasted five weeks. Steve had his hands full. He ran the picket lines. He collected strike funds and fed the strikers' families. Twice he was shot at, palpably by gunmen engaged by Von. He was on his legs almost day and night. And he relished it all. He was a leader.

Toward the end of the fifth week (as Steve put it to me later) old man Von came to his senses. He sent word to Steve, requesting him and the rest of the strike committee to call on him. When they did, he granted all their original demands unconditionally, along with a new demand, that none of the leaders, Steve included, were to be discharged or in any way whatsoever discriminated against.

Steve called off the strike and the machines in Von's shops turned again. Which gave Steve another feeling of elation. The men worked again, at better wages, because *he* had led them!

But a month later Steve was suddenly discharged for "inefficient service," although for four months before his work had been satisfactory. He wanted to call a special meeting of the union, but immediately realized that few of his fellow workers cared whether Von dismissed him or not, so long as they kept their jobs.

Steve stayed idle a few weeks. Seeking employment again, he discovered that he was blacklisted in every machine shop, foundry, and shipyard in Brooklyn, New York, and New Jersey.

He commenced to get sour on the labor and radical movements. He was especially bitter because the men in Von's factory, after he had led them to victory, were indifferent to what the employers did to him. He had a sneaking suspicion that they were laughing at him.

For two or three months he continued to live with his friend Bob Twombley and, idle, read a good deal. At the Public Library one day he picked up a book entitled *Men vs. The Man*, a debate in the form of letters between Robert Rives La Monte, a Socialist, and H. L. Mencken, a prophet of capitalistic individualism opposed to Socialism and Democracy. Steve was inclined to think that Mencken had the better of the argument. His days as a radical were numbered.

One day Bob Twombley was killed in an accident, which shocked and grieved Steve for a while. Thereafter Brooklyn and New York commenced to annoy him more every day. Also, among the radicals, Steve had begun to see much petty bickering and intrigue, which tended to disgust him with the entire movement. When we got together, he talked to me cynically of his recent experiences.

STEVE RADIN

One day in January, 1917, he came to see me. He had no money. I had none to give him. "Aw hell! I think I'll join the army or something," he said.

He did, and I did not see him or hear from him for eight years.

CHAPTER VIII

My Own People in America

I

EARLY in 1916, when my English had improved so that I could translate ordinary news articles from the *New York World* into Slovenian without having to consult the dictionary every half-minute, I was made Mr. Zemlar's assistant in the *Narodni Glas* editorial-room. In addition to translating news, I edited letters of Bohunk workmen written to the paper from all over the United States, describing labor conditions in their localities. My salary now was eighteen dollars a week, which I considered a good deal of money. Delighted with my new job, I worked hard, and Mr. Zemlar was pleased with me. I was not yet seventeen, and to be assistant editor of a newspaper, I thought, was something of which to be proud at my age.

To get the paper ready for the press at nine o'clock, I had to be at my desk at four in the morning every weekday. At that hour downtown Manhattan was dark and deserted. The skyscrapers, with only a window lighted here and there, looked mysterious and lovely, much nicer than in the daytime.

My advancement enabled me to wear better clothes and eat more substantial lunches, and tended to lessen the bitterness about America that had seized me on reading *The Jungle*. The incongruities and cacophonies of American life, as I perceived them, seemed to me as sharp as ever, but I now developed a tendency to be amused by them.

My curiosity about the country increased.

98

MY OWN PEOPLE IN AMERICA

II

Narodni Glas, like most Bohunk newspapers, was perennially in financial doldrums. Every few months it was in danger of going under.

When I had been assistant editor for about three months, and the circulation of the paper was showing an especially swift decline, I suggested to the publisher and Mr. Zemlar that they send me on a "trip around the United States." I proposed to visit the larger Slovenian *kolonije* in the industrial centers, see how our people lived, write of their problems as immigrants, their social and cultural life and their working conditions, and solicit subscriptions. Some of the other Bohunk newspapers had traveling correspondents and subscription solicitors. My chief motive in wanting to travel, of course, was not to put the paper on its feet, but to see the country.

The publisher at first hesitated, then decided to try me out for a month, in which period I was to cover Pennsylvania and Ohio. I first went to Forest City, in the anthracite country of Pennsylvania. Peter Molek lived there. He was glad to see me and we had a long talk.

"What did I tell you?" he said. "America *is* good for you." He was impressed with my English, which by now I spoke rather passably, and the fact that I wrote for a newspaper.

Molek's health was about the same as when he returned to the United States. He was no longer a colliery watchman. He had recently married a middle-aged Slovenian widow with five children. Her husband, a friend of Molek's, had been killed in a mine. Her insurance money had amounted to a couple of thousand dollars, and with this money Molek and she had just started a grocery and vegetable store which promised well.

99

Forest City was then a town of eight thousand inhabitants, Slovenians predominating with nearly five hundred families. Molek was more or less acquainted with all of them, and helped me to get among them, see how they lived, and secure their subscriptions.

Molek also knew many Slovenians in the neighboring coal towns—Carbondale, Pittston, Scranton, Wilkes-Barre—and gave me letters to them or merely suggested that I call and tell them I was a friend of his. They, in turn, sent me to other Slovenians living farther on, in western Pennsylvania and Ohio. Thus I had no difficulty finding my own people in the grimy industrial cities and towns of those states.

All the places were bleak, unharmonious, with immense coal-heaps, cinder-piles in front of houses, and stinking rubbish-dumps, tin cans and discarded machinery everywhere. But, of course, more than in the looks of places I was interested in the manner of living among my countrymen, the Slovenians and other Bohunks.

III

The great majority of immigrants who plunged into the turmoil of America, from the most intelligent to the least, were naturally bewildered, or numbed by the impact of the country upon their senses and their minds. Their first concern upon arrival was to find people of their own nationality, in whose midst they might orient themselves. One could seldom, if ever, get a job in one's old line. In America there was no stability, which was almost the keynote of life in the European countries before the World War. With machinery being improved from day to day, the job that one found carried with it no security. One might lose it from week to week, almost from hour to hour, and one could seldom base on its continuation any

100

plans for the future. The more pronounced the difference in language, ways, and conditions in America and in the immigrant's own country, the more urgent it was for him to seek out his countrymen.

In the case of the Slavic immigrants eighteen or twenty years ago, at which time they came over in a steady stream, the first, although not the most important, difficulty arose in making the people here—native-born Americans and aliens of other nationalities—understand who they were and whence they hailed. The difficulty lay basically in the fact that many of them were not clear on the point themselves. If a Slovenian was asked what his nationality was, he very likely replied that he was a Kranjec or Krainer or Carniolan, from Kranjsko (German, *Krain;* English, *Carniola*). Only a few Czechs, Styrian Germans, and Italians from Trieste and Giorizia knew what he meant. It was as if a citizen from some such obscure state as Nevada, arriving in Belgrade or Lublyana, announced that his nationality was Nevadan. If he really knew what he was, he declared himself a Slovenian, but that, to the average American, Irishman, or Scandinavian, meant no more than Carniolan.

The poor Bohunk then proceeded to explain, perhaps with the aid of a map, that the Slovenians were a small Slavic nation, first cousins, one might say, to the Czechs, Poles, and Russians, inhabiting a little country within Austria which the Hapsburgs, with their Machiavellian *divide et impera* policy, had cut up into three tiny provinces, Carniola, Carinthia, and Styria. But before he was through explaining, presto! he was an "Austrian," which, in a sense, was correct. Where his people had larger colonies, as in Cleveland, Forest City, Wilkes-Barre, Carbondale, Pittsburgh, and Chicago, they were known also as Krainers or Granners (Carniolans).

101

By a similar process, the Croatians, too, became "Austrians," though, since Croatia used to be a part, not of Austria, but of Hungary, that was never true in any sense. Even the Serbs and Montenegrins, who appeared to speak the same language as the Croats, were labeled "Austrians," and the Yugoslav languages became the "Austrian" tongue. The Czechs, always conscious of their nationality, never hesitated to state what they were. In consequence, though they had been under Austrian rule longer than the Yugoslavs, they were never Austrians in America, but either Czechs or Bohemians.

The Poles, with their dramatic historical background, which included the participation of a number of their countrymen in the American Civil War, had no trouble making anyone understand who they were and where they came from. They were Poles or, at worst, Polacks. American-born Polish children, in some cases even of the second generation, usually showed pride in their origin, and if their family names were at all pronounceable, retained them. In this case they differed from all the other Bohunks save the Bohemians. (I write in the past tense because immigration is ended and immigrants are vanishing in the melting-pot.)

The Serbians, too, with a historical background as bloody, though perhaps not as splendid, as that of the Poles and the Czechs, were a proud people; but most of them never intended to stay here permanently, and so they made no emphatic objection to being called Austrians. On the other hand, the German Austrians who were Austrians before anyone else, insisted strenuously that they were Germans, no doubt because they hated being included with such lowly rabble as the Croatians, Slovenians, Slovaks, and Serbians in the American-made "Austrian" nationality.

102

From that viewpoint the Viennese Germans' objection to being known as Aus*rians was perhaps not unjustified, for Croatia, Bosnia, Herzegovina, Lika, Banat, Dalmatia, Montenegro, and southern Serbia sent to America, for the most part, simple peasants who lacked any definite nationalistic consciousness, and who, next to tilling the earth and fishing, were interested only in fighting, love- and verse-making, drinking, dancing, singing, strumming the *gusle* or *tamburice*, and, last but not least, keeping on the good side of Yahweh. They thought of themselves as fighters, lovers, poets, dancers, singers, and children of the Almighty before it occurred to them that they were also members of definite national and political groups. They were very proud of their endurance at hard physical labor, their reproductive powers (their women were used to very frequent child-bearing), their singing voices, and their ability to carry liquor like men.

The Slovenians, the smallest of Slavic nations, were, next to the Czechs, the most cultured and civilized of Bohunks. Many of those who came to America, even among the peasants of the lowest economic order, were well aware of their nationality and cultural superiority, and, like the German-speaking subjects of His Apostolic Majesty, resented being classed with the "Austrians." But in the United States census figures they were counted, along with the Croatians and the Yugoslav groups, as Austrians.

Ten or fifteen years ago, if one came to an American city and inquired for the Croatian or Slovenian colony, one found that no such thing was known. When one explained that one really sought the "Austrians," the stranger consulted would, with a gesture of disdain, direct one to take such-and-such street-car, ride to the end of the line, and then walk a few blocks; there, in "Hunkytown," lived the "Austrians," or Bohunks, in low, unpainted shacks or bleak-looking apartment-houses along unpaved streets that swarmed with unclean children in torn garments.

The Bohunks indeed were "dung." But their natural health, virility, and ability to laugh served, from time to time, to help them transcend their lowly status in the American scheme of things. On Saturday nights and Sunday afternoons the men got together, and, apart from the prim and proper "better element," sang, played their stringed instruments and accordions, drank, fought, shouted, laughed, and roared to their hearts' content.

IV

Two decades ago most of the Bohunks came to America intending to stay two or three years, four at the most, work to the limit of their endurance at whatever they might find, save every cent possible, and then, returning to the Old Country, pay the debt on the old place, buy a few additional fields and head of cattle, and start anew. But actually only a small proportion of them went back.

In the Old Country the man probably had a wife or a *punca* to whom he had sworn everlasting fidelity and promised to think of daily. But he was invariably a strong, virile he-man, and if he remained true to his vow (and as a rule he did), his womanless existence soon became intolerable. He yearned for his fair Marichka or Yova with a great yearning, and, sooner or later, he sent her a ticket to join him. She came, perhaps with two or three little Bohunks; if she was only his girl and married him here, she soon bore him a few. In either case, saving anything from his wages immediately became a difficult matter. Working conditions often changed overnight; there were strikes and lockouts; the family, which increased regularly every ten months, had to be moved from one state to

104

another. To return to the Old Country thus became a hopeless dream.

He was caught in America and became "dung."

If he had no wife or girl to send a ticket to, he began to look about in the colony or he put a "wife-wanted" advertisement in *Narodni Glas* or some other Bohunk newspaper, which presently led to the same difficulties. And if he took to sin, he spent most of his pay on prostitutes (usually of his own nationality), and the rest—unless he was luckier than he was wise—he had to hand over to venereal-disease quacks for treatment.

In any case, he usually kept on digging coal or ore, or working in the steel-mills, or in the stockyards or forests, or on construction jobs from Portland to Portland. Gradually he abandoned all hope of returning home, even for a visit, and strove solely to make a living, watching for a chance to get out of the dirty, unhealthy, and hazardous work in the mines and mills and into something better. Perhaps he started a saloon, a grocery-store, a butcher-shop, or an undertaking-parlor, or bought a farm. If unmarried, he probably joined the army or became a hobo or a bum.

Unlike most of the other immigrants, especially the Scandinavians, the Irish, and the Germans, most of whom entered the country intending to settle, the Bohunks, with a few such exceptions as myself, had little interest in American events, institutions, and politics, even after they gave up the idea of returning home. Saturday evenings and Sunday afternoons, when they came together, the talk was largely about affairs in their native villages. Their newspapers devoted a good part of their space to clippings from the small-town sheets of southeastern Europe.

105

Of all the Slavic groups, the Slovenians were perhaps the most assimilative, more so than the Bohemians, who, not unlike the hated Germans and Hungarians, were extremely chauvinistic, although as naturalized citizens they usually were active in civic and political affairs. This marked interest of the Bohemian Americans in the public life of their adopted country was perhaps not due so much to their cultural superiority, of which they were very conscious and proud, as to their clannishness, which surpassed even that of the Swedes and the Norwegians, and caused them to live in large, compact colonies whose leading lights were Americanized go-getters (such men as Anton Cermak, who in 1931 became mayor of Chicago).

Before the war, most of the Bohunks had little interest in learning the English language. It was not necessary for them to know it. In the mills and mines the bosses knew their dialects; in the stores they could, if need be, point at things they wanted; in the courts they employed interpreters.

V

For years after the Bohunks began coming to America in great numbers, they were, with scant exceptions, low-paid manual laborers, performing the most dangerous and dirty tasks. There were only a few missionaries, parish priests, office clerks, saloon-keepers, and other such men of dignity and ease among them, and there were not many shoemakers, blacksmiths, and tailors. But some of the laborers who took the trouble of learning English became bosses, and others went into business.

When immigration was at its height, about the time that I came over, the saloon and the church, with the former usually having the better of it, were centers of the Bohunk colonies. The saloon was no mere drinking-place, but a *bordingavz* (boarding-house) equipped to cater to a great many needs of the colony. There one could not only drown one's sorrows, overcome one's weariness from hard and long toil, and meet one's fellows; one could also buy steamship tickets and money-orders for folks in the Old Country, play poker, eat, dance, have one's letters written, enjoy a girl, subscribe to newspapers, pay one's lodge and club dues, and—if the saloon-keeper was on friendly terms with the priest, which was not unusual —even one's church dues!

The saloon-keeper often was a go-getter of no mean order. He was a jolly fellow who knew all the members of the colony by their first names, had a glad hand for the humblest workingman, and if the latter got into trouble with the police, intervened on his behalf. The unmarried men with no permanent addresses received their mail addressed in his care. Usually he was a notary public. He had his own accordion-players and saw that his customers had female company. Sometimes he acted as matrimonial agent, and wedding festivities usually were held in the hall above his saloon.

Most colonies were split into two antagonistic camps— the church members and the unbelievers, mainly Socialists. Each had its own lodges, clubs, singing societies, and social affairs. The unbelievers, of course, were in a minority and largely ineffective. On election day, if they happened to be citizens, they voted for the Socialist candidates, and on their club-room table lay such subversive publications as *Proletarec, Prosveta,* the *Appeal to Reason,* and *The Liberator.*

In the other camp, life revolved entirely around the church. The alien Catholic parishes, with their parochial schools, were strongholds of mediævalism. Unlike in the Old Country, where the priesthood included men of learning and superior character who commanded the respect of their antagonists, the Bohunk-American priests were usually of an inferior order.

There was a third group or, rather, mob—perhaps stronger numerically than the other two put together, but unorganized. It was made up of lost souls, not exactly infidel, but who had no use for the church—yokels inflated with the conceit born of the American idea of equality, distrustful of everything but the most obvious fakes; an uneducated lot in whom ignorance and prejudice created a formidable combination.

All these groups were reflected in nearly a hundred small Bohunk-American newspapers and magazines; with one or two exceptions, as I now see them, all very dull, afraid to print a line that might disturb any reader's prejudices. The American hundred-percenters who periodically cried out against the sinister radicalism of the foreign-language press did not know what they were talking about. Most of the Bohunk papers were conservative and stupid, without program. They discussed only the most obvious phases of American life. Even the most advanced and liberal among them, including *Narodni Glas*, for example, were unaware of what was going on in the field of American letters. A few knew of Upton Sinclair and Jack London, but this was largely through translations printed in the Old Country. In the same way, the Bohunk editors betrayed only the vaguest knowledge of American politics. They wrote nothing likely to put a strain on the brains of their hard-working, tired readers. Most of them—Mr. Zemlar, for instance, as it occurred to me later—were ordinary men, but slightly above their readers intellectually.

108

VI

The month that I traveled through the coal and steel-mill cities of Pennsylvania and Ohio was, on the whole, a depressing one. My countrymen lived hectic, uncertain lives in shabby houses. Their children, instead of playing on the grass as children did in the Old Country, played on cinder-piles. The women had to wash their window curtains almost daily. It was impossible to keep them clean. They got dirty if hung to dry on the line outside.

I was glad when my trip was over.

It was a fairly successful trip. I secured several hundred new subscribers and wrote a daily letter to the paper, describing the conditions in the Bohunk colonies—not as I do here, of course, but to please the readers, without being untruthful.

In the end, however, my trip did little good to the paper. Late in 1916 it ceased publication and I was out of a job.

PART THREE

The Crusade

CHAPTER IX

To Make the World Safe——

I

AFTER the *Narodni Glas* went on the rocks, Mr. Zemlar, with his long editorial experience, received an offer to become editor of another Slovenian paper, in Chicago. He tried to get me a job there, too, but failed. So the Zemlars and I parted.

Suddenly I found myself alone in New York. I wrote to Peter Molek that I wanted to come to Forest City; perhaps I could get a surface job around the mines. Molek replied that he did not want me to come there. There were too many of our people in Forest City. He advised me to sever all contact with our countrymen here; since I would stay in the United States permanently, I should mix with Americans and become an American.

Taking Molek's advice, I then bumped for two months against the harsh actualities of American industrial life, first in New York, then in Paterson, New Jersey. Despite the war in Europe, which enhanced manufacture in the United States, work did not seem plentiful. I got only the worst kind of jobs—digging up pavements, loading trucks, sweeping immense stretches of floor space in a silk-mill.

My fellow workers were unlike the workers I encountered years later on jobs in California. Most of them were foreigners—short, squat, illiterate Italians and French Canadians, only a few of whom spoke English. I felt, successively, sorry for and disgusted with them. The bosses had them cowed. Their wages were low, but they would have worked for even less. At the end of the day they trudged home, silent, uninspiring, a heavy smell of hopelessness about them. They did not belong in America. They knew nothing of the country, nor had the ability or the desire to learn about it. They lived from day to day, from hand to mouth, driven by narrow selfishness.

The women workers in the Paterson silk-mill gave me oppressive feelings. They worked from seven in the morning till six in the evening. Sometimes they worked overtime, for straight pay, till midnight. Few looked fresh in the morning. By evening, after a day's work amid roaring, clattering machines in huge rooms charged with harsh, insistent activity and breathing dust-filled air, they were all flat and unattractive.

II

I quit the job in the silk-mill. I was strong and healthy, but obviously not cut out to be a worker, one of many docile and unimaginative little cogs in the industrial machine. I had no idea what I would do with myself.

The next day a trim-looking, ruddy-faced recruiting sergeant stopped me on a street corner in Paterson. It was in mid-February. The United States had severed relations with Germany and the German ambassador to Washington was on the way home. It was expected, said the sergeant, that before long America would be "in the scrap for fair." Now was the time to join the army. A bright-looking young man like me, even with my imperfect pronunciation of English words, would be a corporal in two shakes of a lamb's tail; maybe even a sergeant. My English would improve. In the army I would have all sorts of chances for self-improvement. The sergeant noted the magazine in my coat pocket. Did I like to read? As a soldier I would have a great deal of time to read and study.

Many foreigners joined the army for the sake of self-improvement. Besides, I would not have to worry about making a living. Uncle Sam would provide me with clothes, food, and a place to sleep.

The sergeant was a friendly fellow, and for days after the first interview I came by his post daily, and we talked. One day I told him that I could use a typewriter (I had used one working on the *Narodni Glas*), whereupon he became enthusiastic, painting the opportunities that awaited a boy of clerical ability in the military service. I would be made a company clerk, which was but a stepping-stone to becoming a battalion or even a regimental sergeant-major—positions of great dignity.

When, finally, I was down to my last five dollars, I went to the sergeant and told him to take me to the recruiting-office. I was not yet a citizen, but had taken out my first papers, which was all that was required for a foreign-born applicant for enlistment.

I was sent to Fort Slocum, New York, to be examined and sworn in. I stayed there, undergoing recruit training, for about two months, or till the end of April.

President Wilson made his speech before Congress, urging a declaration of war on Germany and her allies for the sake of democracy, the rights of small nations, and many other ideals.

A few days after the declaration of war I was called to appear before the commanding officer of my provisional recruit company. At enlistment I had given Austria as my native country, and now the captain questioned me, in compliance with orders from higher up, as to my political views and my loyalty to the United States. Did I believe in the American form of government? I said, "Yes, sir." Did I know why the United States had declared war upon Germany? I said, "To secure the rights of small

115

nations, like my own people in the Old Country, and to make the world safe for democracy." This brought a smile to the captain's stern face, and he dismissed me with the admonition to be a good soldier.

Recruits poured into Fort Slocum. To most of them the army was scarcely more than a convenient meal ticket and a "flop," or an escape from everydayness; but there were also dutiful, ignorantly patriotic lads touched by war hysteria, eager to lay their hands on the enemy or a spy in their own midst. Somehow, word got about that I was an Austrian, and before my comrades-in-arms accepted me as a stanch and loyal soldier in the Crusade for Democracy, I was compelled to take two of them, a week apart, "behind the butts"—a spot in back of the quarters where matters of honor were usually settled with fists. The first one got the better of me, but the second one, who was more my size and less deft with his mitts, I beat up rather thoroughly. Thereafter it was understood at Fort Slocum that some Austrians were Slavs, racially kin to the Serbians and Russians, and Austrians in name only.

III

While I was having difficulties on account of my Austrian birth, I struck up a casual friendship with the boy who had his bunk next to mine.

His name was Lonie Burton. He was an American, nineteen years old, with a handsome, pale face. He had a nicely cleft chin and mild gray-blue eyes, wavy brown hair, a high sloping forehead, and delicate hands with long fingers.

After my second fight "behind the butts," he asked me to tell him more about my nationality. I told him about the Yugoslav Movement before the war, the killing of my

116

friend Yanko Radin by the Austrian cavalry, and my expulsion from the Austrian schools because of my anti-Austrianism.

Thereafter Lonie Burton and I were together a good deal of the time after drill periods, evenings, and on Sundays. He told me about himself. He was from Milford, a little town in eastern Pennsylvania. His mother, a widow, had a summer boarding-house there. He had graduated from high school the previous year.

He had an adventurous, eager mind; a sensitive, responsive, impulsive nature. He read books and the better kind of magazines. From him I first heard of Theodore Dreiser and Stephen Crane. Just then his chief enthusiasms were Walt Whitman and Woodrow Wilson. Whitman, he had recently discovered, and kept a copy of *Leaves of Grass* under the mattress of his bunk. We read the book together. The poem that appealed to him most was "Thunder on! strike on, Democracy. . . ."

For Wilson he had a passionate admiration. He could scarcely express his feelings about the man. Wilson was a poet-statesman, no less. He held in his wise hands the fate of mankind and his great soul embraced every nation, big and small. This was a war to end war. "Thunder on! strike. on, Democracy! . . . I have lived to behold man burst forth and warlike America rise. . . ." The United States, said Lonie, had nothing against the Germans. America's purpose in entering the conflict was to crush the inhuman Prussian machine and save the German people from their rulers and from themselves. Lonie knew by heart a great many Wilsonian phrases, which he quoted to me.

Now and then I caught his fire and shared his enthusiasm. But not for long. Most of the time I was too strongly aware of the unadmirable phases of America, of which Lonie, having grown up in a small and quiet non-indus-

117

trial town, did not even dream. The peasant in me gave me the tendency to distrust intangible things, to rely on common sense and keep on guard against high ideals and fancy ideas. Lonie's idealism was genuine and poetic, but at times it was not easy for me to keep from laughing at him. When I walked alone on the sea wall around Fort Slocum, thinking of Lonie Burton and Walt Whitman and Woodrow Wilson, their idealism seemed to me unsound, romantic, verging on the absurd.

But it was pleasant to walk and talk with Lonie in our spare time, if only as a relief from the routine of soldiering. Also, I enjoyed reading Whitman. My favorite poem in the book was "I Sit and Look Out":

I sit and look upon all the sorrows of the world, and upon all
    oppressions and shame,
I hear secret convulsive sobs from young men at anguish with
    themselves, remorseful after deeds done, . . .
I see the slights and degradations cast by arrogant persons
    upon laborers, the poor, and upon negroes, and the like;
All these—all the meanness and agony without end I sitting
    look out upon,
See, hear, and am silent.

IV

Lonie was all stirred up when we read that the United States would presently send troops to France. He hoped he would be in the first contingent.

But toward the end of April we learned that most of the recruits then at Slocum would be sent to the Panama Canal Zone on a transport sailing in a few days. We were to be assigned to the Regular Army regiments there.

Lonie protested; but the company commander told him, in a severe tone of voice, that his first duty was to obey orders and go wherever the government saw fit to send him. The boy then consoled himself with the rumor, which became current among the recruits, that we were being sent to Panama to raise the regular regiments there to full war strength, and after a while we would all sail for France from Panama.

I rather liked the idea of going to Panama.

CHAPTER X

Superman

THE Regular Army regiment stationed at Camp Empire, in the Canal Zone, to which Lonie Burton and I, along with several hundred other recruits, were assigned on our reaching Colon, was on maneuvers near La Chorrera, a town in the jungles of the Republic of Panama.

On arrival from Colon at the garrison's railroad station, we were met by a few non-commissioned officers who had been left behind to take care of us. After a while there appeared on the scene an officer mounted on the biggest and most beautiful horse I have ever seen. Presently he dismounted and, turning the horse over to an orderly, strode to where one of the sergeants was putting us in formation.

His name, as I learned later in the day, was Captain Waldo Dana Blakelock. He was well over six feet tall, weighed in the vicinity of two hundred and thirty pounds, and was built, in agreeable proportions, of solid bone and muscle—a veritable engine of energy and strength, apparently without an ounce of superfluous flesh, although, as I discovered subsequently, he was in his fifties. Before the war, promotion in the Regular Army was a tardy process. If one lacked the professional or personal qualities that were supposed to make one a successful officer and gentleman, or (as I think was Blakelock's case) happened to be, in some vital respect, an unduly superior individual, one was apt to remain a captain till almost ripe for the retired list.

120

SUPERMAN

Captain Blakelock appeared at least fifteen years younger than he actually was; indeed, the single indication that he was past forty was the graying hair on his temples, which, however, was cut so short, according to army regulations, that one scarcely noticed it. Perhaps the first impression that he gave was that of virile maturity. He was erect, supple, almost dashing-looking. There was a scantily perceptible horseman's bow in his powerful legs, but he moved freely, coördinatedly, like a man accustomed to striding over plains and hills, with a slight, restrained swank very unlike the average West Pointer's precise parade-ground bearing and movement.

His face was in complete harmony with his solid physique—a large, hard face, well-shaped, with a few deep character lines which could not be mistaken for wrinkles. The tropical sun had burned the otherwise smooth, almost taut, skin to a rich bronze tint which glinted vividly whenever he tilted his head, and his face came into the sunlight from beneath the wide rims of his huge campaign hat. Under his close-clipped mustache was a regular mouth with lips of moderate thickness; his nose was straight, neither long nor short, slightly blunted at the end; and just below his eyes, clinging to the rather prominent cheek-bones, stretched a band of even deeper brown which at times seemed rusty red.

His eyebrows, darker than his mustache or the hair on top of his head (which I saw later, with his hat removed), penciled a straight line under his wide and unwrinkled brow, which was much whiter than his sunburnt cheeks. His eyes were wide apart, their whites as white as could be, but with a reddish glint in the grayness of the pupils which gave his gaze a cool, scrutinizing ardor. Now and then, as he talked, the gray pupils seemed to dilate till the whites of his eyes became scarcely visible, and the glint

121

turned into a flame as of an algid, suppressed fire: a sardonic humor leaping discomfitingly with inaudible laughter. From the flash of ivory-like teeth, his speech came with strangely penetrating power in even the most familiar words. It had the deep, ear-filling tones that one logically expected to issue from that massive chest.

He was the most impressive animal I have ever seen in human form—impressive in the manner of a stallion, a powerful motor-car, or a trim battle-cruiser; and even before he spoke to me I could not help but feel, vaguely, that within his huge frame functioned cognitive powers to match it.

II

After we had been lined up by the non-coms, Blakelock made a short inspection of the detachment, pausing here and there to speak with the recruits.

Lonie Burton and I stood side by side, and as he neared us, I remember that I felt distinctly uneasy. I was a foreigner, still self-conscious of my English pronunciation; besides, at Fort Slocum we had been impressed with the idea that, so far as we were concerned, an officer of the United States army was a cross between Beelzebub and Jehovah.

Blakelock stopped in front of Lonie. He gazed at him a long moment.

"What was your idea in enlisting at this time, young man?" he asked him, and the air vibrated with the energy of his voice. "Tell me," he urged, as Lonie, all flustered, sought to collect his ability to speak.

"Sir," began Lonie, "I—I ——"

"What?" rang the voice of Blakelock.

"I want to make—to help to make the world safe for democracy, sir," said Lonie.

His answer sounded idiotic to me. I felt ashamed for him.

"So!" exclaimed Blakelock, and his blazing eyes seemed to expand as if with wonder.

He gazed at Lonie a moment longer, then he turned to me.

"And you?" he asked me.

Lord! what *could* I say? Looking at him, I almost heard something click, or perhaps I should say crackle, in his eyes as he gazed at me.

"Why did you join the army at this time?"

"Same reason, sir," I finally managed to say, idiotically, feeling ashamed of myself.

"To make the world safe for democracy?"

"Yes, sir."

He was obviously mocking me and Lonie Burton; all of us.

Then he turned to the recruit on the other side of me—a fat little Jewish youth in a crummy, heavy, ill-fitting woolen uniform, with tiny beads of perspiration standing out in great density all over his face.

"My, what a splendid lad you are!" Blakelock exclaimed, and stared at the fellow with mock benevolence for an endless moment, while the victim, sweat streaming down his flushed face, commenced to fidget, wince, and shift the weight of his body from one foot to another. "How old are you?"

"Twen—twenty-three, sir."

"Twenty-three! Ah, you're a splendid lad! A splendid lad!" Blakelock repeated with great conviction, the devil turning gay somersaults in the cool blaze of his eyes. Then he stooped and, with his great, sunbaked hands felt the recruit's legs, posterior parts, and back and arms, ignoring, however, the slightly protruding stomach. "Splendid!

123

The army is proud to have a promising young man like you! No doubt you also joined the army to make the world safe for democracy."

"Yes, sir," said the recruit.

"Fine! Fine!"

The non-coms behind Blakelock's back were bursting with suppressed mirth.

III

At the mess-table that evening I overheard a conversation between a line sergeant, who sat at the head of the table, and a newcomer who was a reënlisted man and as such entitled to speak with the old-timers of the Regular Army the first day he hit the post. The sergeant, it seemed, had known Blakelock for years.

"Yeah, a queer bird," he declared. "You saw the way he acted this afternoon. He's always like that when there's nobody that ranks him around to watch him. Sometimes he doesn't care if there is. That's his idea of havin' a good time, I guess—kiddin' the troopers, like the fun he had with that comical kike recruit. 'My, what a splendid lad you are! Splendid!'--and then feelin' 'im up and down like he was a horse or a cow or a turkey he was goin' to buy—tryin' to make the poor sap think he looks like Benny Leonard! He's as liable as not to stop the dumbest-lookin' yap, congratulate him on his intelligent looks, and ask him how much the moon weighs or how far off the sun is, or some other crazy question like that. And if you say that you don't know, he'll tell you how to figure it out —he's a regular walkin' 'cyclopædia—and require you to report to him in two hours and forty-four minutes with the answer. It's best just to make a guess; he takes your answer as correct, anyhow. . . . The old-timers 'round here are wise to him, but I bet he'll have lots of fun with

124

these recruits. He always does. Recruits are his favorite
meat. He's nuts. Been up before boards of medical officers
examinin' his sanity I don't know how many times here
and, before, in the Islands; but on the other hand the
man's too smart for the best of them to prove he's crazy.
They say he's one of the smartest men in the army. I
heard it said by officers that he was too bright for his own
good. He's been in this regiment now for two years, and
we never had a commandin' officer that would give him
permanent command of a company. They keep him on
special duty most of the time—post-exchange officer,
provost marshal, or send him on some mappin' detail in
the jungles. Now the Old Man—'the colonel'—left him
behind to drill these recruits—and he the rankin' captain
in the outfit!"

After supper I took a walk through the garrison. Lonie
would not come with me; he was busy checking his equipment, which he had just drawn.

I walked toward the officers' quarters, without knowing
exactly where I was going, when suddenly I saw a tall
figure in white coming toward me at an energetic pace
out of the dusk. Seeing that it was Blakelock in his tropical dress uniform, I thought of evading him, but it was
too late.

He returned my salute with a tremendous snap, stopped
before me, and through the dimness began to contem-
plate me with intense interest from head to foot. The white
uniform and the gold insignia gave his dark face, with
those incisive eyes peering at me, a suggestion of weirdness, which sent a creepy feeling up my back.

"What's your name?" he asked me.

I told him.

"Ah so! a Slav!"

And, vastly to my surprise, he began to talk with me

125

in a mixture of Russian, Czech, and Serbian, which I had little difficulty understanding. He achieved heights of eloquence in praising my appearance. Was I by any chance descended from Kralyevich Marko (a Serbian legendary hero)? No? Well, even so, I was a fine, heroic lad, and America, the land of the free and the brave, was proud to count me among her soldiers of democracy.

His knowledge of Serbia amazed me; I did not know then, as I found out later, that he had been a military observer in the last Balkan War.

Then he felt my limbs and chest, and urged me, in the manner of Bernarr Macfadden, to take care of myself, for a healthy body was a soldier's supreme asset. Did I play ball? Tennis? Did I run well? Ride horseback? Swim? What, I did not know how to swim! "I shall teach you!" And then and there he made me fetch a grocery-box that he espied near by, assume a prone position on it, and go through the motions of swimming. "That is all there is to it!"

Changing the subject, he told me to uncover myself; then he took my chin in his fingers and, tilting my head this way and that, looked at me with the air of a connoisseur contemplating an object of great interest and value.

"You're a fine young man!" he went on in Slavic, his eyes snapping with a mocking kind of approbation, which made me extremely uncomfortable. "You see that brick building across the street?" indicating the post-office.

"Yes, sir."

"How many bricks are there in it, tell me."

I was confused, stumped; then I recalled the old soldier's remarks at the supper-table, a while before. I looked at the house a few moments, and answered: "Two thousand four hundred and twenty bricks, sir," or some such number, and tried to look amused.

Blakelock's eyes clicked as he looked at me. My mouth and throat became suddenly dry. I longed for the ground to open at my feet and swallow me.

"That's right!" he said, and, assuring me again that I was a considerable asset to the armed forces of the United States, he left me standing in the dark.

When I recovered from the impact of his personality, I laughed to myself in the darkness.

I went back to the quarters and told Lonie about my encounter with Blakelock.

"He's crazy," said Lonie. "What does he mean by mocking us like that?"

I said: "I don't know, but he may not be so crazy as he seems. He certainly is a queer one, though."

IV

During the next three weeks Blakelock put us, with the assistance of a few sergeants, through a strenuous program of recruit drills, field games, swimming lessons in the post pool and hikes: constantly kidding or mocking one man or another, or all of us together; flattering us extravagantly, admiring our beautiful frames and intelligent faces, never reprimanding anyone, asking fantastic questions, venting his tremendous energy in many unique ways, and incidentally shaping the shabby lot of rookies —ex-farm boys, hoboes, petty criminals, factory hands, clerks, and drifters, native and foreign-born—into presentable soldiers.

Somehow I was unable to classify him as a mere nut; indeed, the more I saw of him the more astonishing he grew in my young eyes. To all seeming there was nothing he did not know or was unable to do. I began to suspect

127

that he was a genuinely superior person—woefully out of place in the army—to whom this collection of young soldiers was little more than a source of temporary amusement. With all his eccentricities, he never really jeopardized his dignity; indeed, he steadily maintained what, to me at least, was a fascinating aloofness.

At times he positively awed me. One night he came by our barracks where a number of us sat on the steps, and after wishing us good evening and bidding us remain seated, began to examine us in astronomy. The sky was close to the earth and thickly strewn with stars; and as none of the boys knew much about the constellations, he asked those of us who wished to do so to come with him upon a hill near by, where the view of everything visible above was unobstructed. He kept us there for over an hour, pointing out the various groups and single planets, telling us their size, weight, and composition, and explaining how it was possible for scientists to determine these things. It was apparent, too, that to him they were not mere facts; at the end of his lecture he recited a long poem, which I recognized years later when I read George Sterling's "Testimony of the Suns."

He not only spoke Slavic with me, but Swedish with Swedes, Italian with Italians, and Yiddish with Jews. One evening I even heard him discourse in Chinese with the Chink waiter at the post canteen.

He swam superbly and cut an impressive figure on horseback. The magnificent mount he usually rode was his own property. In a huge holster depending from his belt and tied around his thigh with a leather band he carried a weapon which was no mere side-arm, but a miniature machine-gun of his own invention and design, of which he owned the only copy and with which he was able to hit without fail a baseball tossed into the air.

When he walked the ground shook within a radius of fifty feet. His appetite was Gargantuan. One evening I saw him bolt down two regulation-size vegetable-dishes full of *chile con carne* and beans, with a platter of boiled rice and a bowl of yams, which he considered capital food, and wash the whole mess down with seven cups of coffee by exact count.

One was told that some years before, at the age of forty-five, when the sporting world of America was looking for a "white hope" to defeat Jack Johnson, Blakelock offered to meet the mighty Negro, but that the War Department objected on the ground that to do that would be unbecoming an officer and a gentleman. He would have had to resign his commission, which, for reasons that I found out later, he was unwilling to do.

Stories and rumors about him, I also learned subsequently, were afloat from one end of the Canal to the other. He was unmarried, and extravagant tales of his amours, past and current, while for the most part, no doubt, untrue, were heard and repeated all over the Zone, in Panama City and Colon. One story concerned a magnificent yellow wench from New Orleans, formerly a maidservant in a colonel's family in Balboa, whom Blakelock was credited with keeping in a mysterious cabin in the jungles beyond the Zone line. He was, it seemed, a tremendous lover.

He was one of the highest four or five ranking captains in the army, and he would have been a major years before but for the fact that, at various times in his career, both at home and abroad, he had indulged in "stunts" which in the eyes of his superiors and subordinates alike had marked him as an unmilitary and ungentlemanly, if not downright crazy, individual. All of which, in the course of time, had a blighting effect upon his efficiency record

and promotion. Moreover, he disdained officers' hops and
bridge evenings, which in peace time were integral parts
of the life of every normal officer and his wife. He had
been court-martialed three times, investigated and examined by all kinds of boards, and on several occasions
demoted on the list by a number of files.

Then, too, he was given to frequent criticism of time-
honored military tactics and customs. A great part of the
army drill regulations he considered obsolete since the
Spanish-American War. He had very definite opinions
about West Point and the War College.

In the Army List, some time later, I saw that Blakelock
was a native of Virginia and a graduate of West Point
ι nd the War College. From other sources I learned that
soon after the Spanish-American War, in which he had
participated inconspicuously, he had spent four years on
a language detail in China; then, while still a lieutenant,
he had served, between tours of line duty in the States
and the tropics, as military *attaché* to the American
embassies at St. Petersburg, Berlin, Rome, and Constan-
tinople, and more recently, when a captain, as a war observer in the Balkans, as I have mentioned.

It was widely believed that he was wealthy, and that
during Republican administrations he had had a powerful friend in Washington, now dead—which accounted for
the fact that, from time to time, he had been sent to desir-
able positions in foreign capitals and elsewhere, notwith-
standing his eccentricities and the resultant unfavorable
marks in his service record.

v

One afternoon the acting top sergeant of the provisional
recruit company directed me to report to Captain Blakelock at his quarters. Speculating with much perturbation

on what might befall me, I approached his dwelling at
the end of the Officers' Line—a huge frame house intended
to accommodate four bachelors; but it was no secret that
Blakelock preferred to be by himself, which, on the other
hand, coincided beautifully with the disinclination of most
of his brother officers to live with him under the same roof.

The building reverberated with the staccato noise of
a punching-bag, which ceased as I rang the door-bell. In
a few moments Blakelock appeared to ask me would I care
to be his striker for a week or ten days. His Chinaman had
been taken ill, but was expected to be well again in that
length of time. Blakelock added that while working for
him I would be excused from certain regular duties and
that he would pay me three times the customary fee provided by Paragraph 17, Sub-Paragraph E, of the post
regulations.

Motivated more by the desire to know the man better
than to earn the extra six bits a day, I replied in the
affirmative and became his "dog-robber"—a disparaging
Regular Army term for striker.

They were typical officer's quarters except for the little
gymnasium improvised in one of the rooms, and the library. One day while Blakelock was out I could not resist
the impulse to examine the unlocked bookcases. One contained volumes on military matters in English, French,
and German; in the others were publications in perhaps
a dozen different languages, Western and Oriental, on a
great variety of subjects. There were numerous biographi-
cal studies of such characters as Bismarck, Napoleon,
Justinian, Frederick the Great, George Washington,
Garibaldi, Ivan the Terrible, and Peter the Great. There
were books and pamphlets by Shaw, Emerson, Nietzsche,
and a few contemporary American writers. Perhaps half
of the titles were in languages of which I was ignorant.

131

On the wall hung an immense detailed war map of
Europe, with pins in several colors and tiny flags of the
warring nations strung across the two fronts.

Blakelock often spoke to me, but always in that half-
mocking way, giving me all sorts of crazy problems and
riddles to solve, warning me against the evil women of
the notorious Coco Grove in Panama City, and reiterating
his infinite confidence in my abilities as a soldier.

Only once he ventured an apparently serious remark—
he hoped the regiment would soon be ordered to Europe.

One morning I found about one-third of the books removed from the bookcases and piled up on the back porch.
My wonderment turned to astonishment when Blakelock
directed me to carry the volumes to the incinerator and
burn them. I did as I was told, unable to work up enough
courage to ask him what it was all about. He seemed
unusually abrupt and curt. In the evening he took me
with him to a junk-shop in Panama City, where he bought
a large sackful of old Western and detective novels, cook-
books, Bible commentaries, sermon anthologies, and a set
of Elbert Hubbard's works for a few dollars, and asked
me to lug the trash to his quarters and put it on the
empty shelves in the bookcases.

The whole thing struck me as very peculiar, but months
later it was revealed to me as an example of his sardonic
humor. I was told by a man who was in his confidence—
Michael Koska, of whom more in a moment—that the
day before I burned the books he had received a visit from
the Department Intelligence Officer, who, after putting
him through a long cross-examination about his ideas of
Nietzsche and the other Hun monsters, had ordered him,
in the name of the commanding general, to get rid of
certain volumes in his library without delay.

132

CHAPTER XI

The Man with the Big Head

I

WHEN the regiment returned from the jungles, Lonie and I and about a dozen other recruits were assigned to Company M, and I ceased to be Captain Blakelock's "dog-robber." His Chinaman was well again.

Paying me for my services, Blakelock said to me: "You have been put in a very good company. Very good indeed. When you report to your organization, tell your first sergeant—Sergeant Koska—that I should like to see him soon."

"Yes, sir."

Immediately after joining the outfit, I went to the orderly-room and gave the first sergeant the message.

"All right," he said. "Thanks." Then he looked at me. "You're one of our new recruits, aren't you?" he asked.

"Yes, sir."

"What's your name?"

I told him.

"Your nationality? Where were you born?"

"Slovenian—Yugoslav," I said. "Born in Austria."

He nodded his head, looking at me. His speech had a slight foreign accent, but his English was smooth. His name—Michael Koska—suggested to me that he, too, probably was a Slav by birth, very likely a Bohemian. "All right, Private Adamic," he said, and dismissed me.

But what I had noticed about him first of all was his head—unquestionably the biggest head I had yet seen on a man—a massive affair of great height, width, and depth, but apart from its hugeness quite normal-looking. The face was high and broad, rather stolid, almost mask-like in expression and mildly Slavic in such details as the cheek-bones, the jaws, and the chin. The small hazel eyes were wide-spaced, giving out an intensely, unnaturally calm and abstracted look, which became a bit disconcerting if he took a notion to regard one with it too long. The nose, too, was rather small, though on a smaller face it would have appeared medium-sized; and the same was true of the mouth, with its compressed, immobile lips which scarcely moved even when he spoke.

The front of the colossal dome was shiny-bald, while in back it was a dense tangle of curly, graying dark hair. The forehead rose high and vertically, with a barely perceptible bulge, from the line of thin, uncurved eyebrows to the slow slope of the skull, and the space between the temples was truly enormous. The ears were big even in proportion to the head, and well shaped.

He was in his mid-thirties, a professional soldier with many years' service.

On first impression, when I saw only his head, there was something startling, titanic, almost formidable about the man; but then, as he spoke to me in his impassive, matter-of-fact voice, much of that impression left me. By-and-by I noticed, too, his short, thick-set body, which just escaped looking dumpy, and his small, delicate hands. His chest was wide and deep, but his shoulders and arms did not exactly suggest power. His legs, also, were thin, and he carried a considerable stomach.

Weeks before I came to know him well, I occasionally got an instinctive notion that there was in him a deep strength that was passive, thwarted, unfunctioning. Somehow, I sensed this as I looked at his great face, on which there was not a trace of flabbiness, but just skin, smooth and brown, stretched taut over the muscles and big round bones, with not a wrinkle anywhere except a few very minute ones around the eyes.

On the whole, he appeared an unharmonized personality, and for a time I was at once attracted and repelled by him. He excited my interest from the first, but he vaguely disconcerted me. I could not decide what it was that made me feel that way about him; possibly his big head; I mean purely its physical bigness; but more likely the intuitive feeling I had about him, that he was a superior man not functioning as such.

Outside the line of duty, he spoke seldom and little. But sometimes when he did speak, the stolid expression of his face vanished instantly before a wry sort of grin that contained a suggestion of melancholy. Now and then he gazed at one for minutes at a time, as though trying to figure one out. At drills and generally in the performance of duty his manner was mechanically alert and efficient; off duty it was a little stiff, or perhaps I should say nervously restrained.

He was a good soldier, neat in appearance, and, as first sergeant, consistently fair and reasonable in his attitude toward the men under him; but the idea frequently came to me that he merely went through the motions of soldiering and administering the affairs of the company; that soldiering meant nothing to him—nothing real or vital; that the army to him was an escape (from what I did not know); that while he was putting us through formations and tactical movements his mind was somewhere else.

As first sergeant he had a room by himself next to the company office. When as room orderly I occasionally cleaned the latter, I looked into his room, if he had happened to leave the door open, and saw shelves of books

135

over his bunk. He seldom went to Panama City that he did not return with a bundle of reading-matter, and now and then he received packages direct from publishers in the States. He subscribed to scientific journals, which, after reading them, he usually placed on the table in our company recreation-room.

He mixed very little with the men in the company, not even with the other non-coms. Most of the men, of course, considered him a little queer. None of them tried very hard to figure him out. They merely accepted him as a bit eccentric and let it go at that, for more or less unique or lopsided characters were not uncommon among the old-timers of the Regular Army before the war. Everybody was aware of his big head. Outside the company, those who did not know his name, and even some who did, referred to him as "the guy with the big head from Company M."

Some of the older men who had known him for years said that he disliked very much to have anyone say anything about his head, and so everybody refrained from making any reference to it in his hearing. He did not like to be stared at. Whenever and wherever possible, he wore his hat, which was the largest size in the service.

He had other peculiarities which excited comment in the company, and for that matter in the whole regiment. For instance, like nearly everybody else in the post, he occasionally went to the movies evenings, but he never entered the hall until the lights went out and always left just before the final kiss. In the movie-hall everybody was required to uncover, and Koska did not want people to stare at his head.

And after the show he was wont to walk alone through and outside the garrison till after taps, and then, returning to quarters, read in his room for hours. The light in his room was apt to be turned on almost any hour of the night. Later he told me that he seldom slept more than three hours a night; some nights not at all.

But to me, perhaps, the queerest thing about him for some time was his sense of humor. Often I would see him smile or grin at things or situations in which the rest of us saw nothing funny, and, conversely, often his face would remain stolidly solemn when everybody else laughed or smiled.

Another thing that struck me as interesting and significant was the talk in the squad-rooms that the captain who had made him first sergeant was Blakelock, when the latter had been temporarily in command of the company about a year before. Koska and Blakelock, it seemed, were close personal friends. There were rumors and suggestions that there was something mysterious about this. They were often seen together, talking. Koska visited Blakelock in his quarters.

Our present company commander was a rather shabby, incompetent captain—I forget his name—who, before he came to the outfit, had been on some sort of staff duty and knew little of regular soldiering. He let Koska run the company.

II

Soon after the regiment returned from maneuvers, a good deal of reorganization and transferring went on in the outfit. One of the men transferred out of Company M was the company clerk, a corporal, who became a clerk at the regimental headquarters.

For a few days there was some speculation in the outfit as to whom Koska would make his new company clerk. For a few weeks no one was selected; indeed, there were no eager aspirants for the job, and Koska did the company clerical work himself.

137

Then one day he called me into the office. He said: "I see on your qualification card in the service record"—which had been filled out at the recruit depot on my enlisting—"that you know how to typewrite. Would you like to try to become company clerk?"

I had no particular taste for office work, preferring regular duties even if they included kitchen police and endless "fatigue," but Koska fascinated me so that, after a bit of hesitation, I said, "Yes, I think I would."

So I became "acting company clerk"; later, on making more or less good at the job, full-fledged clerk and private, first class. In this capacity, of course, I spent most of my time in Koska's proximity; and I moved my bunk and equipment into another little room next to the office, where I was allowed to burn the light after tattoo and read.

Gradually I began to develop a great respect for Koska. When he learned that I played a little chess (having played a few score of games with Mr. Zemlar in New York), he became mildly excited. Would I play with him? Of course, I said I would. Thereafter we spent several evenings each week in his room or in the office, playing chess. He owned a beautiful set which he reticently told me he had carved out of two different kinds of wood, one dark and the other light, when he had soldiered in the Philippines, years before. Each figure seemed to me exquisitely done, a work of art. He was an excellent chessplayer, and taught me the more intricate moves.

Eventually we talked of other things. When he saw that I would not take advantage of his friendliness, his manner toward me gradually expanded and I began to think of him as a very likable individual.

I told him most of the things about myself, that I tell

138

in the foregoing pages—of course, not quite as I tell them here, but as I then saw them.

In his turn, he told me that he was, as I had surmised, a Czech by birth, but added, casually-like, that that meant nothing to him. Somehow, he did not feel a bit like a Bohemian, or anything else, for that matter; and saying this he grinned and shrugged his shoulders. What he said I felt was true and frank. I was grateful for his frankness. I had a notion that he had never spoken this way to anyone, except, perhaps, to Blakelock (although I think this exception occurred to me later). He must have instinctively felt that I would understand him, or at least not misjudge him.

He had come to America at eighteen, joined the army at nineteen, and been in the service ever since—"over eighteen years," he said, with a fatalistic lift of his eyebrows, and grinned.

His wry smile—when I knew, or thought I knew, what had provoked it—began to appeal to me. Sometimes I thought that I saw in it a great but powerfully restrained eagerness to be friendly or kind, and I began to like him immensely. I remember that when I heard some soldier make a stupid remark about Koska's head I boiled up inside and wanted to do something about it; of course, I never did anything, knowing that whatever I said in Koska's behalf would only be misinterpreted.

In addition to my clerical work, I had to attend drills and perform a few other duties, in respect to which Koska treated me like any other private; but I was always conscious of his good will toward me.

He was frankly, almost naïvely, pleased with my interest in his books, which were for the most part scientific and philosophic treatises—Huxley, Darwin, Spencer, Spinoza, and the like. He evidently had read them all

139

more than once; many of the pages were pencil-marked. His mastery of the various subjects, when he talked to me upon them, impressed me very much. He spoke to me as though he had memorized and digested everything he read.

He had one or two books in his room which belonged to Blakelock; they had his signature inside.

I perceived that Koska liked to talk to me, and I encouraged him by being as good and responsive a listener as I could. I walked with him evenings.

He could reminisce endlessly about things that he had seen and experienced in the army. During the first few months of our acquaintance and friendship he said nothing that I remember as important or thrilling, but he described everything in minutest detail. What interested me most, I think, was the power and vividness with which he managed to present to me every character, scene, and circumstance that he mentioned. His psychological insight into people's motives and actions, as I realized more later than at the time being, was truly incredible. He had an astounding memory and had but little difficulty in finding words to convey his meanings.

But at the same time I was more and more mystified by him. Always there was that tendency or habit of his to smile or grin (he never laughed), as he talked to me, when I could see nothing funny, and to remain serious when I was amused.

Several times I asked why he was smiling, but he always ignored my question. Talking to me for hours at a stretch more than once a week, he really gave me no direct clue to his basic make-up. Sometimes I lay in bed at night, puzzling about him. Why did a man like this spend the best part of his life as an enlisted man in the army?

140

One evening I ventured to put the question to him directly.

He looked at me, startled. His eyes became big for an instant and his small hands came together in a fierce, nervous clasp. Then, suddenly, he relaxed again, grinned, and lowered his eyelids. In another moment the grin went off his face and there was the old stolid expression. He sat that way for several minutes without moving an eyelash, his lips drawn close together.

For a time I did not know what to do or say next. Evidently, I had touched a vital and very sensitive spot in him.

"Don't mind my asking you, Mike," I said. "I'm naturally curious—" (I called him "Mike" evenings, and by his rank in line of duty.)

He limbered up once more; there was a surge of blood under the deep tropical tan of his skin, and he grinned embarrassedly.

"Oh, I don't mind your asking me," he said; "only I think it's a silly question to ask a man. Why does anybody stay in the army? No reason at all. None of them know. They come in and stay in, some of them, that's all. And why not? What's the matter with soldiering, in peacetime or war-time? You always have a place to sleep and you're always sure of three squares a day and a shirt on your back. That's more than can be said for life outside. There's a lot that can be said for army life. Once you make up your mind to stay in, there's more freedom in the army than in civil life. Nothing to worry about. You do what you're supposed to do, and that's all."

"But," I persisted, "a man with a (I was going to say 'a head like yours')—with a mind like yours surely could have done better at something else. Your scientific and artistic proclivities should normally have taken you in

141

some other direction. That chess set you made, I think, is beautiful." By now I managed to express myself fairly well in English.

There was a moment's pause before Koska answered. I saw that he controlled himself with difficulty. He continued to grin, but his face was red and his eyes looked at me mirthlessly.

"That's all you know!" he snapped, glaring at me. "That's all *you* know."

Then, abruptly, he threw up his hands in a vague gesture. "It's silly to talk like this," he said. "Let's play a game of chess."

CHAPTER XII

Blakelock in Command

I

In July, 1917, the line-companies of our regiment were distributed along the Panama Canal, to guard the vital points of the great ditch. Company M was sent to Darien, a large wireless and power station midway between Colon and Panama City. On one side of the place was the Canal, where those who were not afraid of crocodiles could go bathing when off duty; on the other sides was the jungle.

We lived in large tents. Koska and I had a tent to ourselves. It was an interesting life. At last I knew what the jungle was: a chaos of strange, twisted trees, vines, vegetation, fungi, and flowers, scarcely penetrable even in the proximity of Darien, inhabited by snakes, lizards, monkeys, beasts of many kinds, insects, and lovely humming-birds. . . . So this was the analogy of America! . . .

By and large, soldiering in Panama suited me. In my private thoughts I did not care if I stayed in Panama till the end of the war, or longer. I was sure that eventually the Allies and the United States would beat Germany and Austria, even if I did not go to France. Besides, I was assured that, as a member of Company M, —th Infantry, I was doing important military service, anyhow, guarding Darien, while the other companies of the regiment guarded the locks, bridges, explosive magazines, and other structures which seemed in danger of being blown up by Hunnish spies.

Lonie Burton, on the other hand, along with a few

other men in the outfit, fretted more every day as it appeared that the regiment would not be sent to France. Thinking that I as a company clerk might have some inside information, Lonie asked me every few days if there was a chance of getting sent to Europe soon.

I told Koska about him, about his great eagerness to make the world safe for democracy, his reading of Walt Whitman, and his admiration for Wilson.

Koska merely grinned.

I was conscious of a flow of sympathy and understanding between Koska and myself. I wanted to talk with him about Blakelock and, when we spoke out of line of duty, I tried to lead our conversation in that direction. One day I mentioned that a great many men in the outfit thought Blakelock was crazy, and added that I, myself, thought some of his actions strange, to say the least.

Finally Koska said: "You don't know Blakelock. I mean the inside of him. Nor do those who say he's crazy."

"Do you, Mike?" I asked.

He looked at me, hesitating.

"I think I do," he said. "It's a long story. . . . I've known Blakelock for twelve years. I first saw him when he was company commander of the outfit I soldiered in, in the Islands. He was practically the same then as he's today. We've been what might be called friends for ten years. I usually managed to be transferred to whatever station or organization he was sent.

"He's from Virginia. He should never have gone into the army—become an officer of the army. I don't know everything about him, but I think he went to West Point mainly in compliance with family tradition before he was quite himself. My theory is that he is, always has been, too big a man for the army. He stayed in after he dis-

144

covered that army life did not satisfy him, because he commenced to get a perverse sort of pleasure out of annoying his mediocre superiors with idiosyncrasies which he developed out of the abundance of his energy and the fullness of his unused talents—if you know what I mean."

I thought I knew, and nodded.

"Also, he felt that some day there would be a great war in which, somehow, he might get his big chance. That is why he did not resign to fight Jack Johnson. Then, too, perhaps he knew that the conditions in civilian life in the United States were equally unfavorable to a man of his make-up, unless he took to big business, for which he had little stomach. In the army, as I see him, he was caught in a net of mediocrity."

In this connection, Koska explained to me why, some weeks before, Blakelock had ordered me to burn most of his best books, which, as a gesture, he later replaced with Pollyanna literature.

"He should have lived two hundred years ago and been a king, or something. In America—democratic America— such a man is just plain out of luck. In a democratic country like the United States a superior man most of the time can't become anything but a nut or a lunatic. Blakelock became a nut.

"His eccentricities are unfortunate, but not unnatural. Soldiering in peace-time is not enough for his powers. Then, too, like myself"—and Koska grinned—"he served long terms in the tropics, and the sun, perhaps, affected his brains.

"But the point that I want to make is this: Blakelock is not crazy—not really. He acts crazy to keep sane. . . . Most of his life so far has been a vast gesture. See what I mean?"

I nodded.

II

We were at Darien a week or ten days when our regular company commander was unexpectedly ordered to special duty at the department headquarters in Balboa and, probably because there was no other junior officer available, Captain Blakelock was sent to Darien to take temporary command of the company.

For the three weeks that Blakelock was in the outfit, he and Koska spent much of the time together. They tramped over the trails in the jungle. Somehow, from what Koska had told me of Blakelock, I figured that they had a lot in common. I imagined that this friendship, perhaps, had started when they mutually recognized one another's superiority, frustration, and uniqueness, of which qualities I was becoming more and more cognizant in both.

As company clerk I was required to do guard duty only once a week, and one night—an ineffably beautiful moon-night—I was sentry on what was called the long post, which took me from one end of the wireless-station reservation to the other. On my watch from eight to ten I saw and heard Blakelock and Koska sitting and talking on a pile of lumber near which I passed every fifteen minutes. They sat there and talked almost the entire two hours I was on duty.

Once, as I passed them, I could not help overhearing Blakelock reciting poetry. I did not know what it was he was declaiming, but his voice sounded beautiful and weird, amid the owls' and other creatures' hoots and screeches in the jungle all around. (The next morning, when I asked him, Koska told me that Blakelock had recited "Paradise Lost," of which I had not been aware before.)

Toward the end of my watch I heard Blakelock, from

146

'way off, suddenly burst out laughing. He laughed loudly and long. Koska, who still sat beside him, was silent; as I have said, he never laughed. Blakelock's laughter sounded untellably strange to me. It echoed from the jungle across the Canal. Now and then it seemed to have a double echo. (The next day, when I asked Koska, he told me what had provoked Blakelock to such laughter. "We were talking of politicians in Washington," he said. "I mentioned that a short time before William Jennings Bryan resigned as Secretary of State,"—in 1916—"he gave a dinner to the Diplomatic Corps in Washington at which he served grape juice—and this struck Blakelock as enormously funny.")

Koska and Blakelock parted a few minutes before my relief came. I saw Koska go to our tent.

Blakelock came toward me. I presented arms; he returned the salute, and said, "Gorgeous night, isn't it, Adamic?" His voice, of a sudden, sounded vibrantly soft, as if it did not belong to the same man who a few minutes before had laughed so loudly. Its vibrating intonation went through me, yet was not unpleasant. "Beautiful moon."

I said, "Yes, sir."

He left me.

On getting relieved, I went to the tent. Koska was just crawling under his mosquito netting, as I came in.

"Good night," he said.

"Good night, Mike," I said.

Presently I fell asleep. Koska, I think, was still awake when more than three hours later the corporal of the guard came to rouse me. I had to go on post again from two to four in the morning.

Drowsy, drugged with sleep, I was walking the post a quarter of an hour or so, when, passing a little distance

147

from an unused tennis-court, I heard a peculiar sound—as if some one were sobbing, in great distress. The moon had set by then and I could not see clearly. I stopped and listened closely. A light wind blew across the tennis-court in my direction.

Somehow, before I really made out the sound, I knew it was Blakelock. Curious and perturbed, I softly walked across the lawn and stopped near the tennis-court fence. I distinguished Blakelock sitting on a bench. . . . What could be the matter with him? Had the beauty of the night affected him? Or was a deep personal sorrow possible in such a man? Maybe it was an attack of some sort of *Weltschmerz*? His frustration? . . .

By-and-by the sobs ceased. Blakelock remained on the bench. I walked back across the soft lawn to my post. He did not see me.

In the morning I told Koska what I had heard and seen.

"How do you explain that?" I said.

"I'll not try to explain it," said Koska. "I've seen him that way myself. He's capable of almost any kind of mood, though the world at large knows but one—that of being a nut, a clown." Then he added: "I want you to promise me that you won't breathe of what you saw last night to anybody else."

"All right," I said.

After breakfast I purposely hung around the kitchen-tent to see Blakelock come for his breakfast. But when he came he looked as usual. He ate his customary half-dozen fried eggs and platter of potatoes, drank four cups of coffee, and chided the mess sergeant about the swarms of flies on the tables. The sergeant insisted that he was doing everything he knew to subdue them.

"Ah, get a lasso, Sergeant," said Blakelock, his eyes

148

snapping with all his customary vivacity. "Get a lasso and lasso them!"

III

We stayed at Darien till early in August, when another regiment stationed in the Zone was detailed to guard the Canal. We returned to Empire.

Then things began to happen at a swift rate.

The United States had decided to raise a great army and all Regular officers were suddenly elevated in rank by two and even three grades. In our regiment the colonel, a nervous, crabby old sister, was made a general and, along with most of the other promoted officers, ordered to the States on the first transport.

Blakelock, now a lieutenant-colonel, remained and, as the senior officer left in the outfit, assumed command of the regiment, while the battalions and companies were, for the most part, put under newly commissioned former Regular Army non-coms.

Koska was given a captaincy, with orders to go to the States at once, but managed—I don't know how—to get the orders revoked and himself assigned to his old regiment, whereupon Blakelock immediately appointed him adjutant. A little later Koska had me transferred as a sergeant to a semi-clerical position in the headquarters and I saw him and Blakelock almost daily.

Every now and then rumors started that the outfit would soon leave for the States or even that it would sail straight to France. Blakelock had everybody on tiptoe from morning till night, and he himself worked hardest. He spent an hour a day in the office, at the most; the rest in the hot sun or torrential rains, on the drill-field, or in the jungles. His energy was greater than ever.

We were all made to feel that not only was it war-time,

but that he was our commanding officer. Although the Regular soldier is a proverbially lazy and unambitious animal, the entire regiment, somehow, became infected with Blakelock's spirit, and there was comparatively little growling in the barracks or in the officers' mess. No matter how hard he drove us, there was nothing dull about our existence; into everything we were required to do he injected a suggestion of the circus.

Because he was our colonel, the regiment became known in the Zone as "the Dizzy Outfit." The department headquarters, whose swivel-chair Napoleons perhaps felt that Blakelock was a superior sort of individual but preferred to consider him daft, detailed his regiment to the hardest and most disagreeable tasks, or at least it seemed so. Some one would take a notion to have a strategic trail cut fifteen miles into the thickest jungle, and Blakelock was told to have his regiment do it; or the road to La Chorrera had to be repaired, and "the Dizzies" were ordered out with picks and shovels for two weeks.

Even so, within six months Blakelock had one of the best-drilled, hardest-hiking, best-shooting, neatest and healthiest outfits in the army, although perhaps few outside of the regiment would have admitted it. No doubt he knew his stuff; but at the same time the men—Lonie Burton for one—felt that if the regiment remained in Panama, cutting trails, doing guard duty, and fighting mosquitoes, instead of being sent to Europe, it would be chiefly because of Blakelock, or rather because of his record.

In garrison, Blakelock was holding full-field inspections every Saturday, as though he expected to take us to the front the next day. Thrice a week, at retreat-time, he held formal parade-reviews, at which he required everybody to look his best, no matter how hard we had worked during the day; he himself looked neater than anyone else. Adjutant Koska lined up the battalions facing the setting sun, with bayonets fixed on the rifles; whereupon Blakelock, wearing his largest campaign hat, dashed up on his great horse, reined in suddenly at the prescribed distance in front of the center of the line so that the animal reared a bit, and then for several minutes, while we stood at rigid attention, blinking at the blood-red sundown, he feasted his eyes upon his command—his living toy, the tool with which eventually he meant, perchance, to excel himself.

After the review or inspection, he sometimes would have the companies gather close around him, and he would speak to us from the splendid height of his horse, in that superior-democratic, half-serious, half-mocking way, praising us in glowing terms, hinting at the time—"in the not distant future"—when we would be afforded an opportunity to make our little blood-blotch on the pages of history.

But the rumors failed to materialize; instead, with the coming of another dry season the regiment was again sent on maneuvers in the jungley interior of the Republic. We at headquarters knew how impatient Blakelock was at not being ordered at once to take the regiment to Europe, or at least to the States; but on the march to La Chorrera he appeared, none the less, at the top of his glory. He went afoot all the way, while an orderly led his horse.

Before entering the town, he mounted and, with Koska and the rest of the staff, rode ahead to the house of the *alcalde*, waving his hat, greeting the natives profusely in their own dialect as our noble allies—for soon after the United States, Panama, too, had declared war on the Central Powers.

Behind him came the regiment, the band playing a

151

lively ragtime piece, while the men were urged by the company officers, in compliance with Blakelock's instructions, to wave their hats and shout greetings. The poor "spiggs," of course, were overwhelmed by this sudden cordiality of the *soldados Americanos*, who hitherto had treated them, at best, with overbearing tolerance.

IV

The regiment encamped two miles beyond La Chorrera. In the evening we were free to visit the town, and during those five weeks many a future citizen of the Panama Republic was given, literally, a start in life by Blakelock's men. Twice a week our band gave concerts on the *plaza* and "spiggs" came from the jungle settlements for miles around to hear them.

The place was ours. But then an incident occurred that for a few days marred this happy relationship between the allies.

One night a group of us were sitting in a *cantina*, kidding the Chorrera chief of police, who had invited himself to help us guzzle our "white mule" and beer. He wore his gaudy official uniform with epaulettes, brass buttons, and many medals, presenting the general appearance of a character out of a comic opera. His English was too scant, for him to understand our jibes, or else he pretended to overlook them for the sake of the drinks. At any rate, we were having a noble time.

He took a special fancy to a young private from our company who, having imbibed too freely, began to boast of his various accomplishments and finally produced an army pistol and commenced to explain to the chief how it worked. Suddenly the weapon went off, and an hour later the Chorrera guardian of the law died with a terrible hole in his belly.

The young soldier, of course, was immediately arrested by the M.P.'s. Blakelock restricted the regiment to camp for five days, caused a collection to be made in each company, and on the day after the funeral marched the whole command, the band playing, on to the *plaza* in La Chorrera and, amidst trumpet blares, presented the weeping widow with two bags of gold and silver so heavy that she was unable to carry them. He then expressed the deepest sorrow of the whole United States at the unfortunate occurrence, assured the *alcalde* and the townspeople that the man who was responsible for the valorous chief's premature passing would be punished, and promised that, so far as it was in his power to prevent it, nothing of the sort would ever happen again.

On the sixth day the town was again open to us. There was no bad feeling. The new chief of police (the force, incidentally, consisted only of him) wore the same uniform that his predecessor had worn. Now the coat had a little round patch over the stomach and the bloodstains were not yet entirely removed. The women of La Chorrera were even kinder to the men of the regiment than before. Their imaginations stirred by the exquisite luck of the late police chief's widow, they hoped openly, and with charming naïveté, that we might shoot their husbands, too.

All of which caused no end of laughing in the regiment. Blakelock himself laughed. Koska smiled. Even Lonie Burton was amused, although he disapproved of what he considered Blakelock's mockery of the lowly natives.

v

Finally, in the spring of 1918 the regiment received orders to proceed to a camp in Louisiana. But we no sooner arrived there than Blakelock was relieved of its command

and directed to report to Fort Oglethorpe, Georgia, to take charge of a Negro labor battalion scheduled to go overseas at once.

Blakelock, I think, had half expected that they might take the outfit away from him, but the order sending him to a Negro labor organization—not because it was Negro, but because it was labor—was for him a dose a bit too hard to take.

He went hurriedly to Washington in an attempt to retain the regiment or at least to be given a combatant unit, but was told, as he wrote to Koska, that unless he reported to Fort Oglethorpe and took over his new command immediately he would be court-martialed for disobedience of orders and probably dismissed from the service.

On showing me Blakelock's letter, which was brief and matter-of-fact, Koska said:

"Of course, with that unfortunate peace-time record on file against him in the War Department, and being personally known as a freak to many officers on duty in Washington, it is not unnatural that this should happen. In fact, come to think of it,"—sardonically—"it would be almost absurd that a man like Blakelock should be a combatant in the battle for democracy. Since fate made him an American army officer, it is perhaps appropriate to put him in a labor battalion. He'll be a straw-boss over gangs of coons unloading ships in Brest!" . . .

Lonie Burton, the crusader for democracy, now a corporal, to whom I told what I knew of Blakelock's transfer, said:

"Oh, to hell with Blakelock! . . . You and Koska can sympathize with him all you want to; I think he's crazy —no matter how he got that way—and I'd just as soon have a lesser military genius over me."

CHAPTER XIII

Koska and the "Flu"

I

On reaching Camp Beauregard—a tent cantonment—
in Louisiana, our regiment was split into four organizations, to form a skeleton division which, within a few weeks,
was filled to war strength with drafted men.

The draftees poured into camp from New Orleans,
Baton Rouge, Alexandria, and from the "sticks" and
"pine hills," coastal marshes and alluvial plains of Louisiana. Some appeared well-to-do young men, but many
came barefooted, hatless; illiterate, speaking no English
although natives of the United States. These latter were
'Cadians (Arcadians) or Louisiana French—huge, loose-
limbed, wild-looking but harmless, hookwormy fellows.
Some of them, we discovered as we lined them up to make
out their service records, had no surnames, or at least
did not know what they were. When asked, "What's your
name?" they mumbled, "Henri" or "Pierre" or "Olivier,"
and we had to give them names, simple ones, easy to remember, such as Smith or Jones.

Hundreds, perhaps thousands of these draftees—future
soldiers of democracy—were herded into camp by armed
county sheriffs as technical deserters. Unable to read, and
having no interest in Mr. Wilson's crusade, they had paid
no attention to draft notices, until the sheriffs came for
them and took them to camp—not so much out of a sense
of patriotic duty as to collect fifty dollars for each man
from Uncle Sam, which sum the man was then forced to
pay back to Uncle Sam out of his pay.

Many of these soldiers from the hookworm country amazed me. For breakfast they preferred corn bread and molasses to grapefruit and eggs. Knives and forks were useless to them. They did not know how to use modern plumbing in the bathrooms and latrines. Many of them, too, pretended ignorance of English and acted stupid because they had heard somewhere that those who did not speak the language and were dumb would not be sent to France.

II

In the reorganization shuffle, Lonie Burton went to a newly created National Army regiment as a sergeant. I stayed in the headquarters company of the old regiment; but soon after Blakelock had been relieved and a new colonel had taken over the command, Captain Koska ceased to be adjutant and was given a company, whereupon I secured a transfer to his outfit, and he made me company clerk again.

The summer months were a busy, hectic, feverish time for us all. We drilled from morning till night. Obviously, we were being readied for the front. But, off and on, Koska and I talked a little of things not in line of duty.

Once, in the midst of signing a pile of papers I had put before him, he suddenly looked up at me and exclaimed, in a low tone of voice:

"Fantastic!"

"What is fantastic?" I said.

There was no one else in the office-tent.

"Everything," he said. "This war—this country—this army!"

Reading of the war hysteria that had seized America, I had had a similar notion flitting in my brain; but I said:

156

"Why, Mike?"

"Oh——" he said vaguely "here they are, these yahoos—thousands of them, yanked out of the swamps and brought here by the sheriffs—drilling, marching, singing these silly songs—'*Good morning, Mr. Zip-Zip-Zip*' and '*There's a long trail a-winding*'—and after a while we'll go over with them and, the chances are, get shot. . . . What a helluva commentary on the collective intelligence of this breed called human! 'To make the world safe,' *et cetera.* . . ." He smiled.

"Would you rather we didn't go over?" I asked.

"What do you mean?"

"I mean so far as you yourself are concerned."

"No, I don't care. 'Orders is orders.' "

"And as far as the others—as far as the rest of us are concerned?"

"I don't care, either—except that I rather like you. You're fairly intelligent. . . . You understand. . . . You understand me without knowing me. Not that that is important, but——"

"But what, Mike?"

He lifted his eyebrows in a fatalistic frown and shook his great head; then went on signing the papers.

III

The training of the division went on through the summer. Some of the Louisiana Frenchmen commenced to speak a little English. Many of them were treated for hookworm. They began to look like soldiers, almost.

Then, in the first part of August, we had a long spell of rainy weather. Everything in our tents—clothes, bedding, equipment, cigarettes, matches—was damp and wet. The men drilled in mud and slush.

Suddenly, the third day of the rainy spell, two dozen

men in our company went on sick report. The same was true of every company in camp. Some of the men were too ill with a mysterious ailment—"a sort of grippe"—to leave their bunks and go to the regimental infirmary.

It was the beginning of the "flu" epidemic.

Koska came from an officers' meeting at the regimental headquarters and in his usual quiet voice said to me: "I think we'll all be quarantined before the day is over. Over a thousand men were taken to the base hospital this morning, including thirty or forty officers. . . . Here's some money; go to town and get some booze. Take my valise and bring a load." He thought that liquor would be a good preventive—liquor and raw onions. He said he had fought off an attack of grippe with whisky and onions some years before; it might work again.

I went to a near-by town and filled the valise with whisky. I had no trouble bringing it into the camp; the entire place was confused, almost terror-stricken. No one even asked me what I had in the bag.

By night the command was quarantined. There were rumors that during the day there were some three or four thousand new cases. Many of the doctors were ill. Men were dying. There was no more room at the base hospital.

Koska and I drank whisky and ate raw onions. Our top sergeant and several other non-coms fell sick the first two days of the epidemic. Koska urged those who were still well to get hold of some liquor and eat onions, a bag of which he ordered the mess sergeant to place on the company street. But liquor was hard to get; no one could leave the post. And onions were not an inviting diet.

Every day more men went down with the flu. Drills were suspended. The entire camp became an immense hospital. In each of the thousands of tents, spread over two or three square miles, from four to six men coughed day and night. They were dying by the score. I think the average number of dead a day during the two weeks that the epidemic lasted was seventy.

No one in high authority seemed to know what to do. The camp surgeon ordered everybody to wear gauze masks, but this probably was worse than nothing.

In o1r company all the officers except Koska were in the hospital. By the end of the week all the enlisted men but myself were down with the sickness. Koska and I practically lived on whisky and onions, and I believe to this day that this saved us.

We could do little for the company. We cooked for the men whatever the regimental doctor prescribed. We had no cooks and our kitchen police were sick men who could stay up but a few hours.

"Eat onions, eat onions," urged Koska; but few men heeded him.

Before the epidemic ended about one-fifth of the company had died. Every morning Koska and I went from tent to tent and carried the dead into the middle of the company street for the morgue trucks to come and pick them up. One morning, I remember, we had four corpses.

To me the epidemic was a most horrible experience, but Koska took it calmly. We spoke very little. Once in a while I wondered what he was thinking, but I was half afraid to ask him. Now and then I caught him grinning to himself. What was he grinning about? What was there for anybody to grin about?

One evening he and I sat in our company office-tent.

I said: "I hate to listen to this coughing and choking all day and all night." I was vaguely desperate and gulped down half a mess-cup of whisky Koska had poured for me. He was always pouring me whisky.

"I don't like it, either," he said, and grinned again.

159

"What the hell are you grinning about?" I cried, half hysterical.

"Don't yell at me, soldier," he said, grinning some more. "Remember you're talking to an officer."

I knew he was joking. He looked at me a long time. He stopped grinning.

"Don't get upset about this, kid," he said, in a quiet voice, unsmiling. "All this doesn't touch me very much. I don't like to listen to this coughing, either, but it doesn't upset me. I hate it, but no more than I hate any other noise."

His voice was deliberate. He spoke concisely.

"I don't care how many of them die," he said.

"You don't know what you're saying, Mike," I said. I was afraid some one else might hear him.

"Yes, I do," he said. "I suppose"—he hesitated—"I have it in for the whole breed."

He looked at me steadily for at least a minute. He knew that what he had said required explanation. He went on:

"Don't misunderstand me, though. It isn't that I wouldn't do everything I can or am supposed to do to bring this thing to an end. What I mean is that the suffering of these men doesn't touch me at all, doesn't distress me. I know it's unnatural to be this way, but I can't help it."

I was a little drunk from the big drink of whisky I had taken, but I heard and recall everything he said.

"I thought about this last night," he continued, "and I remembered something that had happened eight years ago —in the spring of 1910—when I was stationed on Governors Island, in New York Harbor. Blakelock was there then, too, although he doesn't know about this. . . . A ship caught fire while lying alongside a wharf across from the island. We saw her burn for several days; they could

160

not put out the fire. Great clouds of black and gray smoke rolled out of her. Then she turned over and sank beside the dock. No human lives were lost, but in one of the papers I read a little paragraph stating that part of the ship's cargo, as yet undischarged, was six thousand canary birds in small cages. They had been burned to death, or perhaps suffocated."

He paused and shuddered. His whole body was taut.

"The next few nights," he went on, tensely, "I spent without a wink of sleep. I walked around in New York, trying to keep from thinking about those birds caught in the smoke and fire in the hold of the ship. I thought I'd go crazy. To me it was the most terrible thing that could have happened. Six thousand little yellow birds—chirping and singing! It almost drives me crazy now that I think of it again.—But you can't possibly understand this."

He abruptly got to his feet and walked out of the tent and up the street.

Suddenly, without knowing why, I sympathized with him more than with the thirty or forty thousand men who coughed under the tents. For several minutes I could not move. Then I rushed out of the tent.

It rained a little. I went to Koska's tent, in the officers' line. He was not there. I turned on the light and waited. By-and-by he showed up.

He grinned. "I thought it was you," he said. "I saw the light. I don't know what this army is coming to. Enlisted men walking into officers' tents and making themselves at home!"

"What the hell is the matter with you, Mike?" I said.

"I'm a mistake walking around on two legs," he said.

"I think the trouble with you," I said, "is that big head of yours."

161

He was looking at me; then he looked away, sat on his cot, and said:

"There's more in what you said than you know. You meant that I think and brood too much for my own good. There may be something in that, but"—hesitating a moment—"my real trouble is the physical bigness of my head. . . ."

IV

That night Koska told me his story from the beginning, which in its essentials is this:

He was born in a village near Brno, in Bohemia. His father was the organist in the village church. His mother sang in the choir, but she died at his birth because of his big head, which was already then man-size, while his body was a normal baby's body.

An aunt raised him. He remembered things that had occurred in the first months of his life and told me about several incidents in detail.

At the age of three or four, when he began to go out of the house by himself, he had to wear his father's old hat because an ordinary boy's hat scarcely covered half of his head; and even his father's hat was too small for him. His body was short and thin, and his head looked terribly out of proportion. Being more or less a freak, all the other children in the village picked on him. They pulled off his big hat and tried it on their heads, and they laughed and mocked him. They gave him nicknames which referred, derisively, to his head. Sometimes, in his rage, he struck at them, but his arms were small and weak, and he usually came home with a bloody nose.

He felt an outsider, as one not belonging, early in his life. He was always conscious of people looking at him and talking about his head, and shaking their own heads. He

162

had an adult mind and understood things that an ordinary child of his age could not understand. He overheard conversations between his aunts, who blamed him for his mother's death. His father never looked at him pleasantly; he looked at the boy's head and the boy thought that he, too, blamed him for his wife's fate.

Always his big head, his big head, his big head. . . .

His father sent him to Prague to attend school there, and there again the boys laughed and jeered at him. He became bitter, more withdrawn.

Being always laughed at for what to him was a tragedy, he arrived at the conclusion very early in life that what people considered funny was not funny at all, and, conversely, was inclined to laugh at things that to others were very serious or sacred. In school and elsewhere he got into no end of trouble because of this.

He began to hate everybody. He wanted to leave Bohemia and sever all contact with the place of his birth as soon as possible.

He heard of America and determined to go there. His father, who had remarried, was glad to get rid of him, and gave him money for passage.

But in New York his head attracted the same sort of attention. People were startled and amused by it. His body continued to be small and frail. Clerks in hat-stores remarked upon the size of his head, and smiled. Everybody looked at him everywhere. A landlady once refused to rent a room to him because she thought he was a freak. He had difficulty finding work. He wanted to commit suicide.

Then, starving, he thought of joining the army. At the recruiting depot the doctors stared at him, looked at his head from all sides, tapped upon it with their fingers, but finally decided that, to all seeming, it was sound inside.

163

The first few years in the army were the worst of all. He was a private and the other privates in the company laughed at him, and he acquired more nicknames. Then, toward the end of his first enlistment, he became a corporal and suddenly his predicament improved immeasurably. Privates could no longer laugh at him, while most of the other non-coms had enough sense to refrain from discussing his head. Thereafter his head was referred to in his hearing only when he drew a new hat from the quartermaster.

For seven years he made no friends in the army. Blakelock was his first friend, and for ten years his only one. I was, he said, his second.

He needed feminine company, but seldom could get a girl or a woman to go out with him more than once. He might start out liking her, and she him, but before she was with him very long she invariably pulled the hat off his head and tried it on her own, and then she let out a whoop at the sight of his dome; whereupon he immediately became hopelessly prejudiced against her. He could not help himself. He knew in his mind that his prejudice was absurd; that, indeed, it was the most natural thing for a girl to want to try on a soldier's hat, but he became sullen to her, often felt like striking her (as he had struck boys back in Bohemia who had made fun of him), and that was the end of his relationship with her. It seemed there was not a woman in the world who could refrain from grabbing his hat; and when she did, it was all over between them.

But even so, he felt that to stay in the army was perhaps the best solution of his problem. He reënlisted again and again. He was always a non-commissioned officer, until he was commissioned a captain for the duration of the

164

war, and as such immune to ridicule on the part of those around him.

Intermittently, he experimented in self-expression; tried to paint, sculpture, carve wood, and even write music; but he always discovered that he could not get things out of himself. He was all tied up within, gagged and dammed up, full of blind hate and resentment, emotionally twisted against the world and mentally despising himself for his inability to extricate himself from the complex. Nothing that he did satisfied him.

He had scientific interests; ideas occurred to him, but he never did anything with them. Always something inside of him held him from venturing into anything that might turn attention to him, bring him in contact with people.

His body continued small and frail well into his late twenties. Then, to develop his chest, he took deep-breathing exercises an hour daily for a number of years, and to acquire an abdomen he forced himself to eat excessively, so as to make his body more in proportion with his head and become more normal-looking, less conspicuous.

He understood himself, but his mind, as efficient as it was in some respects, was helpless in the face of his intricate emotional condition. He remained an outsider, looking in on life, hating it for what it had done to him, hating the normal because they mocked him and laughed at him, building up a wall of tense calm and aloofness against everything and everybody, exercising his perverse sense of humor.

When men were dying of the "flu," he was not distressed, but he had suffered agonies over the canaries in the burning ship! He was a curious mingling of hate and resentment and of infinite tenderness.

V

"And that's that," said Koska, finishing his story. ". . . Here I am, a captain in the Army of Democracy, which is sick of 'flu,' talking to a young sergeant who walks into my tent in my absence and—oh, well!" He smiled. "A strange case, you will agree."

I smiled, too, feeling a strong affection for the man. We each took a drink from the bottle.

"I have a notion," Koska continued, "that this country —America—is full of twisted, screwed-up people like me, and that is why it is what it is. Screwed up in one way or another. For decades now—for centuries, in fact—ships have been bringing over thousands and millions of people who for an endless variety of reasons could not adjust themselves to life over there, who were either too strong or too weak, too self-willed or too soft, to make a go of it in their own native countries, or who had something else the matter with them. Some were criminals, or potential pirates, gangsters—misfits of all kinds. All mistakes walking about on two legs—that is, from the viewpoint of the idea of decent, healthy civilization. But for the war they would still be coming over in hordes. After the war more will come, and they will be even worse— twisted by the war. One nationality against the other. They will make matters worse in America. There will be more people to be exploited. More people hell-bent on exploiting others. And the exploited will try to become exploiters. To get on, to get on! In a word, democracy— a system of society operating to abolish quality and sterilize—make ineffective—the superior individual, the man of intelligence and integrity."

"A jungle," I put in. Some time before, when we were still in Panama, I had told him what Peter Molek had told me of America in the Old Country and of my subsequent perusal of Upton Sinclair's *The Jungle*.

"Yes," said Koska. "Everything strives to grow, to get the better of the next thing—thousands and millions of small things combine to ruin a big thing, and *vice versa*—chaos—jungle—democracy: and we're supposed to be fighting to make it safe for the world! . . . But, hell! I think you'd better go to bed. It's late. We have to be up tomorrow in time to lay the dead soldiers on the street for the morgue truck. . . . Good night."

"Good night, Mike."

Stepping out of his tent into the drizzly darkness, I was assailed again by the subdued noise which was the combined coughs of thirty thousand or more "flu"-stricken men in the tents. Some of them were dying. In the morning Mike and I would carry some of them out into the street for the truck to pick up.

My feet made an ominous, sucking sound in the mud. . . . What a strange guy Mike was! Mike and Blakelock! . . . America: what a grotesque, fantastic place! A jungle, indeed. Mike was right. It was full of twisted, screwed-up people.

I shuddered inside me. My head was in a whirl. I found my way to my bunk in the company office-tent. For a minute fear seized me that I would go crazy. I found a quarter-full bottle under the bunk and emptied it. Then I undressed, crawled into bed, and fell asleep.

CHAPTER XIV

Blakelock Makes a Gesture

I

THE "flu" epidemic ended almost as abruptly as it had begun. All at once, it seemed, the men—a little hollow-cheeked, unshaven, with rings beneath their eyes, still coughing—were walking slowly, uncertainly, minus their gauze masks, in the sunshine on the drying mud in the proximity of their tents.

For two or three days I felt as though I was just waking from a ghastly nightmare. I tried not to think of it, nor of anything else. I kept myself occupied from reveille till taps.

By the end of August the outfits, including our own, were drilling again an hour or two a day, doing light exercises, taking short hikes through the fragrant pine woods outside the camp. The quarantine was lifted.

Then, of a sudden, the whole division was issued overseas caps. We were going to France at once, to make room in the camp for the next draft, which had already been called. We learned that we had been scheduled to sail early in August, just as the "flu" had hit us.

During the epidemic the men of one organization had not been supposed to mingle with men of another, except so far as absolutely necessary. I had been wondering about Lonie Burton every day. Was he dead or alive? Now that the quarantine was raised, I went to see him. His outfit was more than a mile from ours.

"I just thought of going to see if you were still alive," he said, smiling, when he saw me.

168

He had suffered a comparatively mild attack of "flu," but the illness evidently had taken, temporarily at least, a good deal of spirit out of him. He had lost much weight. He looked pale, almost green. He spoke little, with a sort of quivering reticence. He seemed thoughtful, unenthusiastic. But he insisted that he was "all right."

"Have you heard?" he said. "But for this 'flu' we'd be over there by now."

"Yes?"

"Now, when—and if—we finally get over, we may be too late."

"Too late for what?" I said.

"Too late to fight," he said. "The war may be over soon."

But his words, I felt, were not vitally sincere. He merely spoke. There was a perceptible hesitation in his speech. His manner was shaky, nervous.

"You know," I said, "it seems to me that not five per cent of the men in this camp really want to go over and much less to fight."

Lonie looked at me, startled, and said nothing. He obviously had been observing and thinking the same thing.

I added: "But I'm glad we're going over, if for no other reason than to get out of this camp. The last two weeks have been the most awful experience in my life— the endless coughing and dying of the men."

"Yes," said Lonie. "I guess that's one of the reasons why I'm glad we're going, too."

I had a feeling that it was the chief reason.

"How's Koska?" asked Lonie.

"All right," I said. I did not want to talk about him to anyone.

As a matter of fact, Koska was anything but all right. He was deeply messed within himself on account of the

169

overseas caps. He could not get one of sufficient size to fit his large head. The biggest one available covered but half of his dome and thus emphasized its hugeness. He wore his campaign hat as long as he could—indeed, until the battalion commander ordered him to discard it and wear a cap. For days, while we were getting ready to leave the camp, he seemed all tied into a knot, scarcely speaking even to me. He signed whatever papers I put before him without reading them. He let the lieutenants and the first sergeant put the company through the formations.

I said to him one day: "Mike, snap out of it, will you? It's ridiculous."

"I know it is," he admitted. "I'll get over it in time."

He asked me to go to some tailor in the town nearest camp and have him make several extra-large overseas caps. He could not bring himself to go. He said he could not stand the idea of a tailor measuring his head. So I went, and the next day Koska had a half dozen caps of various large sizes, one of which finally suited him. It did not hide his head as thoroughly as the old campaign hat, but it was the best that could be done about it.

II

I had thought that we would sail from New Orleans, the nearest port, but after boarding the trains—late one afternoon early in September—we learned, by grapevine telegraph, that we were bound for Newport News, Virginia.

The next morning we were in Tennessee and by noon in North Carolina—beautiful states. For hours I looked out of the car window at the passing landscape—the green valleys and plateaus, rivers and mountains and forests.

Toward mid-forenoon our journey became very exciting. It seemed that the people of towns through which we

170

had passed telephoned to the communities ahead that troop-trains were coming, and so wherever we stopped, and even in places where we did not stop, there were mobs of people along the tracks: small-town Americans, feverish with war patriotism, carrying the Stars and Stripes and white flags with red stars in the center, denoting the number of boys in their families who were in the service. There were lovely Southern girls, dozens of them at every place, passing out sandwiches, coffee, and kisses; giving us their addresses with requests that we write to them "from over there." With most of the men fully recovered from the "flu," there was much laughing and sex-talk in the cars between towns, and much sexy whooping from car windows wherever a smiling young feminine face appeared along the way.

I wished Lonie Burton was on the train; his regiment was on the train ahead of us. I wanted to talk with him; see how he felt and looked. I had not seen him for days.

I did not want to talk with Koska, who was in the same car with me. Stolid-faced, he looked at the passing landscape. I saw him accept a sandwich from a stunning girl with a mere, "Thank you." God knew what he was thinking about. I did not want to know. I wanted to enjoy the beauty of American valleys and mountains, the exuberance of the people, the loveliness of girls.

I was completely over the epidemic nightmare. I worried a little about the crossing to Europe, but I understood that every transport had ample convoy protection against submarines; and then, too, I suppose, my Slavic-peasant optimism, which began to function again, led me to believe that nothing would happen to us at sea; that nothing would happen to me even in France.

I was glad we were going over, although I had no passion to shoot down as many Germans as possible, nor

171

any desire to become a hero. I agreed with Koska that the war, considered objectively, was a dreadful commentary upon the collective intelligence of the human race; that it was stupid and worse, but at the same time I wanted to see things in France. We heard that there were nearly three million American soldiers in Europe already. I had a feeling, induced by things I read in the newspapers, that the hostilities might end before long. Lonie Burton and Koska shared this feeling with me.

III

The voyage was uneventful. We were on one of three transports, with swift naval vessels all about us. There were only rumors of submarines.

Lonie Burton's outfit was on the same ship with mine. I saw Lonie nearly every day during the nine-day trip. We talked. He had entirely recovered from the "flu" attack; he looked well and some of his youthful enthusiasm had returned. He again had faith in Woodrow Wilson. It was true, he said, that but a small percentage of the American people fully shared Wilson's idealism; that most of them were merely infected with war hysteria, but that, while tragic in itself, was unimportant so far as the realization of Wilson's great dream was concerned.

I said nothing to this. By now I was quite skeptical of the whole scheme of what Lonie considered Wilsonian idealism, but somehow I liked Lonie partly because he was naïve and idealistic. Sometimes I thought it would be wonderful if I could share his faith, but I was already spoiled for simple idealistic faith. As a foreigner, always on the alert, trying to know and understand America, I had become, in the preceding few years, aware of too many things that were not in tune with what appeared to be the Wilsonian idea of justice and other such principles.

But, as I say, I liked Lonie and was interested in him. He was so young; a year older than myself in actual age, but really younger, his mind not geared to realities. What would happen to him?

The last day of the voyage I said to him:

"Well, Lonie, I hope you come out of this mess all right. I hope we will meet again—I mean after the war, back in America."

"I hope so, too," said Lonie, eagerly. "What do you intend to do after the war—after we get back?"

The question sort of startled me. I had scarcely thought of that.

"Oh, I don't know," I said, self-conscious. "And you?"

Lonie laughed. "I don't know, either," he said. "Perhaps, as ex-soldiers we won't have much trouble getting jobs. They'll probably show us some preference. President Wilson said something to that effect. . . . I guess as soon as I get out I'll go to Milford, Pennsylvania. My mother lives there, as I've told you."

Koska was rather taciturn throughout the trip. He shared a room on the upper deck with a young shavetail. He spent most of his time reading a battered volume of Rabelais which, oddly enough, he had discovered somewhere on the ship.

Meanwhile he probably was thinking a good deal about Blakelock, who was in Brest with his Negro labor battalion. He had received a note from him a week or so before the "flu" epidemic. He told me he expected to see Blakelock in Brest.

IV

When we reached Brest it was raining.

We stayed aboard the ship for several days, waiting for transportation. None of the enlisted men were al-

lowed ashore. We stuck in the holds of the ship. Some of
us were restless, impatient; Lonie Burton, for one. It was
mid-September, and there were rumors, originating God
knew where, that the war was about to end; that possibly
we would not even land, but would be taken right back to
the United States.

"That wouldn't make *me* mad, big boy!" . . . "To
hell with the war!" . . . Such were some of the remarks
that I heard all about me.

Officers could go ashore, and Koska took advantage of
this to locate Blakelock. He found him and spent an evening with him.

"How is he?" I asked him the next morning.

Koska shrugged his shoulders, then said:

"Not so good. Humiliated. He is still only a lieutenant-
colonel. He sees colonels and even brigadiers come through
Brest who were junior to him a year ago. Now he has to
report to them, salute them. The other day he bumped
into a colonel whom a few years ago he knew as a sergeant. . . . He is hardly more than a shadow of the
Blakelock he was in Panama. His hair is all gray, his face
is getting flabby; there is a hollow look in his eyes, a what-
the-hell note in his attitude toward things. . . . We
didn't talk much. Just sat in his room, which is near the
barracks of his labor battalion about a mile from here,
near the docks. I was uneasy as hell being with him. He
seemed licked. His sense of humor appears to have
cracked. . . . He said he thought we were going straight
from the ship to the front—second-line trenches or something, in a quiet sector, perhaps the Meuse-Argonne,
where several other outfits were sent lately right after
they landed. He thinks we and the Allies are getting ready
for a big push—probably the final one. He believes the
whole show'll be over soon, maybe before the end of the

174

year. Germany, he says, is actually exhausted; it isn't mere newspaper propaganda at home; the prisoners of war that our outfits have been capturing lately are for the most part young boys—kids—who are giving themselves up the first chance they get. . . ."

"Are you going to see Blakelock again?" I asked.

"I don't know," said Koska. "He asked me to let him know our position at the front and he would 'visit' us, as he put it. I guess I'll let him come. He hasn't been near the front yet."

v

As Blakelock had thought, our outfit went straight to the Meuse-Argonne front. We had been issued helmets, gas-masks, and other war equipment at the docks. We were in the second line, and the sector was a so-called quiet one, but even so we were shelled every few days.

The effect of the first shelling upon the men was not unsimilar to that of a powerful physic—which, after it was over, resulted in considerable "kidding" and laughter; but since the first one had produced no casualties and we could nearly always duck into practically shell-proof dugouts, we went through subsequent bombardments almost with nonchalance. At night we sat in the trenches and listened to the terrific roar and swish of large projectiles, the so-called "garbage cans," both American and German, sailing over our heads. Some of them flashed over us with their fuses still burning.

Half of the time Koska had a grin on his face. I never asked him, but I imagined what he was thinking: that the whole thing was a monstrous stupidity: funny. But this, of course, did not affect his being a most efficient company commander, just as a month and a half before in Louisiana, his lack of sympathy for the "flu"-stricken men had not kept him from doing everything possible for them.

We stayed at the front for two weeks, during which time we saw no actual fighting. Our company had only two casualties, "slightly wounded."

Then we went to the rear for two weeks. We camped in dog-tents in a wood some eight miles behind the front.

After that we were sent back to the same sector; only, this time we took over the front line. The sector was still "quiet."

The second day in our new position Koska said to me:

"I sent a message to Blakelock. I guess he'll be coming to 'visit' us one of these days."

On November 4th—a week before the Armistice—Blakelock came. The Germans were sporadically shelling our trenches all day. Those of us who could kept to the dugouts.

It was in the afternoon. Five men, including myself, were in our company headquarters dugout. Several candles and a lantern burned in the place. Koska sat at a little improvised table in a corner, looking at a map. Once in a while, as a shell exploded close by, he looked up for a moment, then turned his attention back to the map again, a faint grin encircling his mouth.

The first lieutenant, a tall young man who had recently joined the company, leaned against a large timber piece at the entrance to the dugout. He was smoking a cigarette and reading a letter from home.

The top sergeant and I sat on a bunk, reading a batch of circulars and general orders that a runner had just brought from the regimental. The other man in the dugout was the company bugler, a New Orleans lad, twenty-two or so, but younger-looking, who also acted as runner for the company commander. I was vaguely conscious of

176

him. He seemed to be doing something with his equipment; as it turned out later, he had misplaced a hand grenade and was looking for it.

There was a voice outside the dugout, "Where is Captain Koska's company headquarters?" It was Blakelock's voice—with a difference; it lacked much of its old vibrancy and vigor.

"Right there, sir," said the soldier to whom he had addressed the question.

"Oh, thank you," said Blakelock.

Koska jumped up and received Blakelock.

"Hello, Koska," said Blakelock.

"How are you, Colonel?" said Koska, rather formally.

In answer Blakelock frowned, then looked around and recognized me.

"Hello, Adamic!" he said. "You're a sergeant, I see. How are you?"

I said, "All right, sir." We shook hands.

He did not know anybody else in the dugout. All the other men had joined the regiment after he had been relieved from its command.

Blakelock was a changed man, just as Koska had described him.

He wore a steel helmet, and a gas-mask was suspended from his neck.

"Well—" he said, looking at Koska.

"Would you like to go around a little?" asked Koska

But the next instant, before Blakelock had a chance to answer Koska, the young bugler, who had found his grenade just as the visitor had entered, let out a terrific yell. I looked at him. I suppose everybody else in the dugout looked at him. He stood in the middle of the dugout with the grenade—a large "pineapple," so called—in his hand. He was terror-stricken.

As it appeared later, the boy—a mere recruit, with scarcely any training in handling grenades—had taken the "pineapple" from its safety-container, to satisfy an impulse of curiosity, and at the same time accidentally pulled out the little safety pin.

He knew that with the safety pin removed the grenade would explode within seven seconds! And now in his terror, instead of tossing the thing out of the dugout, which he conceivably could have done, he let out another desperate yell and dropped the grenade to the floor.

All this occurred, perhaps, in less than three seconds.

Some one else let out a shout. My instinct and training drove me to seek a possible cover, but before I could even turn around I was knocked down by a terrific explosion.

The first thing that I thought of, lying in that smoke-filled hole, and with that awful din still filling my ears to the exclusion of every sound, was how funny it was we had not been killed. Instead, there was a man, the first sergeant, apparently alive, on top of me, and presently I began to hear voices and groans.

Those of us who were not hurt or stunned ran out, falling over one another, and saw that, although without a cut, we were spattered with blood all over.

Koska, as I remember, looked tensely calm. There was a blotch of blood on his forehead. He was trying to wipe it off with his coat sleeve.

All the lights in the dugout, of course, had been extinguished by the explosion. After a few minutes Koska and I, and probably one other man, went back into the dugout, which was full of smoke and stench, and relit a couple of candles.

None of us was seriously injured—except Blakelock, who was blown to pieces.

It was some time before we fully realized what had happened. It was, briefly, this: As soon as the bugler dropped the grenade, Blakelock had yanked the steel helmet off his head and thrown it on the "pineapple," simultaneously hurling himself on the helmet. Then—a second later —the explosion. . . .

None of us could talk for at least ten minutes. I remember that I shook all over, as did some of the others. The first lieutenant, who had not been stunned by the explosion, now swooned. Koska caught him in his arms.

For a moment I thought that I would pass out, myself. I leaned against the soft, damp dirt wall of the dugout.

Then some one said, "Jesus!" It was the young bugler whose carelessness had caused everything. He was hysterical. He threw himself on a bunk and swung his arms in all directions, crying.

Koska laid the unconscious lieutenant on another bunk.

"Give him a shot of whisky or cognac, Sergeant," he said to the "top." Then he looked at me. He grinned, gently, painfully.

"Christ, Mike," I said, for the first time addressing him as Mike in the presence of other men, "he's all over the place!"—or something to that effect.

He said nothing to this. He stepped to the exit of the dugout, staggering a little. There he met a couple of non-coms who had not been in the explosion.

"Can we do anything, Captain?" one of them asked Koska.

"Yes," said Koska; "clean up the mess."

"Yes, sir."

Koska went out. I wanted to follow him, but I was weak in the knees. I reached for a canteen of cognac, unscrewed it, and drank till I emptied it.

I recall that I went to another dugout and dropped on

179

a bunk. I fell into a drunken stupor, then into sleep. In the morning I woke shivering and with a pain in my chest. No one had thought of covering me during the night. When I rose there was a reeling sensation in my head, and finally I swooned. When I came to, every cell and every bone in my body ached.

A Medical Corps man came and stuck a thermometer into my mouth.

"He may have the 'flu,' " I heard some one say. "Get 'im out of here." It wasn't Koska's voice, but I vaguely remember seeing his face, as though in a mist.

I was carried through the trenches to the rear and there put into an ambulance. By-and-by, after a long and tortuous ride over a rutty road, I found myself in a hospital, between two clean white sheets.

I have no idea of what was the matter with me. My temperature fluctuated; if I closed my eyes, my head reeled as though I were afloat in a whirling chaos. Then the pain in my chest diminished and my temperature became normal.

VI

On November 7th, as I learned afterward, my outfit went over the top. There was little "action." The Germans retreated without much opposition. Nevertheless, there were some casualties. One of these was Captain Michael Koska, killed—Mike, dear Mike! . . .

Lonie Burton was slightly wounded. I did not see him again in France.

Then the Armistice—the end of the war, my most vital memories of which are now linked with the names of Blakelock and Koska, and to a lesser extent with the name of Lonie Burton.

PART FOUR

The Land of Laughs

CHAPTER XV

After the War

I

Two weeks after the Armistice I rejoined my outfit in a wood in the Meuse-Argonne region. The country was torn up with shells; rain fell daily, beating down the last leaves from the trees, and the roads were deep with mud.

With Koska dead, we had a new captain. He was drunk most of the time and there was no discipline in the company. The men were restless, disobedient. "When do we go home?" was the general cry.

Lonie Burton's regiment was in the same wood, but Lonie was in a hospital, somewhere near Paris. I thought I might never see him again, and it mattered little to me whether I did or not. Uppermost in my mind was the desire to get out of Europe, especially out of France. As little as I had had of it, I was sick of war and wished I did not have to look at shell-holes and trees with their tops clipped off by projectiles. I wished to visit my people in Carniola—now part of Yugoslavia—but could not procure a furlough.

Finally, in January, 1919, we were on the way back to the States. We landed at Newport News; from there we went to Camp Zachary Taylor, an immense wooden cantonment near Louisville, Kentucky, which had been made a demobilization center for the Southern States.

Having enlisted for three years in the Regular Army, I was not due for discharge till 1920; and so, when the rest of the regiment was demobilized, I and a few other

183

Regulars were made clerks in the demobilization offices or put in charge of the casuals' barracks.

For ten months I worked in the camp finance office, making out final payrolls for men to be demobilized. It was simple work; by-and-by it became automatic with me. I had no regular military duties. I bunked in a room by myself in a former officers' dormitory. I ate excellent meals in a special mess for the demobilization clerical force. My hours were from nine to five, and I had evenings and Sundays to do what I pleased. I read a lot and kept to myself. When not reading in my spare time, I walked through the lovely Kentucky countryside outside the camp.

Thousands of men returning from overseas passed through Camp Taylor weekly. They came by trains in vast, loose organizations and left for their homes within a few days, ex-soldiers of democracy.

I read the newspapers, notably the Louisville *Courier-Journal*, and otherwise kept up with the events, especially with Woodrow Wilson's adventure in Europe and the senatorial opposition at home to his League of Nations idea, but my interest in all these things was not very vital. I suppose I was temporarily exhausted. My contact with Koska and Blakelock had largely disillusioned me in regards to Wilsonism, and I did not care what happened to it.

Then, on a newsstand in Louisville one day, I came upon *Pearson's Magazine*, edited and published by Frank Harris, in which I found a scathing editorial on Wilson the "arch-betrayer." The vigor with which it was written vitalized my interest in Wilson and the Versailles Treaty, and I heartily agreed with Harris' views.

Late in the summer Wilson started on his ill-fated tour
184

of the country to appeal to the people—"to Cæsar"—for his League of Nations program, which the "irreconcilables" in the Senate appeared determined to kill so far as the United States was concerned. The trip, as reported in the *Courier-Journal*, impressed me as rather dramatic. Here was the ruler of the country going to the people!

I had a few hundred dollars saved from my pay, and I applied for a brief furlough, which was granted to me. I had gotten it into my head that I wanted to see Wilson talking to the people. I read in the paper that he would be in St. Louis in a few days, and so I went there.

On the day that Wilson came to St. Louis, I was in a crowd on the sidewalk in front of the town's leading hotel, where he stepped from his automobile. He looked unlike the pictures I had seen of him. He was old and apparently sick; a few days later he broke down completely.

Catching sight of the President, the crowd applauded and cheered; then, abruptly, the applauding and the cheers ceased.

Wilson had brushed aside one of his aides who tried to assist him out of the car, and for an interminable moment he stood on the running-board, his frame bent, his haggard face suddenly tensed by what seemed a fierce hatred. His eyes, flashing like two coals in an ash-heap, swept over the crowd. I thought that in that moment he blamed it for all his troubles. Innately an aristocrat, he had been forced into the rôle of a mob-stirrer, a demagogue. A few months before, the mob of the world had acclaimed him wildly; now his own mob at home, seeing him breaking down against stubborn political odds, only clapped its hands futilely, with a feeble cheer here and there. And he, Woodrow Wilson, with his League of Nations, was offering salvation to the world! He seemed on the verge

185

of bursting out and calling us bad names. The crowd sensing something, ceased to clap and cheer. Then some one touched Wilson's elbow. He regained himself and forced a wan, twisted, demagogic smile; whereupon the people on the sidewalk applauded again.

I had caught an intimate glimpse of democratic America's political soul. It taught me that an even vastly better man than Wilson could not have been President of the United States without being or becoming a charlatan. It seemed to me that Frank Harris did not know what he was talking about—not quite, at any rate. I was inclined to sympathize with Wilson. I did not go to hear him talk that evening. I was too sorry for him; almost ashamed for him—and of him.

I thought of Blakelock, unquestionably a superior man who had died, after a sterile life in the service of his democratic country, to save the lives of a few men, all of whom, including Koska, possibly had been his inferiors. Somehow, in my mind I began to couple the names of Wilson and Blakelock, and their fates. Later they became symbolical to me of the inevitability of superior men's frustration under democracy in America. . . .

II

When I was discharged from the army late in the winter of 1920, I was almost twenty-one years old and a very serious young man, both in regard to the wide affairs of the world and of America, and to my own personal problem.

I had decided, for no good reason, on my release from the service, to go to New York. I had nearly three hundred dollars. I bought myself a suit of civilian clothes, and for several days I felt unnatural in them, which only aggravated my perplexed mind. I had no idea of what I would do in New York. I hoped that as an ex-soldier, and especially with my clerical experience in the finance-office at Camp Taylor during the last ten months, I would have no trouble getting a job, perhaps even a good job.

It was in mid-March, but winter was late in New York. I arrived early in the morning. I breakfasted, then decided to walk around awhile and see if the city had changed much since 1916.

A light rain had fallen during the night and the streets were frozen. Turning a corner somewhere in the Twenties near Third Avenue, I came to a slight incline where a teamster in charge of a loaded coal-wagon beat and cursed his horses for all he was worth in an attempt to make them pull up the slippery grade. Sparks flew from under the hooves; straining themselves and unable to hold ground, the animals were falling to their knees, making scarcely any progress; and as the wagon shook over the cobbles, little pieces of coal dropped onto the streets. They were immediately picked up by two small girls clad, so far as I could see, in threadbare, torn dresses that barely reached to their knees—and I was cold in my heavy army overcoat! They were immigrants' children, no doubt. Obviously, too, they were rivals, each belonging to a different family, for a piece of coal no sooner struck the street than they both rushed for it like two famished animals for a bit of food, frequently endangering their lives by crawling under the wagon.

The sight of them made me shudder, and my attitude toward New York during the next few days bordered upon nausea. The nice parts of the city, somehow, looked less magnificent to me. I noticed the grime on the skyscrapers. The great bridges over the East River were, I thought, more awesome—awful, almost—than beautiful.

I decided I did not want to stay in New York.

187

I thought of Lonie Burton. His home, I recalled, was in Milford, Pennsylvania, which I found out was not far from New York.

But in Milford, a charming little town—perhaps the nicest I had seen in America till then—I learned that Mrs. Burton, Lonie's mother, was dead; her creditors had taken over her home, and as for Lonie, no one knew exactly where he was. One person thought he had gone to California.

I decided to look up Peter Molek. I assumed that he was still in Forest City, which was near Milford. I was pleasantly surprised to find Molek in improved health and his and his wife's grocery-store doing well. He was glad to see me. He said I looked well and spoke better English than many native Americans.

I stayed two days in Forest City as Molek's guest. I saw that not a few Slovenian immigrants there were mildly prosperous. Some of them were building new houses.

"What are you going to do now?" Molek asked me.

I said I scarcely knew; the chances were that I would look around the country for a while. I might go West. Molek thought this was a good idea. I said I might try to write in English some day. This was a vague ambition that had begun to stir in me at Camp Taylor.

I wanted to see Washington, D. C., so I went there. I walked and looked around the city for two days. It occurred to me that Wall and Broad streets in New York had given me a more definite impression of power than the federal government buildings. The White House, where Wilson lay a sick man, was a nice building; everything was quiet around it. The Capitol seemed rather ugly to me.

188

The House and the Senate were in session. I went to the visitors' gallery in the Senate chamber and witnessed a scene that will always stand out in my memory. I looked upon the nation's highest legislative body and listened to a porcine gentleman speak with a voice of great volume and solemnity on a subject which, after listening to him for nearly an hour, I was unable to determine, while his colleagues—not more than sixty of them—dozed or sat in their chairs, staring blankly, or stood about in small groups, chatting.

This was another intimate peek into the mechanism of American democracy. After sitting in the gallery for about an hour, the scene struck me as so funny that, for fear I would burst out laughing, I left. And looking back now, I think that it was then and there that my youthful post-war seriousness took its first good tumble.

I left Washington for Chicago, feeling much better, smiling to myself. But after that I was still subject to long grave spells; my three hundred dollars soon evaporated and, under the bread-and-butter compulsion, I became a "workin'-stiff" with no particular trade. In Chicago I tried to locate the Zemlars, thinking that Mr. Zemlar might be able to steer me to a job, but it seemed that the paper to which he had gone after the *Narodni Glas* had passed out was defunct also, and no one knew where he and his family were.

For a time I hung around the employment agencies—the "slave market"—on Madison Street in Chicago. I got laboring jobs around Chicago which lasted two or three weeks. My last job in the vicinity of Chicago was on a big road-building project outside of Joliet. From there I went with a couple of other workers to St. Louis, and from St. Louis to Kansas City; moving from one place to another as impulse and necessity bade me.

In the spring of 1921 I drifted East again. Unable to get work ashore, I went to sea, and during the next ten months sailed on five different American ships, which took me to Europe and South America. Early the next fall I quit the sea and worked for a while in restaurants, cabinet-shops, shoe-factories, and textile-mills in New York, New Jersey, and Pennsylvania. (I deal briefly with this period in the present book for the reason that I waxed autobiographical, covering it, in *Dynamite*, a volume dealing with labor conditions in the United States; published in 1931.)

IV

Between jobs ashore and between watches aboard ships I read nearly everything that came my way. In St. Louis, for instance, I stumbled on Theodore Dreiser.

At the time, I remember, I was in a specially low mood. I was without funds and the only work in sight was dishwashing. For days I had been walking around the city. I watched the crowds in the streets. In the evening they poured out of countless doorways. They dismayed me. They scarcely seemed members of my own species. Endless rivers of organisms, moving in a fog this way and that way, pushing, hurrying, oblivious of everything outside their own little spheres.

One afternoon it was raining and I entered the public library. On a table I picked up a book which I noticed was marked *Permission*. I had heard or read somewhere some time before that certain books in public libraries were on "permission shelves"—bad, dangerous books that must not be read by everybody. Some careless attendant had apparently left it here. I experienced a thrill—a "permission book" and Dreiser! I had heard of Dreiser before. Lonie Burton had mentioned him to me, and I think there had been references to him in *Pearson's*.

I sat down and began to read *Jennie Gerhardt*. At nine o'clock I was told it was closing time and I would have to get out. I was back the next morning at nine and finished *Jennie*. Then I induced the library girls to let me read, in succession, the other Dreiser novels—*The "Genius," Sister Carrie, The Financier,* and *The Titan*—all "permission books." I spent two weeks in the library reading Dreiser, forgetting that I had to have a job and food; indeed, I do not seem to be able to recall how I managed to maintain my existence.

Evenings after nine o'clock I walked in the streets or sat in the railroad depot, and the countless faces that moved by me, somehow, were no longer in a fog. Now, here and there, I seemed to recognize Jennie Gerhardts and Carrie Meebers, Lester Kanes and Droutes and Hurstwoods among them—moving, rushing, impelled by their temperaments, driven by fate, yet only a few, if any, realizing their true predicaments. There, too, were Eugene Witlas and Angelas, Rubies, and Suzanne Dales. Now and then I thought I spied out a Frank Cowperwood, self-confident, strong-jawed, competent, yet ultimately—actually—no more important or significant, in Dreiser's eyes (and mine), than Jennie Gerhardt or her kid brother. The faces no longer dismayed me. I was fascinated. Finally I became amused at myself and the crowds.

From Dreiser I gained in a few weeks a clearer perception of life in general and of life in America in particular than I could have acquired in any other way, except perhaps by reading *The Education of Henry Adams*, which came my way soon after, aboard a ship. The Dreiser-Adams conception of life and nature as a chaos—a jungle—within which man dreams and strives for law and order,

191

longs and labors for "normalcy" (then a new word and
political slogan in the United States), and simultaneously,
in his blundering human way, does everything in his
power—particularly in America—to prevent their realization, appealed strongly to my sense of the ridiculous;
whereupon my serious spells began to grow less frequent
and lighter.

Then, too, some time late in 1921, soon before I gave
up sea-going, I came upon a few issues of *Smart Set*, a
monthly magazine of clever and vigorous fiction and
pointed, humorous comment, edited and published by
H. L. Mencken and George Jean Nathan. In their "Ré-
pétition Générale" department I read such expressions of
their views as this:

In Europe, aristocracy is founded upon land. In the United
States, it is founded upon real estate. . . .

In such a country as this, with capitalism securely in the
saddle and practically all human values reckoned in terms of
dollars and cents, it is not only hopeless for a man to try to get
on without money, but also a trifle absurd. . . .

The ideal of democracy has been reached at least. It is now
impossible for a gentleman to hold office in America. . . .

Like all other Americans of my education, I have a sneaking
desire to try life in a civilized country. However, life in such a
country, I suspect, is far too placid to suit a man accustomed to
the United States. . . . I have got so used to the show that I'll
never be able to do without it. . . .

The second engineer on the last ship on which I sailed
was a great Mencken-Nathan "fan." He told me he could
scarcely wait for the next number of *Smart Set*. He said:
"I wish those two —— would make the magazine a weekly
or somethin'."

v

Gradually, there began to form in my mind a view of
the United States which some years subsequently—late in

192

1928, after I had begun to write for the magazines—I put down in an article entitled "The Land of Laughs," as follows:

Seen with the proper perspective and with both an objective and a subjective sense of reality, the American Scene . . . is unquestionably the most vitally interesting and amusing under the sun. As a show, life here is beyond improvement: an endless comedy of futility and chaos in which whole hordes of meddlers, busybodies, snoopers, inspirationalists, idealists, crusaders, reformers, rogues, uplifters and nuts of all denominations try with various degrees of subtlety and all too meager success to abolish one another, in their efforts (some of them honest and serious enough) to establish law and order, usher in an era of peace and bliss, make life more worth living, and induce the race to hoist itself to a higher level by its own bootstraps. Each labors frantically according to his own ideas or lack of them, thereby achieving nothing except revealing his petty individual ego and increasing the excitement, which calls from year to year for more and more reformers and crusaders to propagate this or the other swell idea. The show is flavored with enough pathos and dignity to keep it from degenerating into a farce. . . .

CHAPTER XVI

My First Day in Los Angeles

I

EVERY now and then during my sea-going career I had heard sailors and officers aboard ships speak in glowing terms of southern California; and so in mid-autumn of 1922 I signed up in Boston as a mess-boy—there was no other job—on an empty oil-tanker bound for San Pedro, with the intention of leaving the ship there and trying to find something to do in California.

On arrival in Pedro, early in December, southern California was having a spell of so-called "unusual" weather. A cold gale of between forty and fifty miles blew for two days. The sea rolled over the two-and-a-half-mile-long breakwater. The tanker, drawing only sixteen feet aft and eight feet forward, swayed like a balloon as it lay anchored in the Outer Harbor till the pilot is dared to take us through the narrow channels to the dock.

After the wind died down, it continued to rain.

I quit the ship as soon as we were moored. San Pedro struck me as a dead place. Its streets were flooded with rain water. The town was scattered over the bluffs and hills to the west of the bay, as if a crazy hand had flung it out. I did not dream that within a short time I would return there, stay for several years, and find it a delightful community.

I walked off the ship with twenty-odd dollars in my pocket, a substantial army overcoat, and a suitcase containing mostly books and old copies of magazines, including several *Smart Sets*. I boarded a Pacific Electric train

194

and an hour later, after checking my suitcase at the P. E. depot, I was walking in the streets of downtown Los Angeles.

My first impression of Los Angeles was unfavorable. Its business section was like that of any other American city; like a jungle, with buildings being torn down and new structures going up. The people seemed unvigorous. There was a preponderance of old people who had come there for their health or to retire.

II

At noon I stepped into a restaurant. Before ordering my meal I went to the lavatory, which was at the end of a long flight of stairs in an ill-lighted, unventilated basement.

There I came upon two men. They looked at me.

"Hello, soldier!" said one of them. I carried my wet army overcoat on my arm.

The other man flashed a revolver in front of my face. "Come on now, give us what you got—quick!"

I reached into my pocket and grasped the slim bank-roll. I hesitated a few moments, hoping that some one would come down and the men would be frightened. But no one came.

"Come on, soldier, quick! We mean business, but don' wanna bump you off if we don' hefta."

I handed the money to the man with the gun.

He said to the other fellow: "O.K. Now tap 'im one!"

Whereupon the second man "tapped me one" and I fell over. I think I came to almost at once, but on rising I scarcely knew where I was. It was hard walking upstairs. My knees shook and something buzzed in my head.

"Here's room for one," said the waiter to me, when I got back into the restaurant.

"No . . . thanks," I said. "I don't want to eat." I

wanted to ask for the manager and tell him what had happened to me—but what was the use?

In my pocket were two nickels and a dime. I returned to the P. E. station and sat there awhile. Every few moments there was a buzz in my head, and I discovered that my chin ached so I could hardly open my mouth.

I went out walking again. It had stopped raining. I came to Pershing's Park. The benches were wet, but I sat down. I tried to think. What could I do? Something quivered inside me and I wanted to laugh. I tried desperately to be calm.

"This is funny," I said to myself, half hysterical. "It's all a joke."

III

Toward evening I was walking down Main Street again, sniffing at the stew of human life with an aloofness rather out of keeping with my circumstances. I came to the Mexican quarter. I passed through Plaza Park and paused near a lunch-wagon, which emanated a blending of the smells of fried greasy meat and onions, hot tamales, and coffee. I leaned against a lamp-post. In a near-by peep-show a music-box ground out raggy tunes, and across the street from it a Mexican barker shouted the virtues of an old Charlie Chaplin film. A few feet from the lunch-wagon a peanut-machine whistled faintly in the damp air.

A lank, hungry-looking dog of uncertain breed came to me and sniffed the edge of my overcoat. His eyes held an appealing gaze. He obviously longed for a pat on the head, and I was not averse to him; at least not until my response to his advances made him over-affectionate, and then I chased him away.

A moment later an old man with a straggly white beard and the unpleasant smell common to aged people in poor

196

circumstances, stopped before me. He said: "God bless you, brother," handed me a printed invitation to the Midnight Gospel Mission located a few blocks away, and a tract entitled "The Dangers of Kissing." The latter, I discovered, was the heartrending life-story of a girl named Mabel who had gone wrong by way of a kiss in the dark.

" 'Lo, kid!"

Hearing myself thus addressed, I turned and saw a woman who stood on the edge of the dim radius of the lamp-post, with most of her person in full light. She was of middle height, but disproportionately bulky, of an age anywhere between thirty and forty, and shabbily dressed. In the shadow of her nose grew a faint mustache; a hank of dirty-red hair flamed over each of her ears; the paint on her face was of the cheapest sort and heavily applied.

"Hard up, ain't you, boy?" she asked, eagerly. "Ain't you?"—moving a step closer to me.

I resented the intrusion. I wanted to be left alone. Besides, the woman repelled me; her voice came struggling out of mucus. I looked away and made as if to walk off, but she stepped before me and placed her hand on my arm.

"Please don't go!" she said, a strange tenderness in her manner. "I'm gonna have a snack in here," indicating the lunch-wagon, "an' when I dine I likes comp'ny—so wonchya join me, sir?" She giggled unnaturally.

"Aw hell! C'mon," she said as I hesitated. "I can see through you. You're hungry. C'mon!"

I was no little confused as we entered the well-lighted lunch-wagon.

The woman ordered for both of us, and the proprietor lost no time in slamming the food down before us, with a vast indifference to his dishes and us. The hamburger

and onions and German fried potatoes and coffee were not
bad, yet I could not stop wishing I had not come in with
her. I was letting a strange woman buy me food. She was
a street-walker. Very likely, too, I was a bit afraid of her.
What was her motive in picking me up?

"Well, what kinda pie you like?" she asked then. "Aw,
now, don't be bashful! 'Course you wan' pie. I like lemon.
Frank," she called to the man, "two pieces of lemon pie!"

We ate lemon pie. Then she paid the bill, took a few
toothpicks, offered me one, and we went out.

"Rainin'," she observed, picking her teeth. The street
was wet again; the rain came down in a soft, soundless
drizzle. "Got any place to stay?" she asked.

I said no, at the same moment regretting my truthful-
ness. More than a place to stay I wanted to shake my
unlovely friend.

She looked at me, meditating a while.

"I live three blocks up," she said, pointing in an uncertain direction. "Got a room, an' you're welcome t'come up
if you wanna.—Don't get the idea," she added, "that I
wanna make you. You can sleep on the couch an' cover
youself up with a carpet I got in my trunk."

A policeman passed a short distance away and threw
us a long look. I wished the woman would leave me alone.
I regretted that I had let her buy me food; now it was
hard to be rude to her. Besides, I was getting a heavy and
disagreeable feeling in my stomach.

I begged her not to bother with me any more. I was
grateful for the supper; it was nice of her, but ——

"Bother!" she laughed in a mirthless, eager way.
"Bother nothin'. I wanna help you. See? I knew a boy
onct, he was a soldier too. See? He was in the war an' got
killed, an'—well, you look sumpthin' like 'im. That's why
I picked you up. Damn near cried when I seen you

198

standin' there pattin' that dog, you look so much like 'im—I mean like the boy that got killed in the war."

She began to sob.

I went with her.

IV

The house to which she led me was a forlorn wooden tene-ment. In the hallway I was oppressed by a rancid odor, and the unlighted narrow stairway with its worm-eaten, wobbly banister squealed beneath our steps as if in pain.

"Well, this is it," she said, apologetically, as she lit the gas-jet in her room. "Not much, but I guess better 'n out in the rain, huh?" Indoors, her voice had a weird sound.

She apparently was on about the next to the lowest rung on the ladder of her profession. She probably never had been much higher. The room was fairly large, but ill-kept, ill-ventilated, the heavy mustiness pressing upon one from all sides. It contained a double bed, a chair, a huge old trunk, a battered couch, an empty orange-crate; on the walls hung a mirror, a picture of the Virgin Mother and the Babe, a signed photograph of Mary Pickford, and an array of clothes and towels.

I was a fool to come here! Rain or no rain, I would not spend the night in this room. Let her cry! What did I care if I hurt her feelings? She was half-drunk, crying-drunk. I wished I hadn't let her feed me.

I was about to open the door and run out, when in order to get to her trunk, which was on the other side of the bed, she shoved the latter to my side of the room and against the door, thus unwittingly frustrating my plan of escape.

"What's your name, kid?" she asked, removing her coat and hat.

I don't know why, but I said it was Bill.

"Billy!" she bellowed, delighted. "That was his name, too—Billy." She opened the trunk and began to rummage in it.

"Whose name?"

"My kid brother's. He got killed in the war. You look so much like 'im. Here's his pitcher." She stretched herself across the bed and handed me a postcard photo of a boy in army uniform. "I brung 'im up an' put 'im through school," with unconcealed pride. "He was goin' to college."

Thinking of flight, I was not interested in her affairs. Then, too, the food I had eaten was causing me deep distress.

She proposed that we have a drink and lifted a huge bottle out of the depths of her trunk. The stuff was bootleg, she said, but not bad: one could stand it. She assured me it would not kill me and poured me a little in a cup and quite a bit more in another for herself.

"Well, Billy, whoever you are," she said, holding her cup aloft and smiling weirdly, her thickly plastered face assuming, in the dim, flickering gaslight, a weird aspect —"whoever you are, here's to you, to everybody—to the whole shebang!"

Perhaps "shebang" included the unhappy hamburger and pie within me; anyhow, the liquor, horrible and breath-taking as it was, had almost an instantaneous beneficial effect on my stomach.

"Billy," she said, after we had both resumed breathing —"I'll call you Billy—sit down, Billy, there on the couch an' make youself at home." She herself sat on the bed. "My name's Maude. Billy used to call me Mud or Muddie for short. Gee! he was such a kid—always fulla fun. Sideways his face was just like yours is. When I seen you like this, from the side, I damn near screamed thinkin'

200

you was Billy. You was pattin' that dog an' I almost
swore you was Billy; he was crazy about dogs. Just your
age, too, I guess. You're quiet-like, not very sociable to
speak of, but that's 'cause you don't like me. Oh, that's
awright; don't blame you 'tall if you don't like me.
You're young, your whole life's 'fore you. You're kinda
hard up now, but that's nothin'. I guess you got folks
somewhere to help you. I'm a old hooker, a battle-ax, but
I'm your frien', though. I'm for you, Billy, if you like me
or not. I'm tickled pink your name's Billy. I am, for a
fact. 'Course, maybe you don't give a hoot if I am or not.
Have 'nother?"

I declined, and she proceeded to knock the breath out
of herself with a second drink.

"This is what keeps me up—booze and hop. Ever take
dope? Don' never do it neither, Billy-boy. I got the habit
after the kid got killed in the war. I cried an' cried. I was
a waitress then. Worked in a cafeteria, too. Then when
Billy got killed in the war I went to hell in no time—three
years ago. Billy was all I had to live for, an' now I ain't
got nothin'. So I drink and take hop. Hop in the daytime
and nights when I'm busy, an' drink like this when I'm
alone. An' I'm getting uglier 'n hell, ain't I? Las' week a
guy called me a ol' battle-ax—that's what he called me."

Maude took a third drink, which drew her loose features into a sketch of horror. Her large mouth opened
wide as she gasped for breath.

"That's all," she announced, corking the bottle. "It'll
put me to sleep in great shape. An' maybe I'll dream. It
don't start to work on me good till I get to bed. Hope I
dream sumthin' pretty—*hic*. 'Scuse me. . . . Gee! damn'
near forgot the rug—the magic carpet," she laughed, "to
cover youself up with. The magic carpet . . ." She began

201

to dig into the huge trunk. "You sleep on the couch—*hic*. 'Scuse me. You don' like me; you sleep on the couch—but I'm for you, Billy. You're only a kid, anyway, like Billy. . . . Here it is! The magic carpet. Had it for years; kinda like it. Bought it on a auction—a Jap auction— 'bout ten years back. Billy was with me at the auction. Anyhow, it'll keep you warm, an' your overcoat. F'gossake take off your coat—it's all wet—an' make youself at home. Don' be afraid o' me." She laughed. "Don' mind me, Billy—*hic*. 'Scuse me. I may be gettin' a jag on, but I know what I'm doin'."

She took a towel and a bed-garment off the wall and left the room through a door I had not noticed before. I thought of escaping while she was in the washroom, but on second thought I decided to stay. The rain beat against the closed window. I could hear the wind outside. After all, this was better than out in the storm.

Presently Maude reappeared clad in a nightgown and a bathrobe.

"The stuff's beginnin' to work on me in good shape," she observed. Her voice now was a drone; the beating of the rain on the panes helped to drown some of its harshness. "I'll get to sleep in good shape, with rain playin' like this on the window. Wanna 'nother nip 'fore turnin' in?"

I declined. Then she offered me a clean towel and suggested that I wash, too.

In the washroom, I heard her take another drink, and a few minutes later, when I came out, she was in bed.

I turned off the light and proceeded to settle myself on the couch, which creaked in twenty places at every move I made.

Maude began to snore lightly.

V

The effect of Maude's rotgut soon began to wear off and
the hamburger and lemon pie began to distress me anew.
The air in the room was unbearable. I rose and opened
the window a little at the top and hoped the rain would
not blow in.

What a strange, awful day! . . . first getting held up
. . . now here with this woman. . . .

A streak of faint light from a near-by street lamp
reached into the room, and returning to the couch, I espied the outline of Maude's bottle on the top of the trunk.
My hostess snored on. I reached for the liquor and took
a tall drink; and as I bumped and stumbled my way
couchward, the anguish in my stomach gave way to an
inner glow, which beneath Maude's "magic carpet" and
Uncle Sam's overcoat, soon took the form of a pleasant,
reeling drowsiness.

The next thing I knew it was bright daylight.

I looked at Maude—still sleeping, snoring. Then I
realized that my head ached. There was a leaden heaviness
in my limbs, and my heart pounded.

It had ceased raining. The day outside looked inviting.

I dressed and began to push the bed clear of the door,
hoping Maude would continue to sleep and dream of nice
things. There was a suggestion of a smile on her face, but
the woman looked a fright.

At last I had the door clear so I could open it suffi-
ciently to slip out, but as I returned to the couch for my
overcoat, Maude stirred and sat up as though stung by
an invisible bayonet. She stared at me.

"Oh, it's you, Billy, is it?" she said, after a while. Her
voice was husky, untellably awful. "Didn't recognize you

203

rightaway. Thought maybe was sumbody else tryin' to beat it 'tout payin' me. God! I feel awful!"

It was punishment to look at her and listen to her voice. I opened the door and began to stammer my thanks.

"Gee! Billy, wait!" she cried, reaching under her mattress. "You're flat an' I wanna help you. Meant to give it to you las' night. Here's a little money that'll tie you over, an' you can send it back to me when you can if you wanna."

I opened the door and bolted.

"Billy!" she bellowed and came tearing after me. "Billy!"

Doors began to open and heads to appear all about me. Perhaps these people thought I was trying to get away from Maude without paying her! Her breasts bounced beneath her loose nightgown, and her whole appearance was enough to frighten a dragon.

"Billy!"

I stopped on the stairs. Tears ran down her face.

"Take it! If you don't I'll be unhappy. I took such a shine to you. I meant to give it to you las' night. Lissen, boy, I got it easy"—she lied—"stole it from a rich guy. He was drunk an'—" She shoved the money in my pocket. I was paralyzed. "There!" she said.

Then she waddled back into her room.

I ran out. On the corner I saw a street-car and caught it. To the conductor I handed the bill Maude had put in my pocket; he could not change it, but let me ride anyhow. The car took me to Lincoln Park.

It was a fine day, like a young face just washed in the morning, warm and fresh. Drops of rain glistened on leaves and grass blades. Two swans swam on the little lake. The trees along the lake were reflected in the smooth surface.

CHAPTER XVII

The Enormous Village

I

THE bill that Maude had pushed into my pocket was for twenty dollars. . . . (Four years later, when I had more money than enough to cover my immediate needs, I spent an afternoon looking for the house where she had lived. I found it, but Maude was there no longer.) . . .

On twenty dollars I lived in Los Angeles for three weeks, while trying to get a job. Nights I slept in the free bunk-house—so called to distinguish it from the ordinary bums' flop-houses—maintained by a local post of the American Legion in connection with its free veteran's employment bureau. I ate in cheap lunchrooms and cafeterias on Main and Spring streets.

Times were bad. The fall of 1922 was the tail end of the first post-World War economic depression in the United States. The Legion's employment-office was jammed with shabby, frustrated, bewildered, half-starved, and profane ex-service men, many of whom, like myself, had recently come to Los Angeles, thinking the city really was the "white spot on America's industrial map," as advertised by the Chamber of Commerce in Eastern papers and magazines. But jobs were scarce. The side streets east of Main, where the commercial employment agencies were located, teemed with unemployed men, some of them willing to work at anything for any money.

I spent hours daily in the Legion's office or going from one of the regular employment agencies to another. The rest of the time I read books and magazines at the Public Library or walked around in the sunshine.

205

II

Walking about town, the idea that Los Angeles was a fantastic human muddle swiftly crept upon me. Hardly a day passed that I was not stopped in the street and handed a religious tract—"Whither Bound, Heaven or Hell?" or "Wages of Sin is Death!" Old men in shabby clothes, their eyes like cold ashes, slowly paced the sidewalks, bearing sandwich-signs inscribed:

THE END OF THE WORLD IS NEAR
ARE YOU PREPARED, SINNER?

Men and women, young and old, calling themselves "fishers of men," accosted me in the streets or, as I sat in the park, reading a newspaper, to ask whether or not I was "saved" or had heard of this wonderful new lady evangelist, Sister Aimee Semple McPherson, and her great message of the Foursquare Gospel. Or wouldn't I like to hear the Rev. So-and-so at the International Bible Institute next Sunday morning? Or the Rev. Thus-and-thus at the Central "Y," who conducted the largest men's Bible class in the city, barring none?

One rainy afternoon I was sitting in the waiting-room of the P. E. depot, when a neatly dressed middle-aged woman with a pale, drawn face and a tall angular body seated herself beside me.

"May I ask you a question, young man?" she said, looking at me aggressively.

"Yes, of course."

She stared at me for a few moments. Her face was tensely serious. She swallowed heavily.

"Have you been washed in the blood of the Lamb?" she asked in a fervid voice.

I wanted to rise and walk away from her, but as I hesitated she put a trembling bony hand on my arm and repeated her question.

"I don't know, lady," I said. "I wish ——"

She shook her head sadly, then smiled eagerly. "Let me help you, won't you? Oh, I know you're not saved, and it breaks my heart. You're such a nice-looking boy. Look. Can't you see the blood of the Lamb on my hands?"

She released my arm and I rose.

"Don't go!" she cried and seized my arm again. "Don't fight me!"—as I tried to pull myself clear of her. "Don't fight your Redeemer!" she shrieked.

"I'm not fighting anyone," I said; "only please leave me alone."

Several people looked at us. I was embarrassed and annoyed.

The woman stared at me. Gradually her look hardened.

"What nationality are you?" she demanded, in a harsh voice. When I did not answer, she said: "You talk like a foreigner. Are you a Rooshian?"

"Yes, I'm a 'Rooshian'," I lied.

"I thought so!" she said, shrilly. All the softness and kindness had gone out of her. "A Boolsheviki, ain't you?"

"That's right," I said.

"What do you mean by wearing that overcoat?"— meaning my army overcoat.

I jerked my arm away and quickly walked out of the station. I could not help but shudder. Then I wanted to laugh.

On Saturdays I saw church advertisements in the *Times* and the *Examiner* announcing sermons apparently by the leading preachers in the city on such topics as "What Would Jesus Do if He Were a Great Movie Director Like Cecil de Mille?" or "—If He Were President of the Advertising Club?" One minister was self-described as an "ex-gambler, now a mighty hunter before the Lord," and his subject one Sunday was "Who Killed the Dead Sea?" An evangelist advertised himself as "a drunkard, gambler, pimp, and outcast for twenty years; five times around the world as hobo; now a miracle of grace." Still another contended that "millions now living will never die" and that the Second Coming would soon occur in southern California "because here the climate is just like that in the Holy Land."

Now and then I stopped to listen to soap-boxers in the rooming-house district off Main Street and to the argufiers or "nuts" in Pershing's Park and on the Plaza, most of them professional atheists, or "Christ-killers," full of sound and fury, as fanatical in their way as the religionists were in theirs. They tried to surpass one another in blaspheming. They denounced the preachers and made heavy, bitter fun of their followers. They were, for the most part, frowzy elderly fellows, pale imitations of Bob Ingersoll and Clarence Darrow: intellectual vagrants and bandits who liked to hear themselves talk and derived satisfaction from referring to Jesus as "Jerusalem Slim" and describing religion as "cheap perfume for the halitosis of the soul." One atheist spoke nightly on the Plaza, refuting the idea that "millions living now will never die" and insisting that "millions living now are already dead."

III

Finally, by paying a fee of two and a half dollars I got a job through a commercial labor agency. It was a pick-and-shovel, or "mucking," job in Hollywood Hills, where a syndicate of Los Angeles realtors were starting a new and "exclusive" subdivision called Hollywoodland, intended to appeal specially to movie stars, directors, oil

208

millionaires, high-powered evangelists, wealthy widows, and divorcees from the East.

I reported to the labor boss on the job. He was in charge of some two hundred men, most of them engaged in digging ditches, grading roads, laying water, gas, and sewer pipes, building retaining-walls along the hillsides, and the like. The workmen lived in a large tent camp at the bottom of a canyon about three miles from Hollywood Boulevard. The camp was in charge of a bull-cook, to whom the labor boss sent me to get a bunk. I had no blankets, so I had to buy them from the company store and pay for them out of my first wage, which was three dollars a day. There was a cook-house, where the working force ate three meals a day, for which we paid $1.80 out of our wages, so that in actual money I received only $1.20 a day for eight hours' work. But the food was abundant and fairly good.

The labor boss assigned me to the night-shift gang in the stone quarry, which was in another canyon more than a mile from camp. It was the hardest work I have ever done. With a dozen or more other men, under a Swedish foreman, I shoveled gravel into huge wheelbarrows, pushed the wheelbarrows and dumped them into trucks from a platform, and rolled boulders from underneath an overhanging wall of rock. The first night I was in constant terror that a rock might break off the wall and crush me. The quarry was lighted by huge incandescents which cast over the scene weird shadows of trees and moving men. The owls hooted in the holly bushes. The sharp metallic clicks of picks and shovels against stone echoed against the opposite wall of the canyon.

The foreman kept his eyes on us every minute, and the only rest we got was when the "powder-monkey" set off a blast of dynamite and during the half-hour lunch period at midnight. The shift was from five-thirty in the evening till two the next morning.

The first few nights, when I finally hit the bunk at two-thirty or three o'clock, I was too tired to sleep. Every muscle and bone in my body ached. I looked at the sloping canvas of the tent through which the moonlight filtered. When I closed my eyes and fell asleep for a minute, I awoke with a start, shuddering all over. I had dreamed that the sloping canvas above me was the overhanging wall of rock in the quarry, about to crash on me.

I worked on the night shift in the quarry for about a month. Gradually I got used to it. I became acquainted with some of my fellow workers, many of whom were I. W. W., or "Wobblies." A few of these, even if more or less lopsided in their ideas, were intelligent, interesting men. They spoke to me of the class struggle and of the new social order, which the I. W. W. movement would bring about. I enjoyed listening to them. One or two of them were intensely alive individuals, romantic rebels. Now and then I took the anti-I. W. W. position and argued with them, just to hear them talk. I liked their passion and also their sense of humor. They could laugh, and their laughter was strong, proletarian laughter, coming from the guts of them. Their songs, which they hummed while shoveling gravel (but, Wobbly-like, accomplishing as little as possible), were funny parodies of Christian hymns. Their views of Los Angeles and Hollywood were "class-conscious" and not entirely objective, but amusing. Los Angeles was "a nut town . . . a scab town . . . full of scissor-bills . . . run by rich bastards who hate the Wobblies like poison. . . ."

One of the men, who himself was an ex-soldier, tried to make me join the I. W. W. The spirit, the humor, and

210

the drama of the movement appealed to me very much, but I was skeptical about its program. It did not seem feasible to me. It did not appear to be geared to any world movement or epic idea. The whole system of life in the United States was against it. Besides, to join anything was contrary to my personal policy toward America and life, which was that of a bystander and onlooker. I was inclined to agree with Mencken that idealism was "bilge"; that radical movements such as the I. W. W. were slave movements, motivated by the slaves' envy of their economic betters, and as such, while vastly interesting, not especially admirable. I did not consider myself a slave, nor even a "wage slave," as the Wobblies put it. I felt envious of no one; only sorry for a great many people.

After about a week in the quarry the soreness in my bones and muscles left me. I got over the fear that the overhanging rocks might tumble down upon me, and ceased having nightmares. I slept like a man that was dead, and awoke fresh and hungry. Hard work in the open air, even if it was at night, and fairly good food, put me in excellent physical health. I enjoyed the company of my I. W. W. fellow workers.

I was young. I felt fine. I could laugh. And there was no end of things in Hollywood and in Los Angeles— throughout America, in fact—that made me laugh.

IV

Working on the night shift and sleeping, usually, until just before the noon meal, I had all afternoon to walk in Hollywood and Los Angeles. On Sundays and holidays I did not work. And walking around, I came upon all sorts of scenes and experiences.

One Sunday morning I attended a church service at

which Rin-tin-tin, the canine movie star, appeared "in person" as an attraction. One afternoon I wandered into the "temple" of a Hindu *swami* in a side street two blocks from Hollywood Boulevard, and heard several hundred human beings, male and female, yelping like dogs because the Hindu, it seemed, had told them that the sound vibrations of yelping had high curative value. On another afternoon I entered a hall in downtown Los Angeles, where a quack, too fat to stand, sat in a throne-like chair on the platform, and lectured to an admiring audience on "How to Achieve Personal Beauty by Dieting."

I became interested in the various religious and health cults. I discovered all sorts of churches I had never heard of before—churches of Divine Power, of Divine Fire, of the Open Door, of the Blue Flame, of New Thought, of Advanced Thought, of the Higher Things in Life. And there were so-called Pillars of Fire, Temples of Light, Chapels of Numerology, Truth Studios, Truth Centers, and many rescue and gospel missions, and endless lecture halls in which one could listen to dissertations on all sorts of subjects.

In the heart of the downtown business district I came upon a cult called "Maz-daz-lan." Its "temple" was in the basement of an office-building. Its chief prophet, or "Master," was one Otoman Bar-Azusht Ra'nish, who claimed to be a Persian prince, but whose real name was Otto Ranisch, formerly a German-American Mormon from Salt Lake City. Every Sunday morning, arrayed in gorgeous robes, he preached before an audience of several hundred well-dressed people. His "teachings" were a weird concoction of sun-worship, phallicism, Oriental philosophies of all kinds, health and breath culture. His god was Mazda, which, I was told, meant Light, but actually, I think, he took the name from "Mazda" electric lamp. On my first attendance I was given a printed card. It was the Maz-daz-lan Credo, which had forty-eight articles, one of which read as follows:

Maz-daz-lan declares that the Infallible Plan of Salvation lies in the Application of Means of Purification leading unto Regeneration, with the first step essential unto Salvation from Ancestral Ties through the efficacy of rhythmic Prayers and Songs breathed on the breath, the utterance of the language thereof, guided by Thought, imparts freedom to the dynamics of life, assuring more perfect and harmonious operations throughout the body and its corresponding factors, quickening the latent forces to renewed action, effecting restoration, filling the heretofore unclaimed tissues and energies with Galama, the Centralizing life principle, which when retained through increased organic operations induces a higher rate of consciousness, and with it brings about the immaculate conception of man born again and again, and born of the spirit.

I bought the "Master's" pamphlet, entitled "Health and Breath," and read:

When hungry and you do not know where to get your next piece of bread, do not despair. Thy Father Mazda, all-loving, has provided you with everything that will meet all cases of emergency. Place your teeth tightly together, with tongue pressing against lower teeth, and lips parted. Breathe in, close lips immediately, exhaling through the nostrils. Breathe again; if saliva form in your mouth, hold your breath so you can swallow it before you exhale. You thus take out of the air the metal substances contained therein; you can even taste the iron which you convert into substance required for making the blood. Should you feel there is a lack of zinc and copper and silver in your blood, place upper teeth over lower, keep lower lip tightly to lower teeth, now breathe and you can even taste the metals named. Then should you feel you need more gold element for your brain functions, place your back teeth together just as if you were to grind them, taking short breaths only. There is gold all around us.

The services in the "temple" ended with the congregation chanting the Maz-daz-lan Affirmation, which I quote in part:

I am all in One individually and one in All collectively;
I am present individually and omnipresent collectively;
I am knowing individually and omniscient collectively;
I am potent individually and omnipotent collectively . . .

I am Maz-daz-lan and recognize the Eternal Designs of Hu-mata, Huhata, Hu-varashta.

A-shem Vo-hu, A-shem Vo-hu, A-shem Vo-hu.

The cult, or rather its "Master," who was known also as the "Universal Genius," operated under a charter issued by the State of California.

v

On billboards throughout the city I saw large advertisements from which I first learned of one Mrs. Elizabeth Goodwill Randolph, the Marvel Woman, the Human, Helpful Woman; the head and founder of the Elizabeth Goodwill Randolph School of Opportunity, also known as the Traveling University for Men and Women. The advertisements invited all to come to one of the largest auditoriums in the city to hear the lady's "FREE entertaining heart-to-heart lectures." From publicity in the *Times* I further learned that she was a "practical psychologist," "originator of Human Analysis," "teacher of teachers."

I attended several of her free afternoon lectures, which aimed to interest the multitudes who came to hear her in courses, for which she charged twenty-five dollars, upward. She was a statuesque person, not hard on the eyes. Elaborately gowned in velvet and silk, she carried herself like a Balkan queen, a rhinestone band about her brow

214

and coiffure, a string of pearls around her neck, and diamonds on her hands, to enhance her gestures with their glitter. She appeared to be in her mid-thirties, but told the audience she was approaching her sixtieth birthday. That she looked so young, she said, was due to the fact that she practiced her own "science of life." She was "Success Incarnate."

Success, she declared, was easy to achieve. Almost anyone could become a titan of industry, a popular idol, a Don Juan, a Cleopatra. Indeed, it was a matter of personal disgrace if you were not at least one of these. Fame, wealth, power and love were within the grasp of *all*. And the way to achieve success was to sign up for a course offered by Mrs. Elizabeth Goodwill Randolph. She had helped literally hundreds of thousands of people all over the world—"and do you mean to sit there and let this wonderful opportunity go by you."

"Oh, let me tell you what is the matter with this world, today," she said. "Too many people look forward from one week-end to another week-end, while their real *weak* end is up here," pointing with her sparkling hand to her glittering head. (Applause.) "But, folks, I know that you who are here this afternoon are not weak at this end—this is your *strong* end, isn't it, or you wouldn't have come, would you now?"

The audience—which consisted largely of tired, fate-flogged people, disappointed drudges of the home, the farm, the factory and the office—was thrown into a fit of delight.

"Oh, folks, success and happiness are yours for the taking," continued the Wonder Woman. "And now don't try to tell me that you're too old to succeed in business or professional life and be happy in love, for you are not. The time will come when elderly people will run the world.

(Applause.) But you must stop taking the back seat!"
(Applause.) Then, as if it had just occurred to her: "Do
you know that Shakespeare didn't write any of his immortal plays and poems till after he passed the age of
sixty?"

Everybody seemed impressed by this information. The
Wonder Woman herself, perhaps, did not know that
Shakespeare was dead at fifty-two, and she proceeded to
mention Goethe and Gladstone as examples of greatness
in old age.

The woman was in Los Angeles for two months, during which period, according to rumor, she cleaned up
over $100,000. In subsequent years, while I lived in
southern California, she returned to her "favorite city"
every six months, with increasing success.

In my diary, which I began about that time, I wrote:

. . . Such a woman is possible only here, in these incomparable States, where Success is a religion, a fanaticism; where
achievement is measured, for the most part, in terms of dollars
and cents; where everyone is supposed to be the equal of the next
man and as such entitled to the same privileges; where the economic, social, and educational systems are so arranged as to
produce multitudes of failures of the sorricst, most pathetic
varieties. . . .

VI

I was glad I had come to Los Angeles, not so much because of the climate, which was agreeable enough to me,
but because the place was endlessly entertaining and ab-
sorbing. A paragrapher on the Los Angeles *Record*, a
liberal newspaper, referred to the city as "the essence of
America," and, agreeing with this characterization, I
said to myself that since I wanted to learn about America
I could live nowhere else to greater advantage. Early in
1923 I wrote in my diary: "Los Angeles is but a bigger

216

and better Gopher Prairie." (I had read Sinclair Lewis' *Main Street* some time before.)

Three years later my views about Los Angeles crystallized themselves into the following notes in my diary, which I quote despite their sophomoric quality:

. . . Los Angeles is probably one of the most interesting spots on the face of the earth. Some one should write a book about it; an honest-to-goodness book, not a mere booster pamphlet. . . . In its advertisements, the Realty Board calls the town "The City Beautiful," "The Wonder City," "The Earthly Paradise," and other fancy names, none of which is exactly inaccurate. It *is* beautiful and wonderful in spots, and I guess for some people it is paradise. But that isn't coming anywhere near the truth about it. . . .

The people on the top in Los Angeles, the Big Men, as elsewhere in America, are the business men, the Babbitts. They are the promoters, who are blowing down the city's windpipe with all their might, hoping to inflate the place to a size that it will be reckoned the largest city in the country—in the world. Throughout the town one sees huge electric signs—"2,000,000 population by 1930." These signs represent the spirit of Los Angeles. They were put up by the men who own most of the lots and subdivisions.

These men are the high priests of the Chamber of Commerce whose religion is Climate and Profits. They are—some of them —grim, inhuman individuals with a great terrifying singleness of purpose. They see a tremendous opportunity to enrich themselves beyond anything they could have hoped for ten or even five years ago, and they mean to make the most of it. They have their fingers in every important pie, not only in the city, but everywhere in southern California and even below the border. They work hard. I hear that Harry Chandler, publisher of the *Times*, spends sixteen hours daily in his office. They are possessed by a mad drive which—so far as I can make out—is not deeply rooted in their own personalities, but is rather a part of the place, this great region of eternal spring which stretches between the Sierras and the sea, and which, of late years, has begun to capture the imagination of millions of people, who for various reasons have become dissatisfied with what life offers them in Gopher Prairies in the East, in the South, and the Middle West.

And trailing after the big boys is a mob of lesser fellows, whom the former awe with their superior economic advantages and control through the Chamber of Commerce and other *pay*-triotic organizations: thousands of minor realtors, boomers, promoters, contractors, agents, salesmen, bunko-men, officeholders, lawyers, and preachers—all driven by the same motives of wealth, power, and personal glory, and a greater Los Angeles. They exploit the "come-ons" and one another, envy the big boys, live deliriously for business, bigger and better business, while their wives gather in women's clubs, listen to *swamis* and *yogis* and English lecturers, join "love cults" and Coué clubs in Hollywood and Pasadena, and their children—boys and girls in their teens: "beautiful but dumb"—jazz and drink and rush around in roadsters. . . .

Then there are the Folks—oh, the *dear* Folks! They are the retired farmers, grocers, Ford agents, hardware merchants, and shoe merchants from the Middle West and other parts of these United States, thousands and tens of thousands of them. They are coming in by trains and automobiles. They have money. They made it during the war. Not that they are not entitled to it. Most of them worked harder than any one should work through their best years. They were the pioneers back in Ioway and Nebraska. No doubt they swindled a little, but they always prayed a little, too, or maybe a great deal. And they paid taxes and raised young ones. They are old and rheumatic. They sold out their farms and businesses in the Middle West or wherever they used to live, and now they are here in California—sunny California—to rest and regain their vigor, enjoy climate, look at pretty scenery, live in little bungalows with a palm-tree or banana plant in front, and eat in cafeterias. Toil-broken and bleached out, they flock to Los Angeles, fugitives from the simple, inexorable justice of life, from hard labor and drudgery, from cold winters and blistering summers of the prairies. . . .

Of course, there are other kinds—many kinds—of people in Los Angeles, but the Folks predominate in numbers and give the place the aspect of a great, overgrown village. They brought with them their preachers, evangelists, and Sunday-school superintendents. They are half-educated, materially prosperous but spiritually and mentally starving. They are retired; they have nothing to do all day; they are a bit exhilarated by climate— and so they follow any fake who possesses personality and looks in any way strange and impressive and can say words which they don't understand in a thrilling voice.

They have money, these Folks, and so, besides the more or less legitimate real-estate business, there are all kinds of bunko promotion schemes—mining, oil, and others—in which the Folks invest their money and never see it again. The financial editor of the *Times* remarked the other day that a sensible person should not get indignant over the existence of bunko schemes in the city. What's the difference, he said, whether the crooks or the idiots had the money? No matter who had it, the money helped to build up Los Angeles. . . .

Most of the Folks are unwell, old, rheumatic men and women. Next to "Where do you come from?" the most frequently asked question is, "Now, how do you feel today?" Health is a big thing in Los Angeles. Most of the people come here to be sun-kissed and made well, and so healing is one of the big industries in town. Besides thousands of more or less regular doctors, there are in Los Angeles no end of chiropractors, osteopaths, "drug-less physicians," faith-healers, health lecturers, manufacturers and salesmen of all sorts of health "stabilizers" and "normal-izers," psychoanalysts, phynotists, mesmerists, the glow-of-life mystics, astro-therapeutists, miracle men and women—in short, quacks and charlatans of all descriptions. . . . My mind goes back to the Old Country. In Carniola, as I recall, "How do you feel today?" was an unusual question; in fact, I believe that I never heard it asked. There, good health was the rule, rather than the exception, even among elderly people, and so there was little interest in it. . . . In Los Angeles health is the leading topic of conversation.

And Los Angeles is America. A jungle. Los Angeles grew up suddenly, *planlessly*, under the stimuli of the adventurous spirit of millions of people and the profit motive. It is still growing. Here everything has a chance to thrive—for a while—as a rule only a brief while. Inferior as well as superior plants and trees flourish for a time, then both succumb to chaos and decay. They must give way to new plants pushing up from below, and so on. This is freedom under democracy. Jungle democracy!

In Panama, I remember, I once saw a great stretch of jungle country from a mountain top. It was beautiful from the distance. Looking at it, I could not believe that actually it was a dank, unhealthy, dangerous region, into which one should not venture except if properly equipped with mosquito netting and armed with guns and bolos.

The same goes for Los Angeles (*i.e.* America). From Mount Hollywood, Los Angeles looks rather nice, enveloped in a haze of changing colors. Actually, and in spite of all the healthful sunshine and ocean breezes, it is a *bad* place—full of old, dying people, and young people who were born old of tired pioneer parents, victims of America—full of curious wild and poisonous growths, decadent religions and cults and fake science, and wild-cat business enterprises, which, with their aim for quick profits, are doomed to collapse and drag down multitudes of people. . . . A jungle. . . .

Hence, if one lives in Los Angeles—in America—one would best be properly equipped and armed—not with guns and bolos and mosquito netting, but with knowledge and understanding of the scene, with a sense of humor—with laughter. Otherwise the place is very apt to get the better of one, both materially and spiritually. . . .

CHAPTER XVIII

Lonie Burton, Still a Crusader

I

I worked on the Hollywoodland job till March, 1923. Then I was "fired," along with several I. W. W.'s, because the labor boss suspected—on account of my friendliness with them—that I was a Wobbly, too.

During the preceding two and a half months I had saved nothing from my wages. I had spent most of my money exploring the jungle of Los Angeles and buying books and magazines which I wanted to read and could not procure at the Library.

The American Legion free bunkhouse had been discontinued; so, to keep the few dollars that I had for food till I got another job, I spent the nights—often sleeplessly—in a confession-box in the old mission-church of Nuestra Señora de Los Angeles, just off the Plaza. I usually slipped into the edifice around ten in the evening, when it was practically deserted, and made myself at home. Now and then I peeked from behind the thick velvet curtain of the box at the large Crucifix directly opposite me, with a tiny light burning before it, and indulged in compassion for the Man on the Cross, to Whom the atheists referred as "Jerusalem Slim." One night I wondered why some hobo-writer—Jack London or Maxim Gorki—had not written a book about Him, treating Him as a hobo, a vagrant. Perhaps I would write it some day. What title would I give it? "Jerusalem Slim" was too crude. Perhaps "The Man of the Road"? I would make

Him a lowly one; a sort of Wobbly of nineteen hundred years ago. . . .

In the daytime I chased after employment. But jobs were still very scarce. When I tired, I went to the Public Library or sat in Pershing's Park, reading or thinking about what I had read or observed.

II

I was walking around one evening, rather low and blue, with only two dollars left in my pocket, when somewhere on North Main, as I paused to look into the window of a cheap clothing-store, I heard a voice call me by my first name. I turned and faced Lonie Burton, although I did not immediately recognize him. He looked frail, shabby, slightly stooped. He had on a short, worn army overcoat.

"I thought it was you," he said.

I was too surprised at first to say anything; unpleasantly surprised, perhaps a little ashamed that I had almost forgotten him.

"What are you doing in Los Angeles?" he asked.

I shrugged my shoulders. "And you?" I said.

Lonie shrugged his shoulders. We grinned at one another with mutual embarrassment. I noted that he needed a shave, a good meal, and a bath. He seemed ten years older than when I had last seen him in France, not quite four years before.

I mentioned that about a year and a half ago I had passed through Milford, Pennsylvania, in the hope of seeing him.

"Mother died," he said. "There was nothing for me in Milford. I came West and have been in or around L. A. the last two years . . . trying to get something to do."

"Where are you going now?" I asked, to be saying something.

"To the post-office," he said. After a pause he added: "I'm expecting a letter from my uncle in Ohio. I wrote 'im to send me some money. Come along."

Walking with Lonie, I felt more self-consciously a bum than before.

We entered the post-office lobby.

Lonie hesitated. Six or seven people stood in line before the A-D general-delivery window.

"There's a line again!" he exclaimed. "Hate to line up for things. Don't you? In the army you had to line up a hundred times a day—now in civilian life ——"

I had no taste for standing in lines, either, but my aversion to it was not so acute as apparently was Lonie's; his face twitched and he passed a nervous hand across his mouth. I offered to ask for him.

There was no letter.

Outside again, we turned toward the park on the Plaza, near by. There was the lunch-wagon where Maude, the prostitute, had treated me to a supper three months before. For an instant, Lonie seemed to hesitate as we passed it, and drew a nervous hand over his mouth. Plainly, he was hungry.

But, to tell the truth, I was none too generously inclined at the moment; indeed, an hour before I had decided to forego supper that evening. With only two dollars to my name, my immediate future looked bleak. Besides, who was this Lonie Burton, anyhow? As a new devotee of Mencken and Nathan, I remembered him from my army days as a species of idealistic nut. He had believed in the Wilsonian twaddle (a Menckenian term) about democracy. He had fought to make the world safe for democracy.

"Still believe in democracy?" I asked.

"Aw ——!" he said, using an unquotable word.

223

He had evidently changed a good deal. I had never heard him use obscene language.

We walked through the park.

Then, thinking of the probability—the certainty, almost—of my companion's hunger, I got a sudden impulse to do what I could for him, and the realization that I could help him, however slightly, pushed up my own morale several notches.

I asked him, as casually as I could, if he had eaten his supper yet.

"Supper nothing!" he muttered. "Had one last night, though—cheese and bread. This morning for breakfast I tightened up my belt two holes and pressed my belly against a cold radiator in the post-office." He forced a laugh.

I invited him to eat with me, hastening to add that, my funds being only two dollars, we would be obliged to go to one of the less attractive eating-places, perhaps no farther than the lunch-wagon just outside the park.

"Better go easy," he said. "If you want to spend some of your fortune on me, let's get as much for the money as possible. When my money started to run low, I began to eat cheese and bread, and drink water from the fountain in the park."

Well, if that was how he felt about it I would not insist that we go to the expensive lunch-wagon. I handed him a dollar, and ten minutes later he returned with a half-pound of cheese and a loaf of pumpernickel, reporting an expenditure of thirty-eight cents and handing me the change.

We ate our supper on a bench in the park, near a water fountain.

"Where do you stay, Lon?" I asked. Suddenly, I felt a fondness for him again.

"Nowhere—everywhere. Last night I fell asleep on a bench in the Santa Fé depot waiting-room, then a guard roused me and said, politely enough, seeing that I was an ex-soldier, that I'd better remove myself, which I did— to the streets. . . . I wasn't cut out to be a bum."

III

We saved half of our cheese and bread for the next day. Then we talked. The story of Lonie's life since his release from the army, late in 1919, was one of frustration, rather typical of ex-service men without money and family ties in the years immediately after the war. He had washed dishes in restaurants, worked as an extra in the movies, and so on. He had been on the bum almost since he came to Los Angeles. He thought he brooded too much. He was disgusted with life; the world was so "goddamn rotten"—so full of injustice, ignorance, avarice, bunk, and tragedy—and he felt so sickeningly impotent against it. Twice during the last week he had entertained thoughts of killing himself. Only this morning he had had a sudden notion to write his thoughts, make four or five copies, one for each newspaper—a kind of protest to the world—and then commit a sensational suicide by leaping off a roof or from a window of one of the high buildings on Broadway or Hill Street, thereby asserting himself—"making them take notice."

He told me of the slight wound and dose of gas he had received in France, and his complete recovery from both. He could make no claim to the government for disability.

"But here's the funniest part of it," he said, laughing self-consciously. "Going to the rear with my little wound, I happened to come across a wounded French officer, and as he was a little guy, I picked him up and carried him with me. I'd almost forgotten about it; then a couple of weeks ago I got a letter from the War Department, forwarded to me from Milford, Pa., informing me that the French government had awarded me a *Croix de Guerre*. I didn't answer the letter for several days. I thought to myself: to hell with the medal. Then I wrote the A. G. O. in Washington that I wasn't in Milford any longer; that I was in L. A., and my address was general delivery. I haven't heard from Washington since. I don't care if I never get the damn' cross."

IV

I made Lonie Burton come with me to the Nuestra Señora de Los Angeles, and he spent the night in the confession-box next to mine.

In the morning we ate the left-over cheese and pumpernickel and drank again from the water fountain. On a bench we found a morning newspaper. The news of the day was about a sensational mystery murder in the movie colony, a baseball bribe, a senatorial investigation in Washington of certain oil leases, the tomb of Tut-ankh-amen. A column was given to an interview by a foreign author on the all-absorbing flapper question, and nearly a page to "society news."

Lonie remarked that the world was cock-eyed, crazy. "Why don't the papers give a break to your problem and mine?" he went on. "Here we are—bums! Five years ago we were cheered as heroes."

We went to the post-office. There was a letter for Lonie. It was an official War Department communication, mailed at Fort MacArthur, the coast artillery post in San Pedro Harbor, and marked "Important" in large red letters on the envelope. It was signed by the fort adjutant, and as I remember read thus:

LONIE BURTON, STILL A CRUSADER

In compliance with instructions of recent date from the War Department, you are notified that the *Croix de Guerre* with two palms, awarded to you by the Government of the Republic of France, is at this office, and you are requested to present yourself at these headquarters next Saturday, before 9 a. m., in order to have this decoration formally conferred upon you at a review of the garrison.

Please acknowledge the receipt of this letter and indicate whether it will be convenient for you to be here on Saturday at the time specified. Envelope enclosed.

"Aw, to hell with it!" Lonie said.

"Don't be a fool!" I said. "Get the cross; you may be able to pawn it." I laughed.

"What's it made of?"

"Gold, maybe."

Lonie was silent a minute, looking at the letter. Then his face lighted up.

"I got an idea!" he cried. "You're right; I'll get the cross. Say, this'll get us publicity, and publicity will get us jobs or—well, it'll get us something. This is Thursday. Saturday afternoon and Sunday papers will carry stories about us on the front page."

He wrote on the bottom of the letter that he would report to Fort MacArthur at the specified time, put the letter in the self-addressed envelope, and mailed it.

"But what's the idea?" I asked.

"Don't worry about that. Just stick around and leave it to me." He grinned broadly. "Early tomorrow morning we start hiking to San Pedro—twenty-six miles. Maybe some patriot will give us a lift."

Friday evening we were in San Pedro. We had had a lift part of the way. We had walked at least fifteen miles. Lonie had not eaten anything all day. He said he was on a "hunger strike"; it was part of his plan to look as ill and hungry as possible.

227

In San Pedro, he suddenly announced that he needed a dollar. I offered him the bill that I still had, but he would not take it. Instead, he set out to collect it in nickels and dimes from men whom he stopped on the street, while I followed him at some distance, amazed by his nerve. Then he entered a phone booth in a drug-store and began calling city desks of several Los Angeles newspapers.

"This is the adjutant at Fort MacArthur," he introduced himself. "We're having an interesting ceremony here tomorrow morning at nine o'clock—one of the World War veterans is to be decorated with the *Croix de Guerre* —and the commanding officer would appreciate it if your paper would send a reporter and perhaps a photographer. . . ."

Later in the evening, in a dark side street, we came upon a crowd gathered around a speaker.

It was an I. W. W. meeting. The Wobblies were then beginning to concentrate at San Pedro. Several policemen stood about. The audience was mostly foreigners, dock-workers—Italians, Dalmatians, Mexicans—their dark, rough, painfully serious faces turned intently, avidly at the speaker, who apparently was a self-educated workingman of thirty or so. He spoke in an even, calm, persuasive tone, with none of the conventional fire-spitting manner of the soap-boxer. This was, as I learned later, one of a series of lectures on the conditions in the United States and in the world, as viewed by an "industrial slave."

Lonie Burton, I could see, was stirred and impressed.

The speaker appealed for members. "The only salvation of the working class—and of humanity—lies in intelligently facing the facts and the forces that move the

world—in solidarity—in one big union—in the Industrial Workers of the World."

After the meeting we were approached by a workman
selling Wobbly papers, leaflets, and song-books. Lonie
informed him that we were flat broke. Thereupon the
Wobby insisted that we take a paper and some leaflets
free of charge.

"Just get into town?" the I. W. W. asked, interested,
no doubt, in the fact that we were ex-soldiers (wearing
army overcoats) and obviously "on the bum."

"Yes."

"Got a place to sleep?"

"No."

"Wait. I'll fix you up for the night."

And so Lonie and I spent the night in the Wobbly
headquarters in another part of town and met "Red
O'Neal," the speaker of the evening. Lonie and O'Neal
got into a discussion about social injustice and the
I. W. W. movement.

v

A few minutes before nine the next morning we entered
the sergeant-major's office in Fort MacArthur. Lonie had
insisted that I go along.

Lonie was about to introduce himself to the sergeant-
major, when the commanding officer and the adjutant
came in, followed by reporters.

"That man Burton showed up yet, Sergeant?" asked
the adjutant.

"No, sir."

"I'm Burton," said Lonie, handing over his soiled and
crumpled certificate.

The sergeant-major checked the descriptive data on
the certificate and declared them in order.

229

"Ah"—a sound from the colonel, a corpulent middle-aged gentleman in a neat uniform, "—too bad, Mr. Burton, you did not come a little sooner. We could probably have fixed you up a bit—for the occasion."

Lonie smiled.

"The troops are out, sir, and assembly has sounded," remarked the adjutant. "Time to begin," looking at his wrist watch.

The colonel on his right, the adjutant on his left, Lonie walked to the parade-ground, where a battalion was formed to render him honor. He turned his head and winked at me as if to say, "Now watch!"

"Stand right here, Mr. Burton," said the colonel. "I'll tell you what to do."

The ceremony began. . . .

"I went out there," Lonie told me afterwards, "intending to faint right in the middle of the show. To fake it. I figured that would give us publicity. . . . But after those officers began saluting one another, I actually started to feel a bit light and dizzy.

"I glanced at the colonel by my side—a fine-looking old man, big, strong, red in the face. I looked at his shiny boots. . . . I let my eyes wander from one end of the line to the other: rows of soldiers responding to sharp commands with brisk movements. Then the bugles, and the band playing that jazzy march. The whole thing seemed grotesque, unreal. I forgot all about publicity and jobs.

"Then more music—*'Over there, Over there!'*—The band passed up and down. I was vaguely aware of the groups of people standing around, looking at me. And I saw those automobiles that lined the parade-ground."

(The announcement of the ceremony in the morning

papers had brought out a great many people.) "I thought of you—cheese and pumpernickel—the park—the letter from my uncle—reporters.

"Then, all of a sudden, I seemed to hear a voice in front of me—a fellow reading something in a loud speech-making voice [the adjutant reading the citation], how on November 8, 1918, going to the rear, wounded and gassed, I had picked up a wounded officer and, to the everlasting joy and appreciation of the Republic of France and the rest of the civilized world, carried him to safety.

"I heard the colonel tell me in a low voice to step out, go halfway between him and adjutant, stop, and face about. I tried to do as he told me, but I staggered a little once or twice—not faking—and almost fell, but finally succeeded in reaching what I thought was midway between the two officers, and faced about. I tried to make 'about-face' in a military manner, but making a blunder of it—maybe you noticed—I just turned around any old way. If they didn't like the way I pulled off these stunts, I said to myself, they could call off the whole show and go chase themselves! I almost laughed aloud, it struck me so funny. Then I seemed again to think of the jobs that we didn't have, and tried to figure out what I'd best do.

"The colonel was coming toward me. I almost laughed again. What would they do if I told the old boy to keep the cross and walked out on them? . . .

"The old man pinned the cross on my chest and grabbed my hand and shook it.

"Now come with me," he said, and we started for our original position. I was late stepping out, but the colonel slowed down a bit to allow me to catch up with him. I got out of step and the old man hopped to get in step with me. Saw 'im do it? I almost laughed aloud. Once or twice I bumped into him as though I were drunk or something. The whole thing was a comedy.

"Then we faced the troops again. 'Pass in review!' the colonel shouted, and after a while the band began to play another jazz-piece and the battalion moved out in column.

"For a moment I thought I was flying, rising. There was a throbbing in my ears. I could hardly hold my head up.

"The band passed by. I think they played '*K-K-Katy.*' The instruments flashed in the sun, almost blinding me. For a while I felt nothing; everything in me became dull, numb. Then I came back to myself and saw the first company go by—a line of grotesque figures. Like one of those futuristic pictures. I heard the music. '*K-K-Katy, you're the only g-g-girl that I adore.*' . . .

"I hardly knew what was going on. I felt a hot wave sweep over me; then I got cold. I tried not to faint, but the world began to whirl around me in a dozen different directions at once and I hit the ground."

VI

The colonel and the adjutant hurriedly unbuttoned Lonie's clothing and called for water and a doctor, while civilian spectators came rushing from all sides.

I made little attempt to get to him, thinking that he was acting, faking, as he had hinted to me that he might. But somehow the newspaper men discovered that I was Lonie Burton's friend and they got the story out of me, which appeared in the afternoon papers. There were big headlines, pictures of Lonie lying on his cot in the local army hospital, to which they took him; of the *Croix de Guerre*, and of me.

LONIE BURTON, STILL A CRUSADER

When I arrived at the hospital about noon, I found Lonie sitting up, talking with a reporter.

"Say," he turned to me, all smiles, "we're offered a hundred dollars for two articles on our recent experiences as job-hunters. Two Los Angeles papers are starting campaigns to find employment for all ex-service men who have no jobs and want to work."

The newspaper man, who said he would write the articles himself, handed us a hundred dollars. Monday, when he got out of the hospital, Lonie received a letter with money from his uncle.

The Sunday papers also ran short stories about the incident, and during the next few days Lonie received several offers of employment in Los Angeles. Nearly all of them were white-collar jobs. He turned them all down. Since meeting O'Neal and other I. W. W.'s, that was not the sort of job he wanted. "I'm a proletarian," he said to me with intense seriousness.

He got a job on the docks in San Pedro and Wilmington (which is also part of the Los Angeles Harbor), unloading ships and handling freight in the sheds. He joined the I. W. W. and became very active in the local movement.

I took a job as a reporter on the Los Angeles newspaper which ran the two articles about Lonie and myself —mostly Lonie. It paid me twenty dollars a week, and I was required to write not only news items—the knack for which I picked up within a few days—but also movie "criticism," book reviews, and blurbs for department stores; and when a "shoe week" came along, articles on "The Shoe Through the Ages."

For two and a half months I saw Lonie at infrequent intervals.

Late in May, 1923, the I. W. W. dock-workers in San
Pedro called a strike. I was sent there to cover it.

The Wobblies tied up the port almost entirely. For
nearly two weeks not a ship was unloaded. The interests
represented by the Ship-owners' Association and other
friendly bodies seemed to be stunned by the sudden emer-
gence into power of this sinister radical movement. The
Wobbly demands were utterly "un-American"—repeal of
the California Anti-Criminal Syndicalism law, release of
political prisoners, better wages, abolition of the ship-
owners' employment agency, the "slave market" at the
harbor. It was appalling. The strike must be broken. The
chief of police of Los Angeles, who had jurisdiction over
the harbor, received orders to break it, and he proceeded
to comply. But his task was no sinecure. The strikers numbered two or three thousand, and they were a disciplined,
sober lot, determined to avoid disturbance and violence.

It was a tense and immensely interesting situation. I
came to San Pedro on the day that Upton Sinclair was
arrested and jailed there for attempting to read the Constitution of the United States on a privately owned piece
of property. "None of that Constitution stuff here," was
the edict of the chief of police.

The streets were full of Wobblies and uniformed and
plain-clothes policemen. There was no disorder of any
kind. The strikers walked up and down the streets, their
arms folded on their chests, their faces tense, serious,
sober. Policemen told them to keep on moving, keep on
moving!

Lonie Burton was active in the strike. There was no
central leadership; nearly every other Wobbly seemed to
be a leader.

234

LONIE BURTON, STILL A CRUSADER

Lonie looked better than I had ever seen him look before. His eyes burned with a clear, evangelistic light. He admitted to me that he had helped to organize the strike. He thought "Red" O'Neal was a "great guy." He spoke to me freely about himself—of his conception of the I. W. W. movement, his own place in it, and his attitude toward it and toward America and the world. He was a class-conscious worker, and gave me a graphic picture of the Wobbly utopia, which thrilled me, not as truth, but as a grand dream never realizable.

We spent a good deal of time together, and I became acquainted with some of the other Wobblies.

When the strike was about two weeks old, and threatened to go on for another two weeks or longer, the police began to round up the Wobblies, herding them into P. E. trains like so many cattle, and shipping them to various jails in Los Angeles. To belong to the I. W. W. was a crime in violation of the so-called Anti-Criminal Syndicalism law.

While the strike was thus being broken, the Wobblies—rough, strong men; native-born and foreigners—sang their songs. They sang in the prison stockade in San Pedro, on the way to the trains, in the trains, and finally in jails.

"God!" another young newspaper man remarked to me. "One feels like singing with them. They got guts!"

Among the arrested men were Lonie Burton, "Red" O'Neal, and a half-dozen or more other Wobblies whom the police considered leaders.

The strike was broken. The timid, docile "robots" who had quit their jobs for fear of Wobbly bombs returned to work on the dock, and the ships began to move once more. San Pedro Harbor was saved from the "Red Revolution." The chief of police of Los Angeles received a gold watch in recognition of the splendid service he had rendered, as well as many commendations from pulpit and press, while "Red" O'Neal, Lonie Burton, and other San Pedro Wobblies, who seemed to the authorities to possess some intelligence and ability, were "railroaded" to San Quentin for from four to ten years each.

I saw Burton in the county jail a few days before he was to be sent to the state penitentiary. Could I do anything for him? He was an ex-soldier, gassed and wounded in the war, decorated by the Republic of France, and I felt that something could probably be done for him on the strength of his war record. But no, he would not hear of it. Indeed, he resented my suggestion. He did not want to take advantage of his war record; he was ashamed of it; he had thrown away the *Croix de Guerre*. Besides, he did not think it would work, anyway—his sin was too great.

Lonie's case and those of the other San Pedro Wobblies were appealed to a higher court, and two and a half years later the sentences were reversed on the ground that mere membership in the I. W. W. was not a violation of the law. The prisoners were ordered released. I wrote to Lonie that if he planned to return to southern California he must come to see me, but he probably never received my letter. I lost track of him for another year.

VIII

One afternoon late in 1926, walking through Pershing Park, I stopped to listen to a group of economic heretics gathered there to vent their indignation and their wisdom. The center of the group was a young radical, who held forth on labor-unionism—an unpopular topic in Los Angeles—and kindred subjects.

"Now, let me tell you what *I* think," put in a middle-

236

aged, substantial-looking citizen who stood near me, when the young radical paused to blow his nose. "I think it's a waste of time and energy to try to stir up the workin'-stiff. I put in ten years trying to make a man out of 'im, so I speak from experience, and damn' painful experience, let *me* tell you. I was a Wobbly before the war and went up and down this coast preaching industrial democracy and solidarity and one big union. Before that I was in the A. F. of L., but I got sick of their ways, so I got into the Wobblies ———"

"Are you a Wobbly now?" he was asked.

"No. Life's too short to sink more than ten years in a hopeless thing like trying to organize the American working-class. I'm now what this young fellow here might call a capitalist—a contractor, employing labor—and, by God!" he added, reddening in the face with sudden fury, "I pay the stiffs as little as I can for as much work as I can get out of 'em!"

The man's frankness was startling. Everybody stared at him.

"The mass of the working-class," he resumed, "is made up of sorry, stupid animals—not even that, because an animal will go out and fight—bite you or kick you. Your workin'-stiff won't do that, not even if he's got to starve and his kids go in rags. We contractors are organized so we can better screw the public and exploit labor—you see I got the phraseology at my finger tips—but labor ain't got sense enough to organize. There's something lacking in the workin'-stiff—and I don't know what the hell it is!"

I felt a touch on my arm and, turning, beheld a bruised, swollen face staring at me with a pair of half-closed, watery eyes.

"Hello!" he said.

I recognized the voice of Lonie Burton.

"What in the world's happened to you?" I asked.

"Got beat up," he answered, abashed, and looked away.

I pulled him away from the group of argufiers. We sat down on a bench.

He told me that he had been working with a construction camp near Glendale. A week before, he had decided to quit and was told by the timekeeper to report to the company office at ten the next day for his pay. He and a half-dozen other men who had also quit the previous day were there at the appointed hour, but the manager, who was to sign the checks, did not appear till some time in the afternoon.

To Lonie this was another example of the capitalistic abuse of the working-class. "We were told to be here at ten to get the checks," he said to the manager as the latter stepped from his car; "now it's twelve, and I think you should pay us for the two hours we've waited."

"What the hell d'you think I am!" barked the manager. "Think I got nothin' t'do but worry about your checks?"

"No, but——"

"Aw shut your —— mouth!"

"It would only be right——" Lonie started to say.

"Right hell!" and the manager struck him squarely in the mouth.

Then one of the labor bosses on the job jumped at Lonie and pounded his face and body till he knocked him out and broke two of his ribs.

I asked what the rest of the workmen present were doing while the labor boss pounded him.

He looked at me, startled.

"Why—what could they do? They stood there——" He looked away.

I think it was only then that it occurred to him that

238

his fellow workers could, and perhaps should, have come to his aid in that one-sided fray.

I asked him if he had overheard the contractor talking under the tree a while before. He nodded.

"What did you think of it?"

He stared before him, without answering. I was sorry. What was the sense of asking him this? I observed how aged he had grown. He was getting bald and his teeth were decayed, no doubt because of the poor food he had had in San Quentin.

He stared at the pavement without moving or saying anything. Finally it occurred to me to offer him some money. He took it.

"Come to see me, Lonie," I said. I gave him my address.

"All right," he said.

I knew he would not.

We parted. He walked in one direction, I in another. I looked after him. He was an old man at twenty-eight, his face battered, his ribs fractured; shabby, bent as though weighed down by a vast burden—a defeated crusader.

That evening I wrote in my diary:

Saw Lonie Burton. . . . He is a living proof to me (perhaps soon to be a dead one) that one cannot afford to plunge too far into the economic and social issues of American life. One is too apt to be caught in their ramifications, overwhelmed and crushed, without beneficial result to anyone. . . .

CHAPTER XIX

The "Assassin" of Woodrow Wilson

I

DURING the Wobbly strike in San Pedro, as I have said, I became acquainted, through Lonie Burton and otherwise, with a number of I. W. W.'s. One of these was a tall, gangling fellow, forty-five or so, sharp-featured, with deep-sunken brown eyes and bushy eyebrows, and his left leg stiff in the knee, which in walking made him swing it out sideways in a semicircle. He was obviously unwell, but still energetic; always coughing slightly, clearing his throat. He had a suggestion of the Indian in his leathery, long face and black straight hair, which was beginning to gray over the ears; later, when we got acquainted, he told me he was quarter Indian, and a native of Colorado.

One day Lonie Burton introduced him to me as Jack Kipps. "He's covering the strike for *Solidarity*"—a Wobbly newspaper published in Seattle.

A day or two later some one else pointed him out to me and said, "That's Jack Kipps, the guy who assassinated Woodrow Wilson."

I took this as some sort of Wobbly joke and thought little of it at the time. The I. W. W.'s were full of wild stories. They were, on the whole, a rather romantic, lopsided lot; as outdoor men in the great open spaces, they had a tendency to exaggerate things, to let their imaginations expand and run riot.

240

Woodrow Wilson was then still living.

I met Kipps several times in Lonie Burton's room and elsewhere, and in the course of a few talks learned, in snatches, probably all there was to know about him— or so I thought.

As a very young man he had been a miner in Colorado. Early in the 1900's he became a socialist and developed into an agitator for the radical Western Federation of Miners. He had known "Bill" Haywood and liked to talk of him. He had had but a few years' schooling; was self-educated and read, unlike most Wobblies, not only radical literature, but everything else that he thought worth while and could lay his hands on.

In the so-called Ludlow massacre in 1913, in which thirty or more people were killed in a labor dispute, Kipps was shot in his left knee; hence his stiff leg.

During the war he laid low. Having trouble with his chest, he went to the Mojave Desert in California and read Plutarch's *Lives* and reread Dickens and Fielding's *Tom Jones*.

His health strengthened after the Armistice and he drifted to Seattle, where, in the spring of 1919, a powerful I. W. W. movement sprang up almost overnight. Ole Hanson was mayor of the city and immediately gained national prominence as a 105 per cent American by his efforts to suppress the Wobblies. The country was being swept by the first wave of anti-Red hysteria. There were great strikes along Puget Sound. The Wobblies tied up the port of Seattle, and American Legion boys warred upon them.

Kipps soon attained to a sort of leadership among the Seattle I. W. W.'s. He wrote pieces for *Solidarity* and other Wobbly sheets, which often printed his portrait, playing up his part-Indian ancestry in an attempt to offset the patriots' charge that the movement was un-American and appealed only to "foreign scum." He was a leader of the faction that opposed dynamite, arson, gunfire and slugging; he advocated, instead, what he called "non-violent violence" or "the force of numbers."

II

One night toward the end of the strike I came upon Kipps in a Greek eating-joint on Beacon Street in San Pedro, and sat down at his table.

Not knowing what else to say to him, I remarked that I had heard Wobblies refer to him as the man who assassinated Woodrow Wilson. What did they mean by that?

I expected him to laugh at my question, but he did not, though I knew him to have an active sense of humor. He just sat silent, evidently reluctant to talk about it.

Curious, I urged him to explain to me what the I. W. W.'s understood by "the assassination of Woodrow Wilson."

Then he began:

". . . It happened in Seattle in 1919. As you may know, in August of that year, Wilson went on his swing around the country, to appeal for his League of Nations which the 'pigmy minds' in the Senate were determined to kill. He spoke in all the bigger cities, and wherever he came the mob cheered him—not quite as wildly, it is true, as he had been cheered in Europe a few months before, but still. . . . [I remembered seeing Wilson in St. Louis at that time, as I tell in a previous chapter.] . . .

"According to his schedule, Wilson was due in Seattle on September 13th. As you know, the I. W. W.'s were then definitely up-and-coming in Seattle; in fact"—he smiled—"the Revolution seemed to be just around the corner. So about the first of the month we announced that

242

when Wilson came a delegation of Wobblies would call on him and present to him a petition for the release of political prisoners in the federal penitentiaries. Of course we didn't expect him to act on our request, but we figured that presenting the petition would be good propaganda.

"But we no sooner gave out our announcement than the politicians in charge of the preparations let it be known that effective steps would be taken to prevent the Wobblies from 'annoying' the President. That was the word they used—annoying him. It appeared that we were unworthy of consideration from anybody in authority. We were an 'outlaw organization' made up of un-American, low-down foreign scum—an ulcer on the fair and otherwise immaculate body of the Republic.

"Naturally, although scum, we didn't like this sort of treatment, but we knew that if they wanted to, they could keep our delegation from coming near Wilson.

"For two or three days we didn't know what to do about it. But we couldn't let Ole Hanson and his gang of petty politicians lick us.

"Just then, we were talking a good deal among ourselves about 'non-violent violence' and the force of mere numbers. I was hot for that idea myself, and still am. So I began to figure how we could get the best of Ole. I hated the little squarehead—not because he was against us, but because he was such a small-time opportunist. I had nothing much against Wilson, and that was true, I guess, of most Wobblies.

"We had numbers. Some of the biggest unions in Seattle were I. W. W. organizations.

"Then I got an idea—an inspiration.

"The idea seemed wonderful to me, and so I got together about a dozen Wobs who were sort of active on the agitation end of the movement, and I said to them: 'When

Wilson is driven through the streets in a machine so that the mob can see him and cheer him, why don't we—thousands of us—line up along certain blocks on the route, all of us dressed up in our working-clothes, sleeves rolled up, arms folded on our chests? It'll be Saturday afternoon and all the work will be suspended for the occasion, and some of us aren't working, anyhow. We can get out thousands of workers and mass them all together, occupying, say, five or six blocks. We can get out early so that the scissor bills can't get those blocks. And when Wilson comes by, we don't give him a tumble; nobody lets out a sound of cheer and nobody claps his hands. We just stand still, all of us, thousands of us. Just stand still like this, our arms folded—nobody moves and everybody looks straight ahead, not at him, but at nothing at all—just stares past him—everybody still and silent.'

"The idea caught on right away. Everybody thought it was a great stunt. It spread around in no time and all the Wobblies in Seattle got excited about it, and they also heard about it in Tacoma, Spokane, Centralia, Walla-Walla, and as far down as Portland and Eureka. They even heard about it in the woods hundreds of miles inland.

"We only had about a week to organize the stunt, and it had to be done more or less in secret so that it would hit them as a surprise. You see, we still weren't thinking of playing a trick on Wilson, but merely of getting even with Ole Hanson and his bunch.

"Days passed. Monday or Tuesday somebody else, I don't know who, improved on my idea by suggesting that we print thousands of hatbands inscribed 'Release Political Prisoners!,' which we did. We would thus present our petition to Wilson, anyhow; he could read it while he drove past us.

"Thursday and Friday nights we held special meetings all over town to instruct the Wobbly mob where to assemble and how to act when Wilson came by.

"On those two nights I couldn't sleep a wink. As I have said, it was my idea. I was excited as hell about it. I began to see now that this wouldn't be merely getting even with Ole, but that we were pulling a stunt on the President of the United States. I knew how susceptible Wilson was to public response. How would our lack of response affect him? And would it work? You can imagine how a thing like this can flop at the last minute. Would the police interfere when they saw us assemble?

"But it looked great. All day Friday and on Saturday in the forenoon Wobblies poured into Seattle from Tacoma, Spokane, Centralia and elsewhere, including the lumber camps in the woods—hundreds of them, from everywhere.

"Then Saturday afternoon came. Wilson was in town. He had been cheered in Tacoma; in fact, he had been cheered, more or less, wherever he had stopped and given the people a chance to see him.

"In Seattle everything was closed and tens of thousands turned out to see him and hail him. The streets he was to pass along were jammed.

"The reception was scheduled for two o'clock, but we had our mob out long before one. We occupied five long blocks near the end of the route, on both sides of the street. There must have been five thousand of us; some say ten thousand, but that's exaggerated; and we packed the sidewalks from the walls of the buildings to the curb. The Great Unwashed, all of us wearing grimy working-clothes, blue-denim overalls and blue working-shirts with sleeves rolled—Wobblies, outcasts, the scum—some of them six feet and a half, great big fellows, Bohunks and squareheads, with powerful arms and necks, chests like barrels.

"We had the five blocks that we had picked out all to ourselves. The respectable mob naturally steered clear of us. We were pariahs, the ugly big boil that Ole Hanson was trying to cut open and cure.

"At first the cops were excited as we began to mass together, but they didn't know what to do about it. There were too many of us, and more were coming. Thousands of us. And some of the lumber-jacks and dock-wallopers looked as if they could eat five cops apiece for breakfast. Besides, how would it look if they tried to chase us off the streets when, so far as they knew at the moment, all we wanted was to see the President?

"The chief of police was all flustered. He rode by us in his machine several times with a worried and bothered look on his face, but finally—perhaps after a consultation with Ole—it was decided to let us alone. I guess they figured it was for the best. They didn't want to have a riot in the city while the President was there. Also, by being all together we would not contaminate the good people of the town farther up the street.

"Most of us wore the hatbands: 'Release Political Prisoners!' We had many ex-soldiers in the movement; they wore their overseas caps and we put them out in front so that Wilson could see them.

"Well, by and by the bands began to play—there were several of them along the route—and Wilson was driven through the city. The mob cheered him till you couldn't hear the music.

"He was all dolled up as a great statesman should be, and he waved his plug hat and bowed a little now and then, acknowledging the ovation of the people. The President of the United States! It was a great event in Seattle.

"Secret Service men moved along the crowd just a little ahead of the presidential car, which was surrounded by cops on motorcycles. And behind it were more machines, carrying other great men—rolling slowly to give the mob a chance to cheer them a long time. There were ten or twenty blocks of cheering maniacs.

"Then, all of a sudden, Wilson came to a block where everything was quiet. Hundreds of grimy working-men, interspersed with women, stood still and silent on both sides of the street. Not a cheer, not a sound, not a move. Most of the men didn't even look at him; some of them, of course, couldn't resist giving him the once-over, but everybody was instructed to look past him. Only a couple of kids were pushing and yelling here and there, which made the Wobblies' silence and immobility even more terrible.

"I naturally had a personal interest in the thing. I stood on the edge of the sidewalk, between two ex-soldiers in overseas caps, on the left-hand side of the street in the first Wobbly block. A policeman was planted right in front of me, but I could see Wilson over the cop's shoulder.

"He stood in the machine. He smiled as he came to our block. Then the smile went off his face—like that," snapping his fingers. "He knew that we were I. W. W.'s, I guess, but didn't know what to make of it. He looked flabbergasted. Back there the mob had cheered him till you couldn't hear the music; here these dirty bums didn't even move, but stood like statues, and among them were dozens of ex-soldiers.

"He continued to stand in the car, but it was obvious that he wanted to sit down. He looked stern. His frame looked limp and hunched up. The hand holding his tall hat hung by his side. His face looked old and saggy.

"The music behind him now sounded clear and awful. A second before it couldn't be heard for the mob's noise, now you heard nothing but music and the roar of the cops' motorcycles.

"The car moved on—slowly. Then there was another block of still, silent Wobblies in denim overalls, their arms crossed on their chests, printed hatbands on their hats and caps, most of them not looking at Wilson, but straight ahead, past him. Thousands of them. Block after block— five blocks.

"It was dramatic as hell, believe me.

"At the third block Wilson sat down beside his wife. I guess he had to because he couldn't stand up any longer. Those who saw him there said that he seemed to be crumpling up. He put on his tall hat, a little to one side. He had been told that the Wobblies were out, but I guess he didn't expect anything like this. He was white as a sheet, hunched over.

"Beyond the Wobbly blocks there were more cheering people, but Wilson didn't stand up again. He merely waved his hand and smiled weakly to the mob.

"Afterward we heard that the newspaper men who accompanied the presidential party were asked not to play up the demonstration too much; it might only fan the anti-Red hysteria; and most of them reported it with great restraint or ignored it altogether. The *New York Times* man, for instance, saw fit to print only that the

I. W. W.'s had been 'undemonstrative,' which gave the reception a 'sinister note.' I happened to see the write-up and have the clipping somewhere.

"That evening a messenger came to the I. W. W. headquarters with a request from the President for our delegation to call on him at ten-thirty the next morning and, if we desired, to present our petition.

"Of course we informed the messenger that we'd be there. Then we quickly made up a delegation of five men, including two ex-soldiers and myself. The ex-service men wore overseas caps and other parts of the uniform; one had a wound stripe on his sleeve, and we made him Number One of the delegation. He was to present the petition. His name was Harry Link. Each one of us was supposed to make a little speech, and we rehearsed half the night.

"At ten-twenty-five the next morning—Sunday—the five of us went to the swell hotel where Wilson was staying. The place was all in flags. A couple of sentries stood at the entrance to the lobby.

"A young army officer in a snappy uniform—boots, spurs, Sam Brown belt and saber—met us in the doorway. I guess he was waiting for us. He gave us the once-over, especially the ex-soldiers.

" 'You are—?' he began to ask.

" 'We are a delegation of the Industrial Workers of the World,' said Harry Link. 'We have an appointment with the President.'

"Newspaper men began to crowd around us, and the officer quickly ordered us to follow him. We went up an elevator, and then through a corridor, which was banked with flowers, with a couple of soldiers hanging around.

"We entered a small room and the officer asked us to

249

sit down. His neat military appearance was in sharp contrast with our own. He kept on eyeing us.

"We were in the presidential suite. We sat there about ten or fifteen minutes. Nobody said a word. Somewhere we could hear the clicking of a typewriter.

"Then a door opened and a civilian secretary or Secret Service man advanced to us briskly. He looked us over and took our names. Then he said: 'Come this way, please,' in a crisp official tone of voice. He looked like a floor-walker.

"He led us into a great big room. Right near the door was a tremendous basket of flowers, and the rest of the delegation sort of crowded me against it. The top of a fern leaf tickled me under the nose.

"'Step this way please,' said the floorwalker, and we all moved toward the center of the room.

"Wilson stood by a long heavy table, his left hand holding the edge of the table top. I had a funny feeling I can't quite describe to you. I was sort of mixed up, maybe because the fern had tickled my nose and I had almost overturned the flower basket.

"Wilson looked small. I had an idea he was taller. His face was long and his head seemed to be heavy on his neck. And he looked old—*old*.

"Now he sort of took a step toward us and said: 'Good morning.' One of the delegation insisted afterward that he said: 'Good morning, gentlemen,' but I think he merely said 'Good morning.'

"He shook hands with us. His hand felt dry and shaky in mine, like nothing much. His voice shook. He evidently was under a great strain. He could scarcely look the two ex-soldiers in the face. I believe he thought that I was an ex-soldier, too, because of my lame leg; he hardly looked at me, either.

"After shaking our hands, he stepped back to the table and leaned on it with his left hand.

"I was sorry for him. I wondered if he was still under the effects of our demonstration on him the day before. I almost wished we hadn't pulled it.

"Well, we stood there before Wilson, the five of us, all of us, I guess, feeling pretty nervous. Harry Link held the petition in his hand and shifted the weight of his body from one foot to the other. He was a great big six-footer and built like an ox; had been wounded in the war.

"Wilson then nodded to the floorwalker, who stood to one side, and the floorwalker withdrew.

"I guess Wilson waited for us to speak, and there was a long and awkward silence. Harry Link cleared his throat and was going to speak, but couldn't. Instead he just handed Wilson the petition. Wilson took it. His hand shook pretty badly. Harry cleared his throat again, but couldn't get a word out. It was awful. I felt the blood rushing to my face.

"Wilson didn't look at any of us, only at Harry Link for a second. He expected him to say something. Then, when Harry said nothing, Wilson placed the petition on the table and said something to the effect that he would read it immediately. I don't remember his exact words. I watched his face, which looked very bad—long and gray. His long narrow jaw moved up and down, and his voice, while fairly clear, was sort of unnatural, or so it seemed to me. Perhaps the acoustics of the big room made it sound that way. I can't quite describe it. I remember it kind of vaguely. The whole experience was queer, unreal.

"According to the rehearsals the night before, each of us was supposed to make a speech, but I was the only one who managed to say anything. There was another long silence, and then I said: 'Mr. President, attached to the petition are the signatures of over one thousand of our fellow workers, all of them citizens of the United States. We could have secured ten thousand signatures, but until last night we thought we would not be allowed to present the petition to you.'

"Wilson looked at me for a moment. Then he said that he was sorry that obstacles had been placed in our way when we had first planned to call on him. He added that he had been displeased upon hearing of the local reception committee's decision to bar us from him. His voice shook. His right hand shook, too, until he finally gripped the lapel of his coat.

"I almost wished I hadn't come along with the delegation. Man, but I felt lousy! My own voice, when I spoke, sounded strange in that big room. I was pretty well balled up, standing under that high ceiling, the thick, soft rug under my feet, feeling sorry for Wilson. I barely heard what he said; later I had to check up on his words with the other four men. They were all mixed up too.

"I was supposed to have said: '. . . all of them citizens of the United States, and, sir, many of them ex-soldiers and ex-sailors who have served in the war to make the world safe for democracy.' But I forgot to say the last part. I'm glad I did; there was no use rubbing it in about making the world safe for democracy, though, of course, at the time I wasn't thinking of that. I had spoken at hundreds of workers' meetings, but now I was all mixed up.

"Wilson looked pretty bad, but perhaps he was the least flustered man in the room—that is, outwardly. Inwardly, I'm sure he was worse off than all five of us put together. I think it took all his self-control to keep his chin up.

"A couple of times during the interview he closed his

eyes for a few moments and there was a little muscular movement on his face. With his eyes closed he looked even worse than when he had them open.

"I don't believe we were in there more than four or five minutes, and I was glad when it was over. Toward the last I felt sort of weak all over and dizzy in my head. It was the goddamndest experience I ever had.

"Finally, the door opened and in came the floorwalker and stopped at the door, near the flower basket.

"Then Wilson again shook hands with us. He said, 'Thank you,' and we went out. I saw him take a few steps after us, then he stopped in the middle of the big carpet and bowed a little. He looked like a ghost.

"The floorwalker and the army officer got us out into the corridor, which was full of newspaper men. They wanted to know our names. What? . . . why? . . . when? They fired questions at us. But I said to the other four not to talk; to hell with them.

"We got out in the street and jumped on a street car. I almost missed it because, with my leg, I couldn't walk as fast as the others.

" 'Holy mac!' said Harry Link. He was sweating, although it wasn't hot at all.

"We couldn't talk about it for an hour or more. We had been before the President of the United States—and what a mess he was! A pale old man standing in the middle of a big room, under a high ceiling, with a bowed head.

"Everything was a mess. The whole country. I thought to myself that Wilson, in his fine cutaway coat and striped pants, and we, in our working-clothes, were just the opposite poles of the same mess. Here, in this luxurious hotel room, we suddenly met for a few minutes and—well, I don't know. It was pretty queer, the whole thing, believe me. I had no feeling against him. I only thought what a mess he was. A tragedy—the President of the United States, the most powerful ruler on earth, but unable to do anything for us—the workers—although I don't doubt now that in his heart he was for us. He couldn't do anything about the biggest problem in the country, in the world—the problem of the distribution of wealth. Helpless—the President of the United States. Nobody could do anything.

"I felt like two cents for pulling the demonstration on him the day before. It was my idea. It was as unfair to him to pull a thing like that on him as it was for the capitalists to exploit us.

"Well, anyhow, from Seattle Wilson went down to Portland, and from there on to California.

"In a couple of days the Wobblies in Seattle began to discuss the newspaper reports and rumors which were to the effect that Wilson wasn't well, that he was 'fatigued,' and so on.

"Of course, he was sick before he started West, but when two weeks after leaving Seattle he finally broke down altogether, and had to abandon his tour, the I. W. W.'s around Puget Sound developed the idea that our demonstration on September 13th was behind it all.

"We five men who had called on Wilson, of course, told about our visit. I tried to be accurate, but the other four, I think, exaggerated things a little. By-and-by the story of our visit, as it went from mouth to mouth among the Wobblies, was to the effect that Wilson had collapsed while talking with us.

"Very few I. W. W.'s were willing to remember that Wilson was a sick man before coming to Seattle. Almost everybody seemed to be convinced that we—the thousands

of Wobblies who had lined the streets when he rode
through Seattle—had 'assassinated' him. That was the
word they used. And, since I was the one who originated
the idea, I was given the credit for the 'assassination.'

"The idea persists to this day, and I don't believe there
is any way of killing it. The Wobblies argue that I finished Wilson a damn sight more thoroughly than if some
one had shot him dead or blown him up with dynamite.
Had he been assassinated physically, they say, he would
now be a rival for Lincoln as a national hero. In 1919 he
was going through the biggest crisis in his career. A shot
from an assassin's gun would have saved him historically,
whether his League of Nations went over or not, because
such a death would have been dramatic and tragic. Instead, on September 13th he shriveled up before our numbers, and in the next two weeks he degenerated into complete ineffectiveness. He has been of no consequence ever
since. Now he is a futile old man—dead, although still un-
buried. That's the Wobbly idea about it on the Coast."

I asked Kipps what he himself thought about it.

"Well," he said, "I know that Wilson was sick before
he came West in August, 1919. To say that our demonstration assassinated him, of course, is an exaggeration,
but there is no doubt in my mind that it hastened his
breakdown. It was, perhaps, the straw that broke the
camel's back.

"I'm called 'the guy who assassinated Wilson.' I guess
I'll be known as such the rest of my life, though in the
last two years I've heard of two or three other men who
claim to have suggested the demonstration on September
13th. But I don't care. They can have the credit. As a
matter of fact, I often wish I hadn't had anything to do
with it, though I know that as an I. W. W. I oughtn't to
feel that way.

"There is no doubt, however, that the demonstration had a powerful effect on Wilson. Only the other day I picked up a recent *Atlantic Monthly* at the library and there was a little article by him called 'Away from the Revolution!' in which he appeals to the responsible capitalists of the country to lessen their resistance to the proletariat's efforts to improve its lot. The article is almost hysterical in tone; the hysteria of a senile old man just awakened from a nightmare. Read it and you'll see.

"Wilson may live a few years longer and write a few more articles, but you can't convince the Wobblies on the Coast that he hasn't been dead ever since that Saturday afternoon in Seattle in 1919."

III

A few days later the Los Angeles police were beginning to round up the Wobblies and break the strike. Jack Kipps, of course, was among them. Later, with Lonie Burton and "Red" O'Neal, he went to San Quentin for two and a half years.

When I met Lonie in Pershing Park in 1926, I forgot to ask him about Kipps. Then—some time in 1927—I ran into him at the Sunday open forum conducted by the American Civil Liberties Union in Los Angeles.

I scarcely recognized him. He looked definitely ill, all skin and bone, and his hair, what there was left of it, had turned gray. Coughing dryly, he told me with a shrug of his shoulders that now he had T.B. "for fair." The two and a half years in the jute-mills of the San Quentin prison had given the disease a chance to get the better of him. He grinned and said: "Yeah, I'm a short-timer now."

Woodrow Wilson had been dead then over three years.

Kipps was unwilling to discuss the Seattle incident any further. We talked of other things. He mentioned an

256

article or a story of mine that he had read in a magazine somewhere. I asked him would he mind if some day I wrote up the Seattle demonstration.

He thought a while, then he said:

"I'd prefer if you don't. I'm not exactly stuck up over the fact that the idea behind the affair was mine. I never had any bad feelings toward Wilson. He probably was all right in some ways. He was part of the System, helpless to do anything for the workers even if he wanted to. He meant well. The workers must help themselves; nobody else will or can help them; and whether they can or not remains to be seen. That stunt in Seattle was aimed more at Ole Hanson and that bunch of coyotes there than at Wilson. . . . If you wrote a piece about me, I probably couldn't resist looking it up: and I don't want to see it. I can't get the affair off my mind as it is. In San Quentin, when I couldn't sleep nights, I thought about it for hours. I haven't a bad conscience about it, or anything like that; but everywhere I go they say I'm the guy that assassinated Wilson. They called me that in San Quentin. Lately I've started to deny having had any connection with the matter whatever. I don't like it. Wilson is dead now, so why gloat over it? After all, he was President of the United States. I can't help feeling that way, although, perhaps, as a radical I oughtn't to."

He paused a minute, coughing.

"But of course," he said then, "I don't care what you do"—coughing—"afterward. I mean in a year or two. I probably won't last that long."

Soon after this some one induced a wealthy woman radical in Pasadena, a "parlor pink," to send Kipps to a sanitarium at Sierra Madre. He was there two years, a hopeless case, sitting in the sun, reading.

He died in the spring of 1929.

CHAPTER XX

A Soft Job and Mencken

I

THE Los Angeles newspaper on which I worked was an afternoon "rag," as most of the staff referred to it. My workday was supposed to be from six-thirty in the morning until six in the evening, but nearly every other night, after regular hours, I was sent to see some new motion picture or look in on two or three boosters' banquets or similar affairs, and write them up the first thing in the morning. Most of the movies were vile, but we—I was not the only "critic"—were required to praise them all.

When I had sailed on ships or worked on construction jobs, my employer had owned my physical energies for eight or ten hours daily, but even while working my mind was free to do whatever it was inclined to do. Now that I was a newspaper man, the boss owned me completely, all my waking hours. I had almost no freedom or leisure to follow my inclinations in reading. I could not go around and examine the things that interested me. I lived in a small, close room on Crown Hill. Getting but twenty a week, I could not afford anything better, especially since, as a reporter, I had to wear fairly decent clothes. Often I could not sleep nights, my mind whirling in a chaos of the day's experiences and impressions.

The two weeks in San Pedro, when I covered the Wobbly strike, were the only agreeable part of my journalistic career in Los Angeles. On the whole, reporting seemed to me a hectic, unwholesome means of earning one's living. So one day late in June, 1923, I quit the job and, with

fifteen dollars in my pocket, moved to San Pedro. I had
no definite idea what I would do there. During the strike
I had taken a liking to the town. It was so unlike Los
Angeles or Hollywood. It looked sane. There were no
tourists and sick old people from Iowa and Missouri. It
was a normal seaport town, most of its inhabitants work-
ing-people. The architecture was simple in its ugliness;
there were no queer imitations of Spanish, Italian, and
French styles of building, which were general in Los
Angeles, and no Moorish castles with moats and draw-
bridges operated by electricity, such as I had seen in
Hollywood Hills. Coming from Los Angeles, with its
phoney beauty, I thought San Pedro was a clean place.
I liked the mingled smells of crude oil, fresh lumber,
oranges, lemons, spices, coffee, fish, and other cargos
which were handled over the wharves.

By and by I got work on the docks and made my living
at it for nearly six months. One week I was unloading
lumber; the next, as likely as not, trucking coffee or
canned goods, or carrying bunches of green bananas off
some boat just arrived from Guatemala. It was hard
work, sometimes, from seven in the morning till past midnight, or until the particular cargo was loaded or unloaded so that the ship could sail. The wages were nothing
to brag about, often I was in physical danger, and there
were annoyances and indignities which every sensitive
laborer must endure; but even so I thought it was better
than being a reporter.

The best part of working on the docks was that it was
not steady. Occasionally there was nothing doing for four
or five days on the wharves where I usually worked. This
gave me a chance to rest, to loaf around, walk on the
breakwater, and go to Los Angeles—for, as much as I
disliked it, the place continued to fascinate me. Also, now

259

I had time to read. There was a decent, if small, public library in town and after a while I became acquainted with the local bookseller, who, within a few days, was able to procure for me whatever book I desired.

Then, too, among my fellow workers I came upon men who interested me, at least temporarily; some of them as individuals, others as tiny organisms—victims of conditions, case histories—in the great American jungle. Every once in a while I worked for a few days in some gang which was half white and half black. The Negro stevedores were a great lot. They talked incessantly, kidding one another, the while pushing their trucks. And they sang and laughed. Their laughter was marvelous.

I lived in the so-called "Balkan States" section of San Pedro, where the inhabitants were mostly Dalmatians and other immigrants from the Balkans, who made their livelihoods as fishermen, fish-peddlers, dock-wallopers, and bootleggers. The place swarmed with small, boisterous children, and the air, despite the breeze from the bay, was always keen with the odors of drying fish-nets and strong wine. Nearly every other house had a cellar, which the police did not disturb.

My bungalow was a small but comfortable one-room affair, simply furnished, on the edge of the bluff overlooking the outer harbor and the breakwater.

II

Toward the end of 1923 I noticed, on the bulletin board of the Public Library, an announcement of the city of Los Angeles' Civil Service Department that an examination would be held for the position of "municipal port pilots' clerk" in San Pedro. The brief description of the job gave me the idea that it might suit me and that, perhaps, I was just the fellow for it. So I applied, passed the examination first, and soon after New Year's received the appointment.

Thus began four very pleasant and peaceful years in my life. The position of municipal port pilots' clerk was ideal for me.

The pilot station was a small building on the edge of the outer harbor, near the entrance to the main channel, with a full view of the Bay of San Pedro, and the powerful telescope which we had in the office was capable, on clear days, of stretching one's vision to the horizon. My work-hours were from eight to five, with Saturday a half-day and all Sundays and holidays off. My duties were simple, my salary good, and I was practically my own boss. The chief pilot, a phlegmatic old man, let me run the office. There was about a half-hour of clerical work, which I did the first thing in the morning; then I answered an occasional phone call from some ship's agent, telling me the time of her arrival or departure, so that we would have a pilot available for her. The pilots were elderly ex-sea-captains. They were seldom at the station, and I got along with all of them. When their services were needed, I summoned them by phone.

Alone in the office, I read and wrote most of the day. I wrote short stories and articles, and began several novels. I tore up most of my scripts. Now and then, for exercise, I translated a piece of fiction or an essay from the Slovenian or Croatian, and sent the translation to *The Living Age* (then a weekly published in Boston), which usually accepted it and mailed me a check for twenty or thirty dollars. By the end of 1924 I also sold a few feature articles to a Los Angeles newspaper and one of the "little magazines" on the West Coast accepted a short story, for which I received no payment.

III

In my contemplation of the American scene, Mencken was for a good while the most important light. The end of the *Smart Set* under the coeditorship of Mencken and Nathan and the beginning of *The American Mercury*, in the winter of 1923-24, were events in my life. I read every word in the first number of the *Mercury* and during the next two or three years delighted in the apparent success of the magazine. I seldom missed an issue, although in justice to myself I should add that I was not one of the young men, in Los Angeles and elsewhere in the United States, who strolled around with copies of the green-covered review under their arms, in token of their being "civilized" and of their intellectual superiority to the general run of the inhabitants of America. I delighted, too, in the effect that the success of the *Mercury* had upon the other so-called quality magazines; in all of them there began to appear better articles and short stories.

I agreed with Burton Rascoe, who wrote in a pamphlet that Mencken (I quote from memory) was "like a gust of wind, in the sense in which Romain Rolland speaks of the function of Jean Christophe—a blow of keen, purging air going through stale autumn woods, carrying off withered leaves and giving new movement to the boughs," except that I substituted "jungle" for "stale autumn woods." I liked Mencken's gusto, his prose, and his lightning humor; his laughter—"the laughter of Hercules," as some one called it, which aimed to sweep from American intellectual life the unhealthy delusions of democracy, fake uplift, and other forms of "swinishness." His was "the lightning that destroys while it lights," and I believed that most that it destroyed was only fit for destruction.

With a mingling of amusement and annoyance, I noted

262

the various unfriendly criticisms of Mencken. A preacher called him a "cheap blatherskite of a pen-pusher." To others he was a "cynic," "a gay, irresponsible, reckless fellow who heaves dead cats into the sanctuaries and then goes roistering down the highways of the world," "a clown," "the most egocentric man who ever lived," "a sneerer." Many of these appellations, perhaps, were not wholly untrue, but I thought that all the qualities which these opinions described, if applicable at all, were superficial in Mencken. Fundamentally, as I saw him, reading his books and the *Mercury*, the man was a humanitarian, almost a sentimentalist toward his fellow humans; a reformer who saw the futility of reform in America. As early as 1910, or thereabouts, when he wrote a debate book, *Men vs. Man*, with Robert La Monte, the Socialist, he betrayed his sympathy for the most lowly plodding laborer, and I felt sure that some of his most satiric and polemic articles came from his disapproval of outraged justice and his sense of his own ineffectiveness in the face of the colossal muddle of American life. It was hopeless to try to build a decent civilization on the shifting sands of democracy, for, under democracy, whenever a first-rate man attempted to do something worth while, sooner or later the mob—organized mediocrity—was bound to frustrate him. So, in a sort of self-defense, Mencken was a "cynic" and "sneerer"; he laughed at and ridiculed America, perhaps, because that was one way of preserving his sanity and health in the crazy, unhealthy jungle.

For several years I agreed with Mencken that the sensible thing to do for a sensitive and intelligent person who could not help being interested in the American scene was to look upon it—upon the whole "gross glittering, excessively dynamic, infinitely grotesque drama of American life"—with detachment, as a "circus show." His essay "On Being an American," which I first read some time in 1924, I later re-read at least once a year. Among others, I marked the following passage in the essay:

. . . [In the United States], more than anywhere else that I know of or have heard of, the daily panorama of human existence, of private and communal folly—the unending procession of government extortions and chicaneries, of commercial brigandages and throat-slittings, of theological .buffooneries, of æsthetic ribaldries, of legal swindles and harlotries, of miscellaneous rogueries, villainies, imbecilities, grotesqueries, and extravagances—is so inordinately gross and preposterous, so perfectly brought up to the highest conceivable amperage, so steadily enriched with an almost fabulous daring and originality, that only the man who was born with a petrified diaphragm can fail to laugh himself to sleep every night, and to awake every morning with all the eager, unflagging expectation of a Sunday-school superintendent touring the Paris peep-shows. . . .

The whole essay, I thought, was very funny, typically Menckenese. I laughed when I first read it, and later, when I re-read it. But once in a while, as I enjoyed the "circus," a faint chill went through me. Now and then, walking about in Los Angeles, Blakelock, Mike Koska, Lonie Burton, Jack Kipps, and Woodrow Wilson came to my mind. I could not laugh at them.

I read other American writers. Sinclair Lewis, with *Babbitt* and *Arrowsmith*, helped me immensely to know America in a broad way. I continued to read Theodore Dreiser. *An American Tragedy* impressed me powerfully. I came upon Sherwood Anderson, Ben Hecht, James Stevens, Van Wyck Brooks, Ruth Suckow, Eugene O'Neill, Cabell, and others. Of the foreign writers, I read Anatole France, Joseph Conrad, D. H. Lawrence, Knut Hamsun, Thomas Mann, and Romain Rolland.

264

IV

I had a good job and comfort—for the first time since my arrival in the United States. I began to make friends among men and women and girls whom I met here and there. They were, for the most part, simple people, fine in their various ways—native Americans and foreign-born. There were dinner parties and informal lunches at various homes in San Pedro and Los Angeles.

When I had saved some money, I bought an automobile. I took short and long trips, sometimes alone, sometimes with one of my friends. There were drives on the perfect roads to Laguna, to Mojave Desert (in the wintertime), to Santa Barbara, to Carmel, to San Francisco, to Jack London's Valley of the Moon, to Lake Tahoe—all beautiful places, which for a time at least made me forget everything that was not fine and lovely in America. I fell in love with the physical beauty of California, especially the northern part.

In 1926 I began to write a series of articles on Los Angeles for Haldeman-Julius' publications. In 1928 Mencken accepted my first story for the *Mercury*. He wrote me to send him something else. I did. He accepted three or four more articles and stories in a row.

To my people in Carniola I wrote only brief notes that I was well and content. In a letter I could not begin to tell them about America.

PART FIVE

Some People in California

CHAPTER XXI

The Man with a Soul

I

SOON after I came to San Pedro, I occasionally noticed a shabbily dressed middle-aged man with a small mongrel dog pass by my dwelling, headed for the eucalyptus grove a stone's-throw up the road. In time we came to know each other by sight and exchanged conventional greetings and remarks about the weather. The man obviously was a foreigner, perhaps a Slav.

One day I heard him call to his dog, whose name, it appeared, was Complex; and as I casually remarked on the unusualness of the title, he explained, laughing broadly, that the dog was an unusual dog; he had a complex. He had acquired him, he said, a few months before from a friend who used to live in one of the shacks in the grove, and betimes discovered that the trunk of a certain blue-gum eucalyptus near the cottage was, to all seeming, the only object in the world against which——

"Well, sir, it's a somewhat delicate matter," he told me. Three times a day he had to take the dog to the grove, else the poor animal would pass out in agony. It was a problem for psychoanalysis, no doubt, but so far that science had not tackled canine psychology.

We both laughed as though the case of the wretched dog were the drollest thing in the world. Then we exchanged a few personal questions and, to our mutual surprise, learned that by origin we were both Slovenians from Carniola. The man had been in America over twenty-five years, but spoke good English, appeared

269

widely (but irregularly) read, and otherwise impressed me as an uncommon Bohunk.

Before long Lenard Podgornik—his name—began dropping into my bungalow two or three times a week for an evening's talk or a game of chess, or to borrow a book or share a drink with me. Later, when I got the job at the pilot station, he acquired the habit of coming to see me there, to help me "kill time." We became intimate in a loose, detached sort of way. He seemed glad to have me to talk with, and I found him a pleasant, interesting fellow; a professional lazy man who, as I learned by-and-by, had worked hard the greater part of his life and then perceived the unwisdom of labor; a wondering, somewhat befuddled cogitator, the kind that one encounters in the most unlikely places in America; a quaint blending of bum and gentleman.

II

He had come to the United States at nineteen, and for the first five years worked in Pennsylvania coal-mines and iron-foundries. At the end of that time he had saved twelve hundred dollars. A saloon-keeper friend of his urged him to buy an interest in the establishment, but while he was considering the proposition the bank failed and he lost his savings. "Chances are that if I had gone into business," Podgornik remarked to me later, "I'd have lost it, too, and perhaps not as neatly." But in those younger days he was less philosophical, and so, returning from work one evening, he picked up a brick lying in the street, went to the bank, and heaved it through the large window on which the name of the wrecked institution was inscribed in gilt letters. The sound of falling glass made him feel good; but passers-by, thinking he was insane, seized him and called a policeman.

270

In his broken English Podgornik tried to justify his act, but the judge who tried him reacted unsympathetically to his loss of five years' savings and sent him up for six months. Actually, that judge did him a favor, for except for a few short strikes and a brief illness, this was Podgornik's first rest in America. Moreover, in the lock-up he became acquainted with another Bohunk, a young Bohemian poet named Jan Novák, a Villonesque sort of character who claimed to have a degree from the University of Prague, to be a political exile from Austria, and to be sought, in addition, by the police of Paris, Vienna, Cleveland, San Francisco, and Reno. Just now he was in jail for stealing a few books from a shop in Pittsburgh, and he happened to be released at about the same time as Podgornik.

They had taken a liking to each other, and when Podgornik remarked that he guessed he would see if he could not return to work, the vagabond-poet advised him strongly against such folly. Why not come with him? He was going West.

So they became partners, bumming through the West, and working occasionally as farm-hands, as saloon porters, or as laborers on construction gangs; now and then the resourceful poet even pulled a job which temporarily put them on Easy Street.

One night there was a brawl in a saloon in a mining-town in Montana and Novák caught a stray bullet in his chest. He died saying something in Latin, which Podgornik, having had but two years in the *Gymnasium*, did not understand.

Having buried his partner, Podgornik moved on, but soon discovered that bumming alone was not to his taste; he could not hope to find a partner to take the place of Novák. He drifted to sunny California, and in Los An

geles he heard of the breakwater that the federal government was building at San Pedro Harbor. He went to the
port and found work on the trestle, rolling boulders off
flat-cars into the Pacific. San Pedro, although not one-
sixth the size it is now, was even then—in 1906—a lively
town, with Front Street a solid row of saloons, and Happy
Hollow a place dedicated to undisguised sin; but Podgornik's tastes, while not of an ascetic nature, found little
satisfaction in that direction. He missed Jan Novák and
his crazy, highfalutin talk. Among the people with whom
he came into contact he found no one to take the poet's
place. He knew a few Dalmatians, but he could not bring
himself to enter into intimate friendship with any of them.
As for the dagoes, the squareheads, and the native Americans, they were out of the question.

Podgornik was lonesome. He resubscribed to *Narodni
Glas*, which he had been getting in Pennsylvania. One day
he noticed the wife-wanted ad of a Slovene workman in
Colorado, and it occurred to him that maybe it was time
he thought of marriage himself; he would soon be thirty,
and at that age one should settle down. So he composed
and sent off a little advertisement announcing his wish to
correspond with a "good, diligent Slovene maiden or
young widow without children," and, hinting delicately
that he inclined to matrimony, suggested that applicants
enclose their photographs.

To his dismay, several hundred Slovene maidens and
childless widows all over America answered the advertisement and most of them enclosed their pictures. Lenard
spent two months reading the letters and looking at the
portraits, comparing the girls' virtues as described by
themselves, and classifying them under various headings.
At the end he sifted the problem down to six applicants
whose virtues appealed to him about equally, and dumped

the pictures and letters of the rest into the Pacific. Then he donned his best clothes, went to a barber-shop, and thence to a photographer, and a few days later mailed a copy of his likeness, with a polite request for further particulars, to each of the half-dozen Bohunk maidens. Four of them answered, and in about six weeks, after he had given yet more thought to their merits, as set forth by themselves in greater detail, Podgornik wrote to Agnes Judnich, of Cleveland, Ohio, to come to California as soon as she saw fit, and invited her, if it turned out to be agreeable to her, to become his wedded wife. She need have no fear, he assured her; true, he was no angel, but in fairness to himself he must say that his habits were fairly regular, that he had a steady job on the breakwater, which would take two more years to complete, that San Pedro was a nice place to live in, right next to the ocean, with the sun shining nearly every day, and that if she made him a good wife, which he thought she doubtless would, he would do the right thing by her.

According to the best testimony, matrimony was a gamble, and Lenard figured that perhaps this was as good a way of getting a wife as any.

III

They exchanged a few more letters. Agnes was a prudent, circumspect girl. His letters were convincing enough, but how could she be sure the man was not a scoundrel, aiming to do her evil? Four more months passed, and Podgornik, in his lonely singleness, developed a great longing for a sight of his unknown picture-bride-to-be and finally sent her the fare to California.

Agnes decided to take a chance and Lenard took a day off and met her at the station in Los Angeles. A week later they were married by the priest in San Pedro.

True, Agnes was not the good-looker represented in the photograph, but she was a healthy and competent young woman. She had been in America only two years, working as a milliner in New York and Cleveland, but, as Lenard soon perceived, she possessed considerable information about America. After they had become better acquainted, she told him that the reason she had answered his advertisement in *Narodni Glas* was because she had heard so many wonderful things about California (which, Podgornik reflected, had doubtless been the motive of his other correspondents), adding, however, that she had nothing to regret.

By and large, Agnes made Lenard Podgornik a good wife. She was resourceful and industrious, and possessed most of the other virtues she had specified in her letters. Indeed, she was well-nigh everything that a poor man's wife should be. Although her English was still none too fluent, she found a job as a waitress in a lunchroom almost immediately, and worked at it until her first child was born.

Lenard worked on the breakwater till its completion. They managed to save a little and presently bought a lot on part-payments and built a house. From the breakwater Lenard went to longshoring and, although work on the docks was irregular, he managed to keep up the payments on the property and provide Agnes with good medical attention in her annual confinements.

Just before the war he took out his citizenship papers, and in the war-time he worked at the shipyard in East San Pedro, making big money, while Agnes raised the children. He joined the Elks, cleared the indebtedness on his property, and, as the family increased, put up an addition to the house and a shed for the Ford. He listened

274

uncritically to four-minute speakers and bought Liberty bonds till it hurt.

The war over, he stayed in the yard at a smaller wage, which, however, yielded him enough to provide for his family according to American standards and now and then put a little by.

San Pedro was booming, and Lenard and Agnes, lying in bed at night, spent many an hour discussing how they might best take advantage of the boom. They had three thousand dollars in the bank and another thousand in Liberty bonds. Agnes favored buying a corner lot on Pacific Avenue; she had heard that a Jewish merchant downtown had recently acquired several, which surely was a sign that something was soon to happen.

Lenard, on the other hand, was inclined to consider a proposition he had been "let in on" by a fellow named Joe Miller, whom he knew in the yard. A certain shipmaster, Joe, and two other men were getting together to acquire two lumber-schooners that lay anchored in the outer harbor and were for sale dirt cheap; they proposed to start carrying lumber from Puget Sound. It was a big thing: after they got going they would all be making money hand over fist, for there was no doubt that a boom would soon strike the whole of southern California, with the result that shiploads and shiploads of lumber would be required for building.

Podgornik had three days in which to consider the proposition. On the third day Joe Miller happened to pass by him. Well, had he decided yet to get in on the deal or not? Lenard hesitated. Joe shrugged his shoulders; it was immaterial to him one way or another; he could do as he pleased; they could get all the money they wanted in Los Angeles and Long Beach; he had merely suggested it because Lenard was a permanent citizen in San Pedro, and they wanted to give the home folks the first chance.

At lunch-time Podgornik went to the bank, withdrew twenty-five hundred dollars, which was the minimum Joe Miller would consider taking, and, in exchange for a receipt, handed it over.

That was the last he ever saw of either Joe Miller or the cash. Two weeks later he learned that the whole thing had been a bunco scheme, whereby eight or ten other workmen in the yard had been similarly swindled out of their savings.

Agnes, of course, was furious. She told Lenard in forceful terms what she thought of him, and he silently agreed with her. The bunco outfit had no window into which he might hurl a brick, and he brooded over his folly. At home he scarcely ate or spoke; in the yard he hardly knew what he was about. At times he walked in a daze.

IV

This was the beginning of a streak of ill-luck. The week before Thanksgiving, soon after they had lost the twenty-five hundred dollars, Agnes won a live turkey in a raffle conducted as an advertising stunt by a grocery-store downtown, and on the eve of the holiday she sent Lenard to fetch the bird. He set out immediately, intending conscientiously to comply with the command, but on returning he met a fellow he knew who lured him into taking a drink out of his bottle. Prohibition and bootlegging were then—in 1921—still in their infancy and the rotgut which Lenard imbibed presently put him in doubt whether he was going or coming. He managed to walk, but in doing so he held the turkey by its legs, so that its squawking head dragged on the sidewalk.

Then a large automobile drew up alongside and he

heard himself addressed by a severe female voice which for the first half-minute he was unable to distinguish from the turkey's yapping. The lady in the car appeared to object strenuously to the manner in which he carried the fowl. That seemed strange to Lenard, and, uncomprehending, he walked on. But presently the lady's Negro chauffeur came after him and led him back to the car. Meanwhile the woman had ordered an urchin to hunt up a policeman, and when the latter appeared she informed him that she was Mrs. So-and-so of Pasadena, wife of Mr. So-and-so, the financier and philanthropist, and second vice-president of the southern California branch of the Humane Society of the United States. She was also a deputy sheriff of the county of Los Angeles and, opening her beautiful beaded handbag, she produced a gold badge. She had arrested this inhumane wretch, who, on top of his shocking treatment of the turkey, was also drunk. Would the officer kindly take him into custody? She was in a hurry for a dinner engagement at the Yacht Club, but would later call at the police headquarters and attend to the case.

Lenard spent four nights and three days in the San Pedro jail. What became of the turkey remains a mystery; instead of turkey meat, Agnes and the children had boiled beef and potatoes for Thanksgiving dinner; and when Lenard returned home, he found, to his relief, that his wife's anger had reached the point of speechlessness.

He returned to work in the yard, and for days his fellow workers kidded him about the turkey, for his adventure with the humane Pasadena dame had been duly reported in the San Pedro *Daily Pilot*. Lenard was annoyed, but tried to appear to take their jibes good-naturedly. He moved about in a sort of self-conscious stupor and one nice day he stumbled going down a narrow gangplank, fell, landed on a fender-log between the dock and the ship, bumped his head against a pile, and then rolled into the water. They fished him out with a broken leg, two fractured ribs, and a cut on the side of his head.

v

Lenard Podgornik was laid up for three months and had his second rest in America. Agnes toned down her reproaches; the children were told to let him alone, and now and then a few of the fellows from the yard came to see him in the evening or on Sundays. One of them, Jim Culley, a timid-looking, smiling Irish rigger who, if he knew one, liked to "talk about ideas" and was on that account often suspected of radicalism, brought him a little packet of literature, as he called it, suggesting that Lenard give it the once-over.

Podgornik had not been much of a reader. Years before Novák had stolen books from public libraries and bookshops and made him read them, but he had enjoyed only two or three, and these only moderately. Perhaps Novák's tastes in books had been too high for him. He was getting the Los Angeles *Examiner* and the San Pedro *Daily Pilot*, and occasionally he bought the *Literary Digest* or the *Saturday Evening Post*, to sort of keep up with events, although not infrequently he had a sneaking notion that things were happening in the world that were not mentioned in these prints; that, indeed, everything was not as it seemed; that although he was an Elk and the father of five children and had a document to show that he was a citizen of the greatest country under the sun, he was but a paltry bit of nothing within an elaborate scheme; and that this radical talk one heard from Jim Culley and other fellows possibly was not all hooey, as some of the men thought. He felt all this confusedly without ever molding the feeling into the silent formulæ of thought. He had little time for reading and less for thinking. Evenings he was too tired, or there was an Elk meeting; on Sundays, if he had nothing else to do, the kids wanted him to explain the funnies, or take them to the beach and play with them.

He glanced at the titles of Jim Culley's booklets. One caught his eye—"The Right to be Lazy," translated into English from the French of one Paul Lafargue. Podgornik read it. It was a learned Socialistic tract, full of footnotes, references to and quotations from Tacitus, Salvianus, Descartes, Plato, Monsignor Le Play, Saint Matthew, Napoleon, de Villermé, Goethe, and others, most of whom Podgornik had never heard of, unless it was that Novák had mentioned them to him years ago in his discourses on the road, which somehow had failed to touch him very deeply. He read it again; then put it aside and looked at the ceiling.

The right to be lazy! The *right*! . . . Podgornik understood the brochure only in spots, and these were far apart; but as remotely as he perceived the writer's argument, he experienced an inner excitation. A vague thrill passed through his entrails. In view of the arduousness and grimness of his labors in the past and the loss of his savings on two occasions, the philosophy of laziness struck him as very charming and worthy of one's thoughtful consideration. His labors, he suddenly realized, had been unproductive for himself of any beneficial results: here he lay, an old man at forty-four, tired, his body broken, his savings gone. No wonder he had lost his money; no wonder a female busybody could get him locked up for three and a half days for carrying upside down a turkey that had been raised to be killed and eaten! He was stupid. His endless labors had made him stupid, a fit object upon which crooks and busybodies might practice their arts. Suddenly he rebelled against work.

Later he told me: "I was so keyed up over this new notion that I sat up and felt no pain in my injured parts, although I was not supposed to move violently. My mind seemed to be flooded with a light—as if the Holy Ghost Himself had come over with me. I decided that I'd never work again—that is, hold down a job like I used to for twelve or fifteen years. I'd be lazy! Let the others work; they didn't know any better. I laughed out loud. Agnes came in, wondering if I had gone crazy or what. I told her to get the hell out, shut the door, and let me alone. I was a bit surprised at my own boldness, talking to her that way, and laughed some more. She was sure I had lost my mind and for a while treated me not alone with caution, but with gentleness."

Lenard had Jim Culley bring him more literature, both from his own collection and from the Public Library. He read Upton Sinclair's indignations about the stockyards, high life in New York, newspapers, and the religious business; Plutarch's *Lives*, Lecky's *History of European Morals*, Plato, Gibbon's *Rome*, Schopenhauer, Dreiser, Nietzsche, Santayana, and St. Augustine. He read anything and everything.

Long afterward he said to me: "Although I understood hardly one-third of what I read, I felt like a new man. The more I read the more I understood, or thought I did. My English was still very limited, but Jim got me a dictionary, and sometimes when I found out the meaning of some word and all at once things sort o' cleared up in my mind, I experienced a kind of holy thrill. Oh, laugh! I don't care!" he exclaimed, laughing himself. "It occurred to me that I was just beginning to live. Jim Culley, who was a sort of poet, insisted that my soul was reborn;

Agnes, on the other hand, contended that I was just 'queer' because in falling off the gangplank I had bumped my head. In fact, she believes to this day that a screw was loosened in my cranium—which for all I know may be correct."

From Agnes' viewpoint, Lenard's queerness manifested itself in increasingly deplorable ways, the most appalling of which was his announcement, soon after his much-delayed recovery, that he would not return to his old job, waiting for him at the yard. He left the house at eight-thirty in the morning and returned toward evening, having spent most of the time at the Library or in Jim Culley's shack in the eucalyptus grove, reading everything from *Susan Lenox* to *The Winning of Barbara Worth*, from the *Atlantic Monthly* to the *Smart Set*; or sitting in the park on the bluff overlooking the harbor, walking around, dropping into pool-rooms, talking with Jim Culley's friends, most of whom, like Jim, as Lenard learned, were I. W. W.'s, and, by-and-by, became his friends, too. He liked to listen to these fellows and occasionally put in a word of his own newly acquired book wisdom.

"I was beginning to live," he said to me three years later, "*live*, if you know what I mean. I was getting at the under side of life. And I heard and saw things I had not even dreamed of before, although they were all around me. I could watch flying sea gulls by the hour, and enjoy it. I went on the breakwater with bags of stale bread and fed it to the birds; in time they recognized me before I even opened the bag and flew screeching about me. Or, going over to Jim's shack, sometimes I imagined those eucalyptus trees to be living beings, as they actually were, moving, waving their arms, assuming all sorts of shapes in the changing light. My faculties seemed to be keyed to a higher pitch. I was *living*. I was getting acquainted with myself."

Agnes, naturally, could not be expected to appreciate Lenard's new interests. She raised hell. How did he expect the family to exist. Had he no pride? Wasn't he a man? Who would provide for their support? There was but a few hundred dollars left in the bank, the taxes on the house would soon be due, the children needed clothing, she had nothing decent to wear, and he himself walked around shamefully like a tramp. It was a disgrace for a family man to behave that way. Didn't he want to see his children started out right in life?

Podgornik knew that Agnes was right, but he said nothing; just then he was excited by Dr. Freud's findings, or it may have been by Walt Whitman, the poet of loafing, or by Jurgen, the poet-pawnbroker. But when, some time later, Agnes informed him that the bank balance was less than one hundred dollars, he began to look for a job. He drove an ice-wagon for a month, but gave it up in favor of the milk route of a creamery concern, which suited him better; he did most of the work early in the morning and then had time for loafing and reading— "*living*." But the young man who delivered milk for a rival company was a go-getter and soon took most of Lenard's customers. Subsequently Lenard tried lobster-fishing in the bay, running a cigar-stand, operating a pop-corn machine, and so on. In one way or another, in the three years following the accident, or the "rebirth of his soul," as he called it, he managed to earn enough to keep Agnes and the kids in food and clothes, to pay taxes and insurance dues, and to still find time now and then to "*live*"—that is, to read, loaf, feed the gulls, watch the ships, the changing light on the bay, the color of the sky at sunset, and stroll in the eucalyptus grove, smelling the perfume of the trees.

As to Agnes, to his children, he was queer; the older boy, indeed, was a bit more drastic and on occasion declared him goofy, while the girl, who was going to high school, one day came home crying because some urchins in the neighborhood had shouted after her that her old man was a Bohunk and a nut.

This jogged Lenard considerably. He obviously could not be himself and do as he liked; he owed the children a duty, and promised that he would do something.

VI

Several months before I met him, his fortune had suddenly taken a brilliant turn. Favorable circumstances had got him on the good side of Nick Velikanovich, a Dalmatian-American, ostensibly a fisherman, owner of a sizeable smack and a set of purse seines, but really an enterprising member of a booze-running outfit operating a fleet of speed-boats from San Pedro. Lenard suggested that he would like to try the "game," and Nick gave him a long look and said O. K.

For three months Lenard drove a prehistoric Ford truck bearing the legend "Fresh Fish—Caught Yesterday," delivering the stuff to Nick's customers in Los Angeles. It was an ideal job. Ordinarily Lenard made his deliveries by noon and spent the rest of the day in the Public Library or his favorite bookshop next to the police station, where he met bookish fellows in shabby clothes whose pockets bulged with pamphlets and papers, and who now staggered him with their erudition and then caused him to question the soundness of their minds. Occasionally he took in a matinée or a lecture, or mixed with the crowd of sleezy, raucous old atheists and anarchists in Pershing Square, arguing with young students from the Bible Institute.

The "fish business" had in it an element of risk; but then, Lenard understood that Nick Velikanovich had considerable drag, which he used if one of his people got into difficulties. It was interesting work, like reading a good, honest book; indeed, far more revealing of things-as-they-were than the works of America's foremost muckrakers. Almost weekly he came upon some eye-opener. In a bawdy-house which was among his best customers, for example, he once saw the ladies not otherwise engaged sitting in the reception-room, folding the campaign literature of the candidate for reëlection as district attorney.

It was, moreover, the most remunerative occupation Podgornik had ever engaged in. But then, just as Agnes' hope that they might yet own a corner lot on Pacific Avenue was reviving, he again strayed into trouble.

VII

In May, 1923, as already told, the I. W. W. longshoremen of San Pedro called a strike.

Lenard was not a radical in the conventional sense of the word. He shared the Wobblies' antipathy to work, but was attracted to them chiefly because his friend, Jim Culley, was one of the organizers. The idea that then intruded itself most insistently on his mind was that life was a futile, elaborate muddle, but vastly interesting as a spectacle—as a spectacle, indeed, beyond improvement. In the three years since his "rebirth" he had achieved a jovial sort of cynicism and had no great difficulty keeping himself from taking sides or getting violently indignant over things.

Sometimes he sat on some wharf in the outer harbor or

on the breakwater, watching hell-divers and pelicans dive for fish, and somehow he could not help thinking of the I. W. W. The bird shot down, and in a moment came up with a helpless fish wedged in its beak. That was life: bird ate fish, somebody else ate bird, and so on. Among the animals, members of one species did not, as a rule, feast upon their fellows because the law of the survival of the fittest tended to equality, which in turn led to mutual respect. In human society, however, the weak were preserved and propagated; there were classes among humans that had nothing in common with the classes on the opposite extreme; the go-getting capitalist and the poor workin'-stiff belonged to two different species as widely separated as the hell-diver and the fish. Lenard thought there was nothing that could be done about it; the fish, it appeared, were unable to develop any understanding of what the hell-divers and pelicans were doing, or any means to stop them. The I. W. W. movement was merely analogous to the wrigglings of the fish in the bird's beak.

But he liked Jim Culley above anyone else under the sun. Jim was the midwife who had attended at his "rebirth"; and, besides, Lenard thought that they had a good deal in common. At times he suspected that Jim was only a Wobbly agitator out for mischief, for the sheer thrill he got out of stirring things up, rather than a man of deep conviction. It was "the Irish" in him. Several times before and during the strike he tried to make Jim admit that that was the case.

One night in the second week of the strike Lenard sat with him in the latter's shack. They talked of the situation.

Jim smiled wryly and said: "Well, I'll tell you, Len—far as I can make out, and strictly between you and me, we are striking for the hell of it, showing off our power, going through the motions. You had me figured out right. I know that at present it's like throwing rocks at the moon."

Lenard stared at his friend, and was about to let out a whoop of cynical delight, when the door was pushed abruptly open, admitting four detectives of the Radical Squad, who, after placing both Podgornik and Culley under arrest for being Reds, ransacked the shack and seized the small library, everything from the Wobbly song-book to Wells' *Outline of History*, as evidence.

Two hours later they were in a tank at the Los Angeles city jail. Lenard stayed there three weeks and barely escaped being railroaded, along with Lonie Burton, "Red" O'Neal, Jack Kipps, and Jim Culley, to San Quentin.

Meanwhile, Agnes gave the *Daily Pilot* an interview in which she denounced the I. W. W.'s in no uncertain way, came out in favor of American institutions, suggested that all those who did not like this country go back where they came from, and regretted powerfully that her poor husband, once a loyal American citizen and faithful breadwinner for his family, had strayed among these obscene radicals. She blamed his misstep, however, not on his innate evil nature, but on the fact that three and a half years before he had suffered a severe bump on his head, which resulted in his becoming queer and not entirely responsible for his actions.

She made no effort to get him out of jail; indeed, she later admitted to him that she had hoped they would keep him in as long as possible; he was worthless, anyhow.

Instead, she went to Nick Velikanovich and arranged with him to take over her husband's work. And—to make a long story short—by the time that Lenard emerged from the lockup, Agnes was doing five times the business that he had done.

Free again, the first thing that he did was to comply with Jim Culley's request to go to the vacant shack in the eucalyptus grove, find his dog, and take care of it until Jim came out of San Quentin. He found the animal the second day and took it home. But he soon discovered that the mutt had the unfortunate and unmentionable complex already referred to, and renamed it accordingly.

VIII

It was soon after this that I made Lenard Podgornik's acquaintance. We became friendly, as I have said; he told me of Agnes' flourishing business and confessed to assisting her on her busy days; and he seldom visited me without bringing a sample of his best goods. I enjoyed his quaint ways and his talk. Later, one day he took me to the house and I met Agnes, a strapping, capable woman who spoke fairly good English. I came into her confidence and it was amusing to hear her tell me what a wonderful man Lenard had been before and during the war, and propound her bump-on-the-head theory of his present queerness.

As a bootlegger Agnes was a vast success. In a year she was in position to buy a large apartment-house in Los Angeles. So she moved with her family, except Lenard, to the city, and thereafter conducted her operations from there, and with even greater profit.

Lenard remained in San Pedro. He had no particular love for Los Angeles. Besides, there was Complex, who had to be taken to the eucalyptus grove three times a day, which would have been impossible had they taken him to the city. Having promised Jim to take care of him during his sojourn in San Quentin, Lenard was unwilling to turn him over to anyone else. And then, too, he felt that Agnes was just as happy, if not happier, without him. He would have to have been blind not to see that she and Nick Velikanovich had become great friends.

For two years Lenard lived in the old house on the bluff, took walks on the breakwater to feed the gulls, bootlegged just enough to make his living expenses and buy an armful of books whenever he went to Los Angeles, played billiards in his favorite downtown hangout, saw that Complex was happy, and came to see me.

IX

Off and on, I enjoyed him a great deal. Many things amused him and he was always eager to tell me why. He tried to help me at my writing. He was happy when I sent him to the Library to look up things for me. Frequently he came to me, grinning all over his face, with a piece of paper in his hand.

"Here's a good one," he said. " 'Living in America is like drinking champagne out of a rusty tin can.' " He had copied it from some magazine or book. Or, " 'Joy is a fruit that Americans eat green.' "

One day he burst in on me, laughing. "Ah-ha! I got one on your Papa Mencken. I always thought he wasn't a real cynic. Listen—I'll read you something that he wrote in his first book:

> "The light that lies in Dolly's eyes
>   Is sun and moon and stars to me.
> It dims the splendor of the skies—
> The light that lies in Dolly's eyes—
> And me-ward shining testifies
>   That Dolly's mine, fore'er to be.
> The light that shines in Dolly's eyes
>   Is sun and moon and stars to me!"

His life motto, he said, was a sentence from the mouth of a character in *Moby Dick*: "For my part, I abominate all honorable, respectable toils, trials, and tribulations of every kind whatsoever."

X

One day Lenard came running to me. "My God! they're chopping down the trees!" he cried.

"What trees?"

"The eucalyptus trees! Complex—what'll Complex do?"

It seemed that the grove recently had been sold and the new owner was going to build on the site. I laughed and composed a couplet—

> Woodman, woodman, spare that tree;
> It's the only place where my dog can p ——

—but to Lenard the cutting down of the grove was a real tragedy. Of course, even more so to poor Complex. Unable to relieve himself, the dog died in agony a few days after the particular tree was downed.

Lenard grieved for weeks.

XI

Jim Culley returned from San Quentin, and I met him. He was not quite the gay young Irishman Lenard had described to me. He seemed a bit abrupt, distrustful, bitter, impatient; only now and then did his jovial Irish nature come to the surface for a while with the aid of a few drinks. He said he had met me during the strike, but I did not remember him. He, of course, knew Lonie Burton, "Red" O'Neal, and Jack Kipps.

He told me he had enough of America and was planning to go to Mexico as soon as he had made a stake. He had lived there throughout the war, dodging the draft, he told me; he had learned the language and found the

Mexican manner of living, especially in the small, out-of-the-way places, most charming. People there were still human. They lived spontaneously, believed in sin and song. Mexican women knew how to love, and the men were not all wrapped up in business and work.

Then for some time I saw very little of either Lenard or Jim. As I learned later from Nick Velikanovich, they were going hot after the shekels, making a stake. One afternoon they came to say good-by.

"Yes, I'm going with Jim to Mexico," said Podgornik. "Jim tells me it's a real place where a man can live. A man with a soul. I believe him. If I like it in Mexico, maybe I'll never come back. Don't say anything to Agnes, though, if you see her. I told her I'm going, but she doesn't know I may not return. I don't want to make her too happy all at once. She and the kids will be better off without me. They're Americans. Agnes is, too. . . . 'Living in America is like drinking champagne out of a rusty tin can.' Agnes has the American idea. Some day she'll be a rich woman. I—I don't know what I am. I'm nothing, I guess; not even a Bohunk any more. Jim used to say that I have a soul. I don't know. . . . Well, *adios!* you see," he laughed, "I *habla Español* already. *Adios, amigo!*" Evidently he had had a few drinks.

XII

That was the last time I saw Lenard Podgornik. A year or so later I received a short note from a place in the state of Sonora. "Boy, I'm *living!*" he wrote. "Everybody here hates work. People here are wise without knowing it. I'm getting younger. Don't say anything to Agnes if you see her. 'Joy is a fruit that Americans eat green.'—Jim sends his regards."

One day I ran into Agnes on the boulevard in Hollywood. She did not appear particularly happy at meeting me, but I was interested and asked her to lunch. I learned that she had given up bootlegging for more respectable pursuits. She had been caught, but managed to get out of it; and then, as it came to me from another source, she had quarreled with Nick Velikanovich. . . . But she was reluctant to talk of her past. The children were just fine, thank you. The oldest girl was in a school-for-girls in Pasadena. The oldest boy was taking up law. And so on.

"I guess you know that my husband is dead," she said, with amazing . casualness. "Yes, I got a report from Sonora, Mexico. Official report. A snake bit 'im." We finished our lunch. "Say, what do you think of theosophy? I think it's wonderful. Don't you? You heard of Krishnamurti, didn't you?"

I had; but I was more interested in the date of Lenard Podgornik's decease as reported by Mexican authorities. She told it to me. Later I examined the letter I had received from Sonora. It was undated, but the postmark, although slightly blurred, shows that it was mailed after Podgornik's "official" death.

Mexican officials are most obliging. I have not heard from Lenard since then. But I'd not be surprised to get a line from him again some time.

CHAPTER XXII

A Bohunk Woman

I

IN SAN PEDRO it was my lot to experience another Bohunk immigrant, a woman who, in the brief time that she remotely entered into my life, quite indelibly impressed herself on my mind—not so much as an actual person, but as a sort of symbol or composite study of the lives of many Bohunk women in America whose men performed the hard, dirty work in industry, and to whom fate was not so gentle as to Agnes Podgornik.

Her name was Mrs. Tanasich.

She was recommended to me by a Dalmatian fisherman, a friend or acquaintance of Lenard Podgornik's, when—some time in 1926—I was looking for a woman to come and clean my little dwelling once or twice a week. She was *nashka*, I was told—"one of ours"—in low circumstances, and needed work. Her husband had been permanently disabled in an accident while working on the docks two years before, and she supported both him and herself by doing housework by the day and the hour for people in town who were willing to employ her; and they were not many, because she was old and ill. She drove from job to job in a stuttering old Ford, working here a full day or an afternoon, there only an hour or two.

She was a tall, gaunt woman, in her fifties, as I learned later, but older-looking; quite emaciated, almost skin-and-bone, suffering (as I also found out by-and-by) from an incurable ailment. Her angular sallow-brown face, with its high Slavic cheekbones, was intricately etched with a

network of grooves and tiny wrinkles. Her deep-set, lus-
terless eyes had a look of discomfiting calm, a flat disin-
terestedness, a profound monotony. The points of her
broad, slightly up-curved chin and rather longish thin
nose came within about an inch of meeting over the tooth-
less, tight-shut mouth, with its drawn yellowish lips, which
gave her face a flitting suggestion of weirdness. Her hair,
what there was left of it, was ashen-gray and, combed
straight back over the skull, usually hidden under the
dust-cap. Her brown loose-skinned hands were all awry
from too much work. Her long frame, with its stooped
shoulders, curved back, and awkward broad hips, seemed
longer than it actually was because of the outmoded dark
dress, made of the cheapest material, that she always
wore, with the back of the skirt trailing on the floor.

Her manner was apathetic, cheerless, mechanical. At
first I was vaguely annoyed by her (ill-looking people
generally affect me unpleasantly), and perhaps I would
have told her not to come any more had it not been for
the fact that—maybe because she was a countrywoman of
mine—I developed at once an irresistible interest in her
personality.

The work she accomplished with moderate competence,
but without a suspicion of zest. To change the bedding
or empty the waste-basket obviously had for her neither
value nor meaning; there was in her no trace of the fussi-
ness that is characteristic of elderly women. I began to
sense in her an invincible indifference to everything.

For our mutual convenience she generally came toward
evening, and the light by which I most frequently saw
her was, by consequence, either defective or artificial; but
I think that because of that fact I saw her, in a sense,
more clearly than most of her daylight employers. The
dimness of my apartment in which she moved, sweeping

and arranging things, gave me a kind of perspective upon her; it softened the sharp outlines of her personality, endowing them with a slight nebulousness, and at the same time bringing out the suggestion of a death-calm fatalism that, for a moment now and then, lifted the tragic aspect, which was the dominant aspect of her figure, to a rigid abstract quality.

There were no old-woman exaggerations or exuberances about her. She was drudgery incarnate; going through certain definite motions; a drab, cold woman, almost unliving, hovering on the edge of existence, undisturbed by emotional demands or vital communal sympathies. She seemed beyond all that. But presently her very drabness, like that of a banal, bleak old house, abandoned to collapse by itself, offered a sort of beauty and dignity.

Aided by memories of peasant women I had seen in the Old Country in my boyhood, I tried to imagine her as she had probably been in her younger life in Croatia—stalwart, full-built and hard, of the type of women I had watched carrying gracefully and with surety great burdens on mountain roads or working long hours in the fields with a careless, even cheerful, fatalism, yet whose whole beings seemed at the same time fixed upon a purpose of inconceivable importance; decisive, ready, and capable, their faces flushed from the sun, with the honor of freedom and poverty in their words, glances, and gestures.

She evidently had been in America a long time.

II

At first, when I tried to talk with her, "yes" and "no" comprised most of her answers to my queries and remarks. Her voice had a dull, unnatural huskiness which seemed incongruous with the rest of her; it sounded, almost, as if it came from a source remote from herself; but in time I became used to it, too and it commenced to harmonize for me with her physiognomy and her inner character, as it was gradually revealed to me—dulled, unemotional and, little as she spoke, very monotonous.

Sometimes, when I said something, she merely shrugged her shoulders or shook or nodded her head. She showed no annoyance at my questions or remarks; she was just flatly unresponsive, indifferent to my curiosity. Her brief answers came, perhaps, in the same category as cleaning the rug: something one was obliged to go through as part of the earthly ordeal, which she obviously had determined to endure with minimum ado, simply, without elaboration, sentimentality, or impatience.

I came to a kind of instinctive understanding of her, and before long I would look forward to her coming on Tuesday and Saturday afternoons, aside from the fact that my place needed cleaning.

Occasionally Croatian people in San Pedro who had known her for years told me things about her. Her doctor, for instance, who also was a Yugoslav, described to me the nature of her disease, and told me he had been giving her drugs to dull the intolerable pain so that she could get around and work.

Last year, he said, her condition had still held out a little hope, but she had refused to submit to a dangerous operation, unwilling to take the risk of not surviving it. She had to live a while longer; she did not want to leave her husband, who was dependent upon her and whom she expected to die before long. No doubt the drugs helped to dull and mystify her whole personality.

She worked for me about three months.

One afternoon I happened to return to my apartment just as she drove up. I noticed that she parked her Ford a bit uncertainly. It was just before sundown. The rich, reddish California sunlight flooded her somber figure and haggard face as she got wearily out of the machine. Watching her gave me, momentarily, a heavy sensation. She did not seem to belong among the living. Her person emanated a chill mustiness.

"*Dobar vecher,*" she greeted me in Croatian, as was her wont. "Good evening." Her voice was hollow and far-away.

She ascended the few steps to my dwelling with great difficulty, but without a groan or a sigh. Inside, she stopped in the middle of the room and started to sway a little, as if struggling against swooning.

I helped her to a couch. "Can I do anything for you?" I asked.

She shook her head. Her eyes were closed; her arms lay limply by her sides.

I managed to reach her doctor by telephone, but he said he could not possibly come before an hour and suggested that meantime I give her some liquor if I had any; it could do her no harm. He said she was so far gone that the drugs he was giving her had scarcely any effect upon her. He did not think she was in pain, but perhaps was very weak, and a strong drink might do her temporary good.

I had recently procured a bottle of fierce Jamaica rum from the steward of a British vessel that had been in port, and, in vague desperation, I gave her a big drink of it. It nearly knocked the breath out of her, but after a while it seemed that a little color appeared in her face.

Sitting by the couch, I was wishing the doctor would come sooner than he had promised. Now and then a creepy feeling seized me. She might die here and now!

I turned on the light. Then she opened her eyes and

296

looked at me a long time. Her eyes now were large and somehow seemed faintly luminous.

A twitch that perhaps was meant to be a smile passed across her lips and, with a sort of quick, out-running impulse, a jerky, sudden movement, she took hold of one of my hands with both of hers, which were cold and dry.

"Thank you," she said in Croatian. "You are kind to me." Then, after a pause: "I should have gone home instead of coming here, but I thought I could hold out another hour. I am very sick. So weak."

It was the longest speech she had yet spoken to me. Her voice was low and very remote.

I gave her another drink of rum. It was almost pure alcohol; it choked her a little and deepened the color of her cheeks.

For several minutes she lay very still, her eyes closed. She scarcely breathed. Now and then her left hand twitched a little.

Then she made a move as if to rise. "I feel much better now," she said. But she could not move herself, whereupon she was still and silent for several minutes once more.

"I can't move," she said, "but I feel very good. Very good," she repeated. "Indeed, I don't feel anything, just a queer glow all over. What was that you gave me? Rum?" Her face twitched again in an attempt to smile. Her voice seemed nearer; her eyes shone with a low, quiet light, "My head is very clear—so clear. Nothing matters."

Then she was silent again for a while, as if thinking over what she had just said.

"Please touch my hand if you don't mind," she then said.

I complied with her request.

"I scarcely feel you," she said. "As though I wore very

thick gloves. . . . You are kind to me. I like your room.
I always liked to come here. Maybe that is why I came
today, although I knew I shouldn't. You have many
books. Books . . ." She fell silent, as though going over
something in her mind.

Then, again: "People are good, many people all over
the world are good, but the world—I mean life—life is
cruel and evil. People want to be good, but can't. . . .
Strange, isn't it?" she philosophized.

She spoke in very good Croatian, now and then putting
in a word or a sentence in English. "People are good, but
they make a bad world, and the world in turn makes them
bad. It's a circle," and she made a vague round motion
with her hand. "Good and evil . . . but there is too much
evil . . . too much. One is best dead. I should have died
many years ago. I had lived . . . but too much sorrow
. . . too much sorrow . . . Life was too cruel here.
America is big and terrible. I had seven children; they
are all dead except one, perhaps. I had four husbands;
three of them died; the fourth one is still alive, but would
be better off dead. . . . But perhaps nothing matters.
I don't matter. Only life matters . . . life and America.
Life must go on. A terrible process, isn't it? America must
become great. . . . We all came over from the Old Country to help America become great and terrible."

"Dung," I thought to myself.

She closed her eyes and was silent for a long moment.
Then she looked at me again, then around the room. Her
lips twitched with some success into a fugitive smile.

"Everything is so—so lucid," she said. "I have never
seen things so clearly. Nothing matters. Nothing. . . . I
can't feel anything, just a glow—the rum you gave me,
perhaps—, but I have never been so alive . . . so
sharply alive and conscious of everything . . . you and

298

this room. I wish I could stay here forever. I hope the
doctor never comes. He can't do anything for me. I don't
want him to do anything for me. He told you to give me
rum; that was all I needed. Everything is all right.
Everything is clear and . . . and kind."

I gave her more rum. She could hardly raise herself to
drink it. I had to hold the glass.

"You are good to me," she said after a minute. "Rum
is good. I never felt this way before. I can't move my
body, but I don't care. I hope you don't mind my being
here a while. My body . . . it doesn't matter. I have
loved four men—they entered into me—and borne them
seven children. Four and seven . . . four and seven," she
repeated. "Four and seven . . . just numbers. One, two,
three, four . . . one, two, three, four, five, six, seven.
Numbers."

I had an eerie feeling, quite indescribable. I went to the
telephone to get the doctor, but could not rouse the oper-
ator. I hung up and, not knowing what else to do, put
a record on my gramophone. It was a gay Croatian national song.

Mrs. Tanasich listened to it with her eyes open, lying
very still. Music made the situation even weirder, but I
let the record play out.

"That was nice," she said. "I barely heard it . . . far
off."

I sat down again by the couch.

She continued talking to me; the doctor was late, and
before he came she told me of her life in America—facts,
essentials, stripped of all emotion. "Can you hear me?"
she once interrupted herself. "I can scarcely hear myself.
Very strange." Her voice was low, but I had no trouble
understanding her in the stillness of the room.

Several of the facts in the story that follows had come

299

to me before, and others I learned later from people who knew her; most of them she gave me herself.

Twenty-seven years before, in the Old Country, she had been in love with a young man whose first name was Mato. They were poor peasants in the same village. Mato came to America to earn some money and in two years return to Croatia, whereupon he would buy some land, build a house, and marry her. Milla—her first name—waited for him. But in the 'nineties there was a long panic in America, and Mato earned little more than he needed to keep soul and body together. He worked in the mines.

He went to Idaho and found work in the mines there. He wanted her; she wanted him. Two years went by. They were writing to each other. Then he sent her money to join him, and she came.

Milla arrived in Idaho just as the long strike started in the Cœur d'Alene mining district, in the latter half of the 'nineties, when the Western Federation of Miners was coming into being. There was a bitter war between the miners and the mine-owners. Men were shot dead, openly and in the dark, on both sides. There were frequent battles between organized groups of armed workmen and company guards and the militia.

Mato married Milla. A week later he and two other workmen were found dead in a gulch. The miners' union buried them. They were heroes; the "company gunmen" had killed them.

A month later a Serbian, whose name was Dushan, asked her to marry him. She accepted him. He was good to her and to Mato's child when it was born. He worked in the mines; she ran a boarding-house for unmarried miners, and each year, of course, gave birth to a child.

300

A BOHUNK WOMAN

She bore Dushan four children; then there was a cave-in and two weeks later they dug him out of the mine, dead, with five others.

She married the third time. He was a Dalmatian; his first name was Ivan. He was a fine man, too fine; a good worker, intelligent, aflame with resentment against conditions under which he and other men in his circumstances earned their living in America. He read many books and papers, and made Milla read them. He had gone to a city school in the Old Country. He was an active radical. His English was good, and he often spoke at workers' meetings.

But, being an agitator, a class-conscious under dog, he frequently had trouble finding work; and when he found it he seldom kept a job very long. He was blacklisted far and wide.

The family was compelled to move from place to place. From Idaho they went to Nevada. There two of Dushan's children died of scarlet fever. The company doctor was not interested in the case, and they could not afford to send to Reno for a good doctor.

Milla had two children by Ivan. He was good to her and all the children, but it was a trial to be married to him. As soon as the company found out that he was an I. W. W. agitator he was discharged.

From Nevada they went to Arizona. Ivan found work in the mines near Bisbee. Milla begged him to curb his radicalism, and he heeded her plea. But he always read and studied and meditated. Nights he could not sleep, brooding over the injustices of the industrial system.

Then, suddenly, he turned away from radicalism. He had discovered, it seems, that Socialism, I. W. W.-ism, and all such organized movements were futile. He became an extreme individualist. He read Tolstoy and studied

301

his life. He went daft on the subject of Tolstoy, non-resistance and individualism. He made Milla read all of the master's works. Then he proposed that the entire family withdraw from the evil world and live "the simple life," go back to nature, "into the wilderness," away from the perversions of industrialism and wage-slavery. He would take them to the mountains somewhere, he said, and there provide for them from what nature offered. They would use nothing produced in factories, for that was helping to continue the terrible slavery of millions of people, many of whom did not realize they were slaves. Every intelligent person ought to do that, said Ivan; then all the ills of life in America would vanish. The factory system must go. People must return to the simple life. Tolstoy was right.

But Milla, feeling responsibility to her children, would not go with him. She begged him to be sensible; after all, he was but a tiny grain upon an enormous sand-beach. But Ivan had seen the great Truth; it became an obsession with him, and, Tolstoy-like, he left Milla and the children and went off to lead the simple life by himself.

He pitched a tent near Bisbee and worked just enough to exist. He chopped wood and did other odd jobs that people had been doing before industrialism descended upon the world. He visited the family and begged Milla to join him; but Milla couldn't if she had wished to. The children were growing up and thought the man was crazy.

So she ran a boarding-house for miners and supported herself and the children that way for a number of years.

Then Ivan disappeared altogether. He walked all the way to New York, as Milla learned later; actually walked. He would not ride in a train, even if he had the price, because railways were part of the evil industrial system, nor would he steal a ride, for the same reason. Besides, he was too proud—an individualist.

302

He reached New York, and there got in touch with some Dalmatian fishermen who had just purchased an old American sailing-ship and were about to sail for the Old Country, and fish there. Ivan had no objection to fishing and fishing-boats, and he went with them.

He got back to Dalmatia just before the outbreak of the war. He was determined to live according to his Tolstoyan ideas there. People in Dalmatia, he thought, were unspoiled, and would not laugh at him.

Ivan was a pacifist; Tolstoy's *Ivan the Fool* was his favorite book; and so when the Austrian government ordered him to report for examination for military service, he refused to go—and a few days later he was shot.

Milla heard of his execution, and then she married the fourth time, her present husband. He, too, was a Dalmatian, a miner in Bisbee, a good, simple, middle-aged man. His name was George Tanasich. She had a child by him in Arizona, her last.

Her first son, growing up, became a miner, too. He was Mato's son. The second year in the mines he was killed in an explosion five thousand feet underground.

Then Milla began to hate the mines with everything that was in her. She wanted to leave Bisbee at once and get away from the mines forever. She heard there was a large Dalmatian colony at San Pedro, in California, and induced George to quit his job and take the whole family there.

They went. George was getting old, but he found work in a shipyard in San Pedro. The children were growing up. The eldest two—Dushan's boys—went to work too. They were strong, ambitious boys. They were Americans, getting ashamed of their mother, a Bohunk woman, and her aging, inarticulate Bohunk husband.

America entered the war, and the boys joined the army.

303

One died of influenza in a camp on this side, the other went across; he came back to the United States after the Armistice, so far as she knew, unharmed, but she never heard from him again. Telling me of this, she said matter-of-factly: "America swallowed him. America is so big."

Her two children by Ivan also died of influenza during the war, and her last-born—George's—of infantile paralysis soon after the Armistice. Thus all her children went. Seven of them. She had long since given up hope of hearing from Dushan's boy who had disappeared upon leaving the army.

During the war George Tanasich made good money, but most of it went for doctor's bills and funeral expenses. They bought and paid for a small house.

Getting old, the best George could do was to work occasionally on the docks as a stevedore. He made enough for them to live on. Then something fell on him and he was crippled for life. That happened two years before I met her.

Milla was in ill health for many years. First her teeth went bad. Then rheumatism. Then she developed terrible agonies in her womb. She had borne so many children without getting the proper care.

George's compensation for his injuries was not sufficient to keep them alive, so Milla went to work to support herself and her man. She went from house to house in her old Ford wherever people would give her work. She was through with life, but she wanted to go on till after George died; she did not want to leave him alone. After all, he had been her best husband.

But now, it seemed, she was done for altogether. The drugs that the doctor was giving her were becoming futile. "But," she said, "no matter. George can't live more than a few years longer. There is the house. He can sell it. He will have enough."

IV

Finally the doctor came.

She opened her eyes once more and managed to make me understand that on a certain table in her house was last month's gas bill, and would I please see that it got paid. George could not leave the house. There was some money in a certain bowl over the sink in the kitchen.

She thanked me for the rum; it had made her feel very good. She thanked the doctor for all his trouble with her, and asked him to keep an eye on George. She had arranged with some neighbor woman to feed him and see that he did not die in his own filth.

We called an ambulance, but she died before it came.

CHAPTER XXIII

Steve Radin—(Concluded)

I

ONE Saturday afternoon early in 1925 I stepped into my friend Stanley Rose's bookshop in a side street off the Boulevard in Hollywood.

"There was a man in here yesterday who said he knew you," said Stanley. "A countryman of yours. Looks like Napoleon and acts a little like a nut. Steve Rodin—Radin, or some such name. . . . He saw an article you had in a magazine and noticed in the 'Notes About Contributors' that you lived in southern California. He took a chance, I guess, and asked me if I happened to know you. I said you came in every once in a while. Then he gave me his address. He's anxious to see you. He lives at the Marco Polo, seems to have money, and is trying to get into the movies as an actor. . . ."

I telephoned Steve at the Marco Polo. He asked me to come to the hotel and have dinner with him.

He had changed considerably. He was now thirty, dark-faced, and strikingly Napoleonic in features as well as in stature and posture. A little lock of hair curved over his forehead. When on his feet he had the habit of putting his right hand between two vest buttons on his chest. I could not help laughing at him the moment I stepped into his room. He grinned, himself.

"Hello, Bonaparte!" I said.

This greeting, obviously, pleased him. His manner was affected, self-dramatizing. He seemed to be "Hollywood" from head to feet.

306

"So you're becoming a writer in English!" he exclaimed. "Pretty good for a Hunky, I'll say. Some day, perhaps, you'll write me up. Some day I'm liable to be material for a—what you call it?—biography."

I thought he was either joking or crazy.

About the rooms were scattered books entitled *I Can —I WILL!* and *Success Is Easier than Failure*, and copies of film fan magazines, the *American Mercury*, Haldeman-Julius' *Monthly*, and *Cosmopolitan*.

I stayed with him the rest of that afternoon and all evening. By-and-by I became fairly certain that he was neither crazy nor joking; certainly no crazier than a lot of other people in Hollywood. Realizing that he was serious, I was amused by him all the more. My laughter was anything but displeasing to him.

Hollywood was full of pompous, ridiculous people, inflated with their own egos. Steve's vanity, however, while in many respects typically Hollywood, was inoffensive because not untempered by his own humor. Also, I began to feel that his egoism was not wholly baseless.

He impressed me as a crude, chaotic character, secretly aware of his crudity, which he strove hard to abate or, better, translate, with his broad sense of humor and natural bent to act, into clowning. I recalled his buffooning in Mrs. Schmidt's parlor, in the prize-ring, and as a soap-boxer in Brooklyn, back in 1914, '15 and '16. Now he was more an actor, a buffoon, than ever before; a diverting pantomimic, who enlivened whatever he was saying with exaggerated gesticulations and facial expressions. He spoke good English, but when at a loss for a word he cut a gesture or a face, either straightforwardly funny or mock-serious, which was more vivid than any phrase.

307

"I came to Hollywood to become a star in the pictures," he said.

In some respects he was the same Steve that I had known nine years before, and since almost forgotten. He had an avid, untrained, undisciplined mind, burdened with some of the subtler brands of hokum prevalent in America, and from the start interesting to me for its efforts to grope its way out of the muddle of its short-comings, conceits, complexes, and inadequacies; and achieve—somewhere, somehow, sometime—some kind of effectiveness. He was in the grip, as I presently recognized, of a great ambition to be appreciated by millions of people and be felt in the world, preferably as an actor. He was driven to the fulfillment of this ambition by a defiant optimism and confidence in his luck and personal qualities, which he knew were yet uncrystallized but doubtless ordained eventually to hoist him to success.

"Success, that's the thing!" he cried, dramatically, walking before me up and down the room.

II

But to resume the story of his life where I have left it off in a previous chapter:

Steve was in the army throughout the war, went to France, and returned as a corporal, undamaged. In France he had gambled a little on pay days and, with luck and "science" (by which, I think, he meant crooked methods), won several hundred dollars a month.

He had become thoroughly convinced that the ideas motivating the radical movements in America were "hay wire." Somewhere he had come upon Mencken's book about Nietzsche and, partly in consequence of reading it, developed the notion that he was a superior individual.

Another idea that seized him was that money was the

important thing in America—for that matter, anywhere in the world. To be somebody one had to have "dough." Without it one was a back number. There was nothing in being a workin'-stiff.

On his return from France he continued to gamble. He won regularly and saved the money. On the expiration of his first "hitch" he reënlisted, with the intention of continuing to gamble. He developed what he considered a Nietzschean contempt for the great majority of soldiers and had no scruples about taking money from them. They were a bunch of "morons" or "boobs," anyhow.

In connection with his acquaintance with the writings of Nietzsche and Mencken, another notion began to buzz in his head, namely, that he was a sort of carbon copy of Napoleon. He looked like one. Other soldiers in his outfit told him so. He studied himself in mirrors. He commenced to think that he not only had the exterior of Napoleon, but was Napoleon inside as well. He was conscious of a vast ambition within himself to become somebody and get at the vitals of the world. He read books about Napoleon and it dawned upon him that he was Napoleonic not only in the large, fundamental aspects, but also in some of the smaller, psychological details. For instance, when Napoleon rode at the head of his army through newly conquered places, he had the habit of counting the windows on houses by the roadside. He (Steve) had the same habit; he always counted windows on buildings he passed. On campaigns Napoleon needed only a few hours' sleep a day; and while leading the strike in Brooklyn in 1916, he (Steve) had scarcely slept at all for weeks.

After his reënlistment Steve stayed in the army another year, then—early in 1921—purchased his discharge, and with several thousand dollars—all gained by gambling—returned to Brooklyn.

There he "looked around" awhile. He met fellows he had known in his pre-socialistic days—Joe Riley and his friends. Riley's saloon, of course, was closed, now that prohibition was in effect, but the Saturday Night Club was still going strong, and Joe was doing well. He operated a "blind pig" not far from the Club and was getting on as a bootlegger. Bootlegging was then in its infancy, but Joe believed that gradually it would become a "big thing." Steve agreed with him. Joe had no hard feelings against him.

At election-time Steve contributed a "grand" to the campaign fund of the Democratic party in the borough of Brooklyn and thus began to develop swiftly into a local politician of considerable potency. He was given the "privilege" of investing in a trucking company and a contracting business which had the good will of politicians in and out of office who ruled the borough. He also took an interest in Joe Riley's booze racket, and began to make money in a big way.

For four years after his discharge from the army his popularity and influence grew. At political gatherings he was asked to make speeches; and when he spoke, he aimed always to be amusing, to make people laugh. He declined offers of appointment or nomination to minor offices. "I didn't want to get stuck in some two-by-four office," he explained to me. "Besides, the big shots were impressed by my refusal." He had no definite plans. He was young yet—just twenty-five. He meant to be an opportunist, always on the alert; to reach for the immediate and let the future come; to "play the game." That was the American way.

"Had I remained in Brooklyn and kept on the way I started," he told me, years later, "I would of gone far, and no maybe about it. I had got rid of all my socialistic boloney. To hell with the masses! I agreed with Nietzsche and Mencken that their only excuse for existing was to serve superior men in satisfying their urge to power. I had no trouble with my conscience." He laughed. "Beyond good and evil—savvy?"

III

In the fall of 1924 Steve attended a semi-political banquet at the Astor in New York. He was asked to speak, and spoke for ten minutes in his usual clown-Napoleonic way. Everybody laughed. He was the third or fourth person to be called upon to speak. Others followed with short addresses or remarks. The speeches went on well toward midnight.

Then the chairman introduced a woman by the name of Mrs. Elizabeth Goodwill Randolph, "a lady of high charm and distinction," as he described her, "famous throughout the country as a practical psychologist, an expert in the science of success, a vocational analyst, who is and looks younger at the age of sixty-two than most women look at thirty-two." He suggested that Mrs. Randolph give the gathering a practical demonstration of her science.

Mrs. Randolph complied with the request. She took men and women at random, and it seemed that everyone was a square peg in a round hole, or *vice versa*. Analyzing a preacher, she said he should have been a bond salesman or a floorwalker at Macy's. A captain of police whom she picked out possessed "the soul of a poet" and a "potential" talent equal to that of Edgar Guest.

Then she stopped in front of Steve Radin.

"And here, ladies and gentlemen," she said, "is doubtless the most remarkable man in this room tonight."

Steve was embarrassed. She was kidding him, no doubt.

"I don't know what he is doing," Mrs. Randolph went on, "but I heard him speak here this evening, and if he is not an actor, he is, I have no hesitancy in saying, in the wrong profession. If not actually, then potentially, this gentleman is an equal of Charlie Chaplin, Harold Lloyd, and Larry Semon—a great comedian."

Everybody laughed.

Later some one—perhaps Mrs. Randolph's secretary—brought Steve her card, on the back of which was a note suggesting that he call at her hotel for a closer analysis.

He called the next day, and one of the first things that the woman said to him was that he looked "the spittin' image of Napoleon"; and did he know that Napoleon had been one of the greatest actors in history? She studied Steve's palm, asked him for the date of his birth and his birthplace, and then told him that he was Napoleonic also from the viewpoint of palmistry and astrology. Indeed, he very likely was a reincarnation of the Little Corporal! Analyzing him further, she pointed out, first, his shortcomings, which, true, were numerous, but not fatal, and then his virtues.

To Steve's utter amazement, she "hit the nail on the head in every statement she made." ("She read me like a book," he told me in Hollywood. "She struck me as the smartest person I'd ever bumped up against. I suddenly realized that nearly everything I'd done so far—prize-fighting, talking from soap-boxes, and after-dinner speaking—had been motivated by a blind tendency of my innate 'aptitude,' as she called it, to be an actor.")

Mrs. Randolph said to him: "I urge you to go to Hollywood at once, for you are now almost thirty and you have no time to waste. Muster all your courage, determination, aggressiveness, stick-to-it-iveness—all your moral and material resources—and become a star in the

films. If you do what I say you will be a phenomenal success—phenomenal!"

IV

Steve's faith in Mrs. Randolph's "analysis" was so complete that in the next two weeks he hastily sold out his
interest in trucking and contracting companies, severed
his connection with Joe Riley's booze racket, and gave up
his two mistresses. His personal, business, and political
friends in Brooklyn and Manhattan thought he was crazy,
but all he told them in explanation was that he was bound
for Hollywood.

In Hollywood—with some two hundred thousand dollars to his name—he put up at the Marco Polo. For several days he remained undecided with which company he
wanted to affiliate himself. On the Boulevard he recognized famous stars, whose splendors (he smiled to himself) his own fame was about to eclipse. Walking about,
he would not have been surprised if some director, spot-
ting him, suddenly let out a whoop and waved a $7,000-
a-week contract in his face. He took it for granted that all
movie executives and directors were adepts in character
analysis, and would recognize him instanter for the great
actor he was. But nothing happened.

The second week in Hollywood, he paused for brief
periods in front of studio entrances, expecting that some
director with seeing eyes would surely discern his talent.
But still nothing happened. Stars and directors drove up
in Hispano-Suizas, but remained oblivious of him.

Growing impatient, one day Steve succeeded in forcing
himself into the office of a casting director, who, he
thought, ought to recognize the actor in him the moment
he saw him. The casting director gave him a deep look,

313

then pressed a buzzer under his desk. A minute later two husky guards, employing force, had Steve in the street.

This was strange, to say the least. But at the other studios Steve had no better luck. He became acquainted with extras and "bit players" who hung around the casting-offices. All of them appeared to consider themselves no lesser actors than Steve considered himself. They spoke of their art, and Steve learned that "crashing" into the cinema—they did not use the word "movies"—was usually a slow and heart-breaking process. They advised Steve to take his chances with them; register at the studios and various screen bureaus and wait for a call. Some of the most famous stars had risen from extra-playing. So, since that apparently was to be his fate, too, Steve took their advice and registered at all the large studios, and in several agencies.

v

It was at this point in his Hollywood adventure that I met Steve.

Thereafter I saw him frequently in Hollywood. Now and then he visited me in San Pedro. At times he interested me even more than Lenard Podgornik, or Lonie Burton, or Mrs. Tanasich. He was possessed by success— the spirit of America.

Every other week or so he received a call from some studio or agency to play a "bit" as detective, sailor, waiter, "tough guy," or Austrian army officer, at from five to ten dollars a day. But no matter how conspicuous he made himself on the lot, no one in authority in the film industry noticed his "phenomenal" talent.

Waiting for calls in his hotel room, he continued to read such books as *I Can—I WILL!*, and Nietzsche and

Mencken, and other books which he bought—some on my suggestion—in Stanley Rose's bookstore.

He complained of the ignorance in the studios which kept him from realizing himself as a big actor. He was quite serious in his complaints. He took lessons in pantomimic dancing and enrolled in dramatic schools. The instructors encouraged him, but that was as far as he got.

Whenever we came together, he had some scheme whereby he figured he might "go over." Once he wanted to make me his publicity man, offering me a good financial arrangement, which I was tempted to accept. But too conscious of my shortcomings as a ballyhoo man, I hesitated. Instead, I put him in touch with some publicity men whom I had met during my newspaper days in Los Angeles, and he received a few mentions in the local movie columns.

But to no avail. For a whole year after I had met him he was still playing only "bits." These were small and far apart.

One day I chanced to hear that at the S. O. B. studios they were casting a comedy picture called "Napoleon's Cook," to be directed by Maurice Thiers, whom I knew slightly, having met him some time before at Stanley Rose's. I called up Thiers and induced him to give Steve Radin a test to play Napoleon, a minor rôle.

Thiers, when I saw him several days later, was mildly enthusiastic about the outcome of the test. "But, of course," he added, "I haven't the final word in casting and Hollywood is full of Napoleons."

But at the end nothing came of this.

"Well, that's that," said Steve, with dramatic restraint, when we read in the papers that some one else had been cast for the part. "I'm through with the movies. Too many pants-pressers in the studios."

I asked him what he was going to do now.

"I'm going to San Pedro."

VI

For months previously, as I have said, Steve had been coming to see me at San Pedro. There I had him meet Lenard Podgornik, and through Podgornik he had become acquainted with Nick Velikanovich, boss of the Hunky booze ring at the harbor.

Now Steve came to San Pedro and put "fifty grand" into Velikanovich's business, and they ordered built immediately two large seagoing speedboats equipped with airplane motors, faster than any rum-chaser. "What the hell!" said Steve with a gesture of recklessness. "Why not?" He and Nick, he added, were going in for booze-running in a big way. The sky was the limit in America. By-and-by they would work up a big "racket"—then a new word in California—and get a grip on the lucrative Hollywood "trade," which he knew was not yet organized. He promised eventually to work me in "on a safe spot." "You'll have an income," he said, "and you'll go on writing without having to worry about your ham and eggs. See?"

I saw Steve every few days. He had a fast and beautiful car, and I frequently went driving with him. He loved to speed, and every now and then we had narrow escapes. "An inch is as good as a mile," laughed Steve.

Once a week or so he came to the pilot station at five in the afternoon, when I was through for the day, and an hour later we were eating dinner in a delightful Spanish café at Laguna Beach I had discovered some time before. Off and on we had Lenard Podgornik with us. I had told Steve's story to Lenard, and Lenard's story to Steve. They were amused by one another, and the three of us

316

occasionally had a grand time together. We laughed ourselves red in the face.

Thus for about a year.

One day in the early fall of 1927 Lenard Podgornik
mentioned to me that Steve was "sweet on" Josie
Velikanovich.

"Nick's sister?" I said.

Lenard nodded. "I think it's serious. Matrimony."

I knew Josie slightly. She was a neat, healthy girl, not
good-looking, but not unattractive, either; twenty-one
and fairly bright. She had been graduated from the San
Pedro high school three years before.

I burst out laughing. It occurred to me that, while
Steve probably liked Josie a great deal, he was marrying
her partly because her name was Josie—Josephine. Napoleon and Josephine!

Next time I saw Steve I laughed out again before I
could say a word.

"Well, what's struck you now?" said Steve.

I told him of my Napoleon-and-Josephine theory.

Steve laughed, too. "But it's about time I got married,
isn't it?" he said. "Keeping mistresses is sort of nasty.
. . . Go ahead and laugh! It's funny, all right. Sometimes I get off all by myself and park the car somewhere
where nobody can see me, and unbuckle my belt and laugh
for fifteen minutes at a stretch, thinking of how I got to
San Pedro."

VII

Steve and Josephine were married late in 1927. They
went to Honolulu on their honeymoon trip. Then Steve
bought an elaborate estate in Palos Verdes Hills. Booze-
running was highly profitable to both Steve and Nick
Velikanovich. As Steve put it, money was "rolling in."

The movie bug was still buzzing in Steve's brain. Once he said to me: "When I make my first million, I'll try to crash the pictures again. I'll be producer and actor, and I'll put you in charge of the scenario department. See?" And he laughed.

He gave big parties at his home, to which he invited Hollywood people. Most of them were mediocre actors, assistant directors, and writers. They came to drink Steve's excellent booze. Josie managed the parties, but was not very happy about them. They upset the house so. She wished both Steve and Nick would quit the booze business and go into something more respectable. But neither Steve nor Nick would listen to her.

Steve was restless and hectic. Making ten or fifteen thousand dollars a month, he bought one new car after another. He continued to call for me at the pilot station and take me for rides halfway to San Diego and back. Josie begged him not to speed. She was pregnant and would not go riding with him. He asked me to lie to her that he had gone only forty miles an hour.

VIII

Now and then Steve was in the habit of going outside the twelve-mile limit in one of the speedboats which brought in the liquor. Nick and he had men to operate the boats; some of them, in fact, were members of the ring; but Steve joined them because he was restless and loved speeding. The boats ran without lights, of course. Josie always implored Steve not to go out, but he seldom listened to her. "I can't sit home all day and all evening long!"

One night, in the summer of 1928, the boat that Steve was on ran into a fog and crashed into an empty oil-tanker, bound for San Pedro. There was a gasoline explosion on the boat. Instantly the whole craft was ablaze.

318

In their panic, the regular boat operators leaped into the sea. They did not notice that Steve was caught in the wreckage of the little pilot-house, where he had been steering. It took Steve, perhaps, two minutes to extricate himself and jump into the water, too. Meantime his clothes had been doused in flaming gasoline and he was burned all over his body.

The crew of the tanker fished the men out of the ocean. The speedboat sank with some $50,000 worth of liquor.

Steve was broiled. He fell unconscious soon after they pulled him out of the sea. He died before the tanker reached port.

Josie was in the eighth month of pregnancy. On learning of the accident and the death of her husband, she suffered a miscarriage.

CHAPTER XXIV

America and Myself

I

THE deaths of Mrs. Tanasich and Steve Radin occurred within two months of one another. For a short while they had a depressing effect on me. Six months after Steve's death Lenard Podgornik, as I already have told, departed for Mexico. I missed the old boy very much.

For a time these three people were in my mind a great deal. But after a while they ceased to figure in my thoughts as persons I had known. They became case histories and symbols, which to me were acute comments on life in the Land of Promise.

Mrs. Tanasich, to say nothing of her several husbands and her American-born children, of course, had been "dung"—in the sense that Peter Molek had used the word—from the day of her arrival in the United States to the day she died in my room. She had derived scant joy or satisfaction out of her years in America. In all likelihood, I said to myself, she would have been better off had she remained in the Old Country.

Slavic immigrant women of Mrs. Tanasich's class, which meant the overwhelming majority of them, were faded and wrinkled at thirty and aged at forty-five. Back in Slovenia, Croatia, or Dalmatia women stayed young longer. There they worked outdoors most of the time. They were spiritually alive and stimulating even at the age of seventy or eighty. They belonged there. I remembered seeing peasant women in Carniola, young and old, with large baskets of eggs or berries gracefully balanced

on their heads, walking barefooted ten or fifteen kilometers to the market-place in the city. Strong pride, pride
in their poverty and physical well-being, was inherent in
their every stride. Returning home, they often sang.
Their lives were simple. Their country was primarily
agrarian and depressions in the world's economic life did
not seriously affect them. They and their menfolk unquestionably had a hard time coaxing meager livelihoods out
of their little patches of soil and scraping together enough
money twice a year to keep the tax-collector in good temper; but their struggle had a certain dignity. There they
were pitting their strength and wits against nature and
the elements. If drought and hail destroyed their fields,
they assumed an aspect of tragedy. They accepted their
misfortune fatalistically and tried again. The community
spirit came to their aid almost as a matter of course. Mis-
fortunes due to natural causes seemed to make them even
hardier.

In America, Bohunk women were indoors most of the
time. They were part of the industrial system. They ran
boarding-houses for unmarried immigrants in grimy coal
or steel towns, or worked in silk or hosiery mills. They
worried about accidents in the mines and their men's and
their own uncertain employment. Their daily intimate
lives in America lacked charm and grace and the simple
amenities that were the rule among peasant people in the
Old Country. Their love affairs here were not what love
affairs were in the villages of Carniola and Croatia. Their
existence here was rootless, too hectic to allow for tender,
romantic feelings. Here they felt, consciously or unconsciously, the essential and ceaseless unfriendliness of
American industrial and social realities to their and their
children's welfare. A financial panic hit them every now
and then. They could not understand these things. The

American system was too complex for their simple minds. The strain of life in the industrial, chaotic, unsettled America—which was not greater than in the Old Country, but different—told on them. It aged them and robbed them of the best human qualities.

Mrs. Tanasich had been one of these Bohunk women. She had died a mere shell of a human being, useless even as "dung," although at a period of her life when, in the Old Country, her middle age would have just begun. America had squeezed her dry. Both in its details and in its essence, her life in America had been so awful that, when she came to my notice, she was incapable of feeling and knowing the full horror of it.

Steve Radin, on the other hand, had not been "dung." Unlike Mrs. Tanasich—and, in fact, unlike most immigrants of the working-class—he had belonged in the United States from the start. He had been the exceptional kind of immigrant, so constructed that it was all but inevitable for him to "make good" in America. He had been adventurous, strongly egoistical, recklessly selfish, realistic and pragmatic (a "wise guy"), but at the same time capable of deluding himself and swallowing the less transparent species of hokum; a go-getter, a schemer, an opportunist, a racketeer, with a will to power and desire for grandeur and acclaim. His values were the values of democratic America; the values of the moment. Using his wits, and being by nature attuned to American psychology, he had risen to comparative wealth before he was thirty. "Playing the game" in the American way, he had accumulated, when still a young man, enough money to make it possible for him to live in comfort and with grace, had he known how, for the rest of his life. But, American-like, he had had to push on for more and more money, and for acclaim. But toward the last, with his growing fortune, his estate, and his Packards, Lincolns, and Cunninghams, he was hectic and restless. Despite his dream to try to "crash" the movies again when he made a million dollars, he had felt, I think, that he would never realize himself as an actor. And I felt that even if he had become a famous film comedian or had attained to a great fortune in booze-running or in some other field, he would have been a frustrated man, anyhow. There were motion-picture stars in Hollywood and rich people elsewhere, men and women essentially like Steve, who, wallowing in wealth and amidst other symbols of success, were unhappy and frustrated people, spiritually starved, personally disgusting; making fools of themselves in their diverse ways; incapable of living gracefully; decaying in the vast jungle, in which they had quickly grown to great size with little effort on their part. . . .

I had liked Steve, personally, but now I most frequently thought of him as a ludicrous, odd, fantastic figure. Occasionally I could scarcely believe that I had actually known him. Had he remained in the Old Country, his life would not have been so drastic, although he had been innately a wild, impulsive, garbled nature. In Europe, where life was more set and channelized, less jungly and with fewer opportunities in which all sorts of people might find avenues of expression for their urges, he would have been forced to fit himself into some conventional, more sensible mold. In America, "the sky was the limit." America was a free country; a rich soil in which anything was apt to take root for a while, quickly grow and develop, and then suddenly rot and end.

Steve represented to me the whole American success idea; the idea that urged, lured, and pushed millions, native and foreign-born, to great material achievements for the sake of these achievements, while—actually—as individuals and as a class, these success-bent men and women, most of them innately unfit to handle wealth and position, were headed, sooner or later, toward some such fate, metaphorically speaking, as had finished Steve Radin—a crash in the dark.

Of the three, Lenard Podgornik appealed to me most, both as an individual and as a symbol. Like most Hunkies, he, too, had been fertilizing the roots of America's material greatness. But then he had experienced his sudden and amusing "rebirth" and perceived the stupidity of working himself to death in order to live. Suddenly he had turned against the great American god Work and the brutal tendency of the grinding, ill-adjusted mechanism of American life to destroy the best human qualities in men and women. In this rebellion, laughter was his chief weapon. He believed that the important thing to him was to save himself spiritually, as a human being, as man; and he was proceeding—awkwardly, gropingly, and humorously—to accomplish that end.

These three people—along with Blakelock, Koska, Lonie Burton, and Jack Kipps who still repeatedly came to my mind—began to represent, or symbolize, to me life in the United States. Haphazardness, chaos, violence, and accident had ruled their lives. Even the "rebirth" of Podgornik had been accidental and violent; to be "reborn," it had been necessary that he fall off a ship's gangplank, bump his head on a fender-log, break a leg, and almost drown. All life in these "free," democratic, individualistic, capitalistic, complex, fantastic States was haphazard, violent, accidental.

It was wrong and grotesque, to my mind, for Steve Radin to die a frustrated "successful" young man, and it was equally wrong and absurd for Mrs. Tanasich to die years before she had actually closed her eyes on my

324

couch. It was wrong, not from any conventional moral
point of view, but because, so far as I could discern, both
of their lives had been devoid of charm and grace in any
real sense of the word. And their lives, I thought, were
symbolical of millions of lives in America.

On the other hand, Podgornik, when I considered him
symbolically, was to me a promise of a possible spiritual
and intellectual awakening and flowering of America. I
believed that, if such an awakening occurred, it probably
would begin with the immigrants and their children—the
Hunkies, the Jews, the dagoes, the Germans, and others.
The early American stock (numerously represented in
Los Angeles and its suburbs) was, I feared, emotionally,
spiritually, and intellectually flat. For generations the old
stock had been pickled in the sour juices of Puritanism, or
dried over the sacrificial fires on the altars dedicated to
the great god Work. I thought, too, that if the awakening
ever began, it would start in some such way as had come
in the case of Podgornik. The people—those still capable
of suffering—would have to suffer a serious accident and
severe pain. The nation would have to be bumped and
jarred out of itself. Then, with luck, perhaps, there would
be a long period of awkward groping after new spiritual
and intellectual values and realities. . . .

Thinking thus about Mrs. Tanasich, Steve, Lenard,
and the others, I decided that eventually I would put them
all in a book, along with myself.

II

As for myself, I had no complaint against America.

I had not come to America, like Steve Radin, to become rich; nor, like Koska, to escape from myself or
something or other; nor, like most immigrants, to slave
at whatever task I could find. Rather, I had come to ex-

perience America, to explore the great jungle, to adventure in understanding—and here I was. I had found the adventure exciting and worth while; and there was more to come. I was not yet thirty.

I had a hungry mind, and there was plenty in America to feed on. Too much. Off and on I suffered with mental indigestion. But never for long. Things clarified themselves, or, if not, I dismissed them as phenomena in the jungle, in which much was yet inexplicable. I read and observed. Now and again, here and there, I came upon vital, stimulating people with whom I exchanged notions and ideas, and compared notes on America. There was, for instance, Carey McWilliams, a young Los Angeles lawyer and writer friend of mine, with whom I met once or twice a month for an afternoon's or an evening's talk. He had a vivid, acute mind, and his general attitude toward things in America was that of good-humored contemplation. There was Edward Adams Cantrell, also of Los Angeles, a man of great wit and erudition, older than myself, to whom I am indebted for many glimpses at the under side of the American civilization. And there was Upton Sinclair, of Pasadena, whom I had admired for his early works, especially *The Jungle* and *Love's Pilgrimage*, but whom I now considered more precious as a person than as a writer; and who, in turn, believed it unfortunate that I was not a regular Socialist, but a "Menckenite." There were others: Paul Jordan Smith, Ernest Paynter, Joe Jackson, Stanley Rose, Miss Frances Wright—many others.

On the whole, I led an interesting life. My health was good. I had a job which was mine as long as I wanted it. I wore good clothes and lived in comfortable rooms. I always had a few hundred dollars in the bank. I had a small collection of books which I liked to re-read. I knew

326

girls who interested me. There were lovely scenes within short distances of San Pedro. I had an automobile which took me almost anywhere I wanted to go. I enjoyed driving, either alone or with some one else.

I was told that I was getting on as a writer. After my stories appeared in the *Mercury* or elsewhere, I received letters of commendation from F. Scott Fitzgerald, James Stevens, Carey McWilliams, and other, less known, people whose judgment I respected.

I was twenty-nine years old and I had been in the United States half of my life, but so far, I thought, America had scarcely touched me. I liked to think that I had not let her touch me in any vital or devastating way, as she had touched Mrs. Tanasich, Steve, Lenard, Blakelock, and the others. She was neither dragging me down, nor pulling me up. I "played safe," as a sensible adventurer should do in a jungle. I laughed and stayed sane and healthy. To Upton Sinclair, as he told me, I was not as admirable as the emotional, impulsive Lonie Burton, who, without knowing what it was all about, had plunged into the jungle with the idea of clearing it and transforming it into an idyllic place, but the jungle had licked Lonie, and his defeat benefited no one, while I was still here, well and strong. Many people had envied Steve Radin, who had become part of the jungle and grown in it, but he, too, had been defeated in it.

Thus I philosophized in 1928. I was in danger, almost, of becoming smug. Late that year I wrote in my diary:

. . . An astonishing place, America. One cannot love, nor hate it. It is terrible and magnificent and funny, vacillating between the sublime and the ridiculous. A place of contrasts and contradictions. It is scarcely possible to define it, or make any observation about it that cannot be refuted by a change of attitude or surroundings. It changes from day to day in particular spots and respects. It is, I repeat for the nth time, a jungle. It is impossible to really figure it out in any fundamental sense. It is best to laugh at it, though, of course, that is not always possible. But one must never, never take it too seriously—not yet. It is futile to try to change or influence it deeply; it is immune to reform, and within it—within the jungle—operate tremendous economic and other forces that seem to have got out of human control.

Certain aspects of the scene incontestably are depressing beyond words; but then again, even during periods punctuated by such incidents in one's life as the deaths of Steve Radin and Mrs. Tanasich, one is apt to stumble, in the most unlikely places, upon persons like Lenard Podgornik and things that cause depression to vanish instantly.

Liberty, for instance, has fallen into an inferior place in the Americans' habitual thinking, but occasionally one is privileged to see that the will-to-freedom is not entirely dead even among the yokels, as Mencken calls them. Last week I attended a large "community party" in San Ubaldo [near Los Angeles]. There was dancing and moderate drinking, and except for a few old maids, male and female, the townfolk and their guests were having a gay time. But in the middle of a dance the party was raided by federal prohibition agents from Los Angeles, who said that they came to arrest the committee in charge, which included the mayor, the chief of police, the county's sheriff, and a few other leading citizens. The mayor tried to reason with the boys, but they were unwilling to deviate a little from their duty. Then a mob of husky ranchers and railroad men surrounded them, and when the sheriff yelled ,"Up an' at 'em, boys!" seized them, unpinned their badges, fastened the badges on their backsides, and, after propelling them into the street, went on with the dance.

Later the same evening, returning home, I happened to drive through Long Beach at high speed and was stopped by a cop, who proceeded to write me a ticket; but as I gave him my name, he remembered reading something I had published in the *Mercury* that had pleased him, whereupon he tore up the ticket and asked me would I come to his home, near by, for a while and examine some poems he had written! What is more, the poetry was not bad.

I have had other experiences during the last few years, equally

328

amusing and provocative. They perhaps are not typical of America, but I think they are peculiar to it, and not wholly without significance. Hardly anything so tangible is typical of America. There is no typical American. As I say, America is a land of swift changes ("now you see it, now you don't"), not of types or typical things or events. . . .

There is a mocking illusiveness about American life that appeals to my sense of the dramatic. Sometimes I think that there is in America, in her drive and rush, in her cockeyed sense of values and her resultant discontent, a high promise—maybe a false one, but nevertheless it catches and fires one's fancy, and one begins to think and feel in terms of the vast, varied, painful, effervescent, tragi*comic* (emphasis on the comic) life of the country.

True, the border of "Coolidge prosperity" and other influences seem to have reduced the greater part of the American masses to a piggish indifference that is not safely commonplace; but underneath the deadness moves a tide of dissatisfaction with the more obvious characteristics of American life, a blind will to overcome the blight (or whatever one may be inclined to call the combination of anarchic Big Business, Democracy, and organized Christianity) that is responsible for the mediocre quality of American civilization. The tide may not affect the surface much; none-the-less, it is interesting to watch the course. At any moment it may start heaving.

Postscript

Postscript

I HAVE written this book as I planned it in 1929, when my interest was suddenly diverted for two years into other channels.

In their essentials, my ideas about America have not changed since 1929. Physically, the continent is magnificent. Its power is incalculable. It is sprinkled with splendid people. The great financial crash of 1929 and the subsequent events, however, have made of it more an economic, political, and social jungle than it ever was before.

Millions of "successful" people—people like Steve Radin—"crashed" in the dark, not knowing what happened to them. Many of them committed suicide. Sanitariums are filled with men and women who once were wealthy and are now dying of melancholia. Ex-millionaires haunt employment bureaus.

Some ten million workers, including millions of my own countrymen and other immigrants, are jobless. Their number, as I write this, is increasing, with the end nowhere in sight. Now they are not even "dung" any longer. The jungle is too fruitful and has no further use for them. The greatest jungle in the world is inundated with "dung," and no one in the jungle knows what to do about it.

Mencken remarks (*The American Mercury* for January, 1932) that the United States is in a "dreadful mess . . . in a hell of a mess." His diagnosis is no less general and no more inadequate than the diagnoses of other publicists and public men, once honored for their perspicacity.

In 1928, a confident and smooth-faced Herbert Hoover

333

stated in a firm voice that the high aim of American life was to have a chicken in every pot, silk stockings on every woman's legs, and two cars in every garage. Nowadays his face, when it appears on the film screen, is a picture of fear, frustration, and bewilderment. In a few short years the jungle destroyed the great Hoover—a rather typical product of the jungle—and everything he stood for.

But while my ideas about the U. S. A. are the same in 1931 as they were in 1929, of late I find it hard to laugh at things and conditions in the jungle, although I know it is essentially ridiculous, for instance, for shoe-workers to walk ill-shod, for woolen-textile workers to have no warm clothes in the winter, for coal-miners to shiver in cold shacks, and for millions of bushels of wheat and potatoes to rot upon farms and in warehouses when millions of people elsewhere are in deep want. Unlike in 1928, when Lenard Podgornik, Steve Radin, and I roared ourselves purple in the face, the jungle in 1931 is too monstrous, too full of horrors and parasitism, for one to laugh in it, and at it, with amusement. I notice that those who occasionally still laugh do not laugh naturally or pleasantly, but hysterically. Even Mencken is no longer as jolly and entertaining as he used to be.

Hence I bring this story of my adventure in America, which I entitle *Laughing in the Jungle*, only to the end of 1928. Some day, perhaps, I shall continue it in another volume, under a different title. Possibly not.

The crash of 1929, I think, marks the end of an era. Just now we are in a period of transition—of acute and general frustration, bewilderment, stress, and misery. I do not know how long the period will last. Probably a long time. It may be that this is the painful bump on the head that the American people needed to bring them to their senses, to experience "rebirth," to start—Podgornik-like—toward a revaluation of values. I do not know. But it seems to me that many people in the United States nowadays are thinking seriously, asking serious questions, getting acquainted with themselves and their environment. Millions of them were interested only in making money, in chickens in the pots, in silk stockings, and cars in their garages; now they are studying economics and looking into their own souls. Millions of them are deeply and sympathetically interested in the gigantic attempt in Russia to conquer chaos with planning. It may be that the tide of dissatisfaction with the more obvious characteristics of American life and with American values, so boldly glorified and personified by Herbert Hoover in 1928, is beginning to heave. It may be that we are in the midst of a revolution; that before many years this tide of dissatisfaction will seize the crazy overproductive and destructive forces now loose and uncontrolled in the jungle, and try to transform the jungle into a civilization. It may be that we are being hooked up to history, to the epic idea that is behind Russia's experiment.

Meantime, personally, I still have no real complaint against America, the jungle. I have come here for excitement and adventure. I have never been hungry for more than two days since I am here. The jungle has been and is vastly interesting. Too interesting. Sometimes it is overwhelming in its complexity and melodrama. And as I say, lately I find it difficult to laugh. But I stay and intend to remain here.

New York,
January, 1932.

THE END